FANTASTIC PAINTINGS OF
FRAZETTA

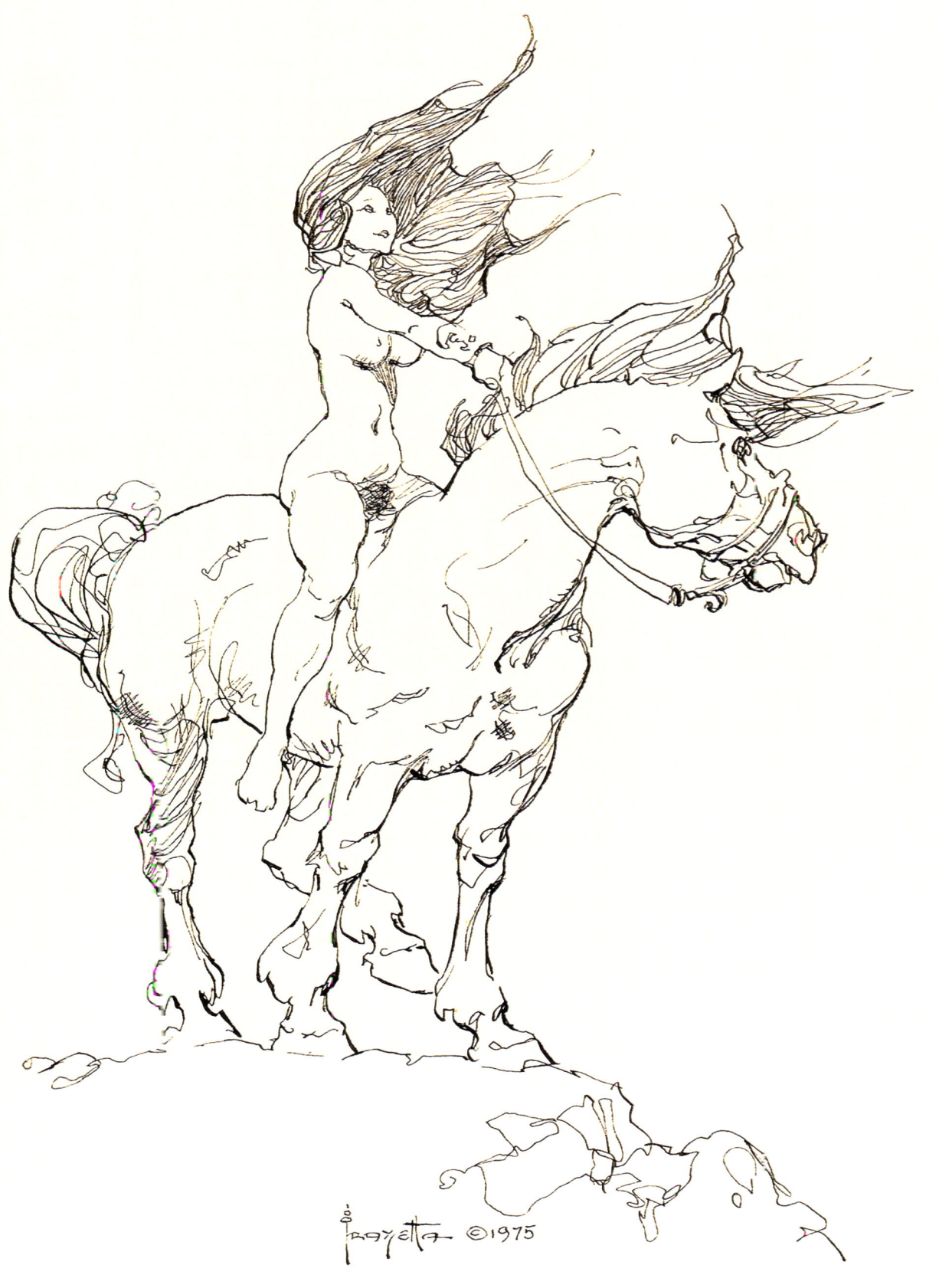

Frazetta ©1975

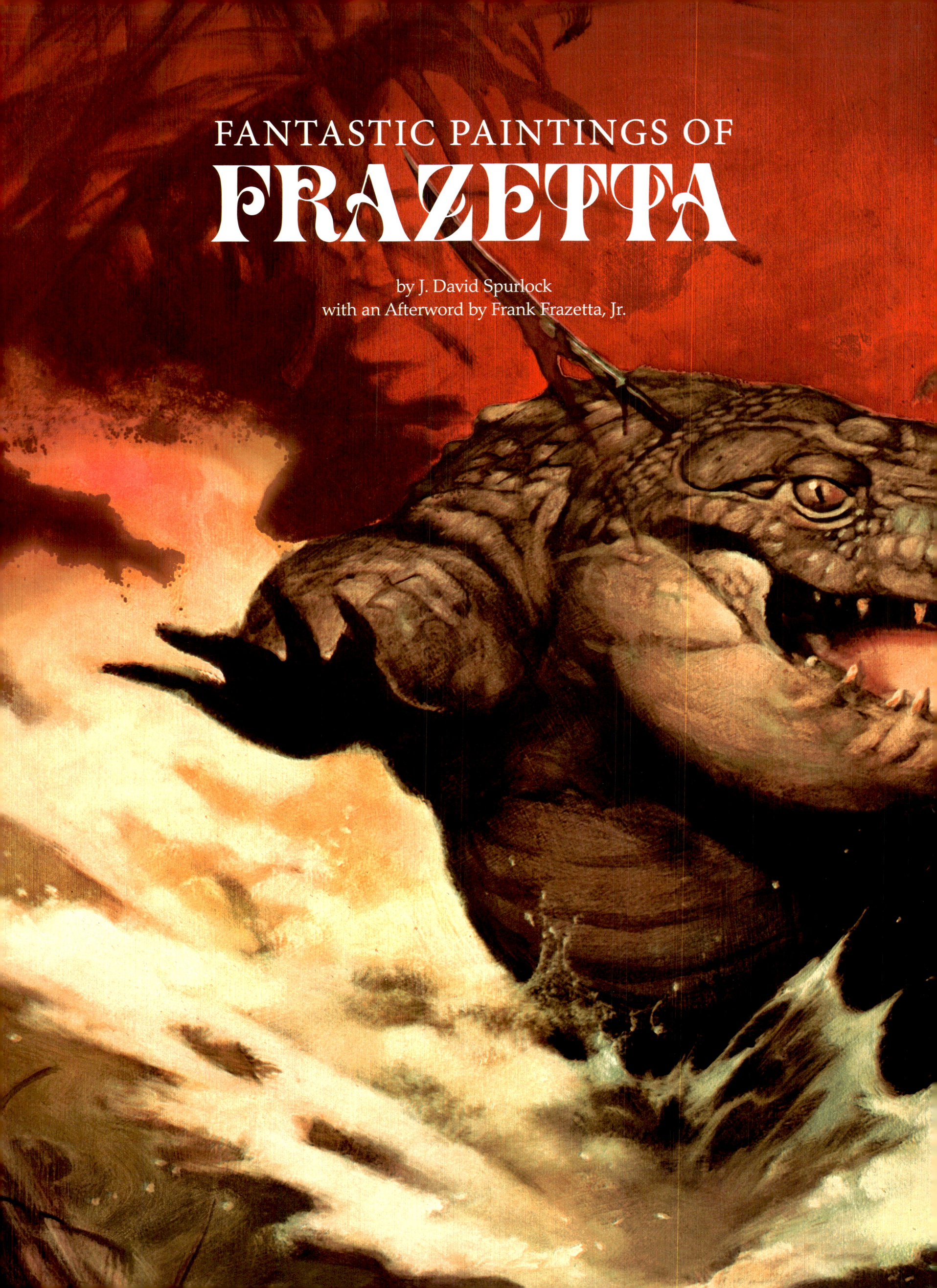

FANTASTIC PAINTINGS OF
FRAZETTA

by J. David Spurlock
with an Afterword by Frank Frazetta, Jr.

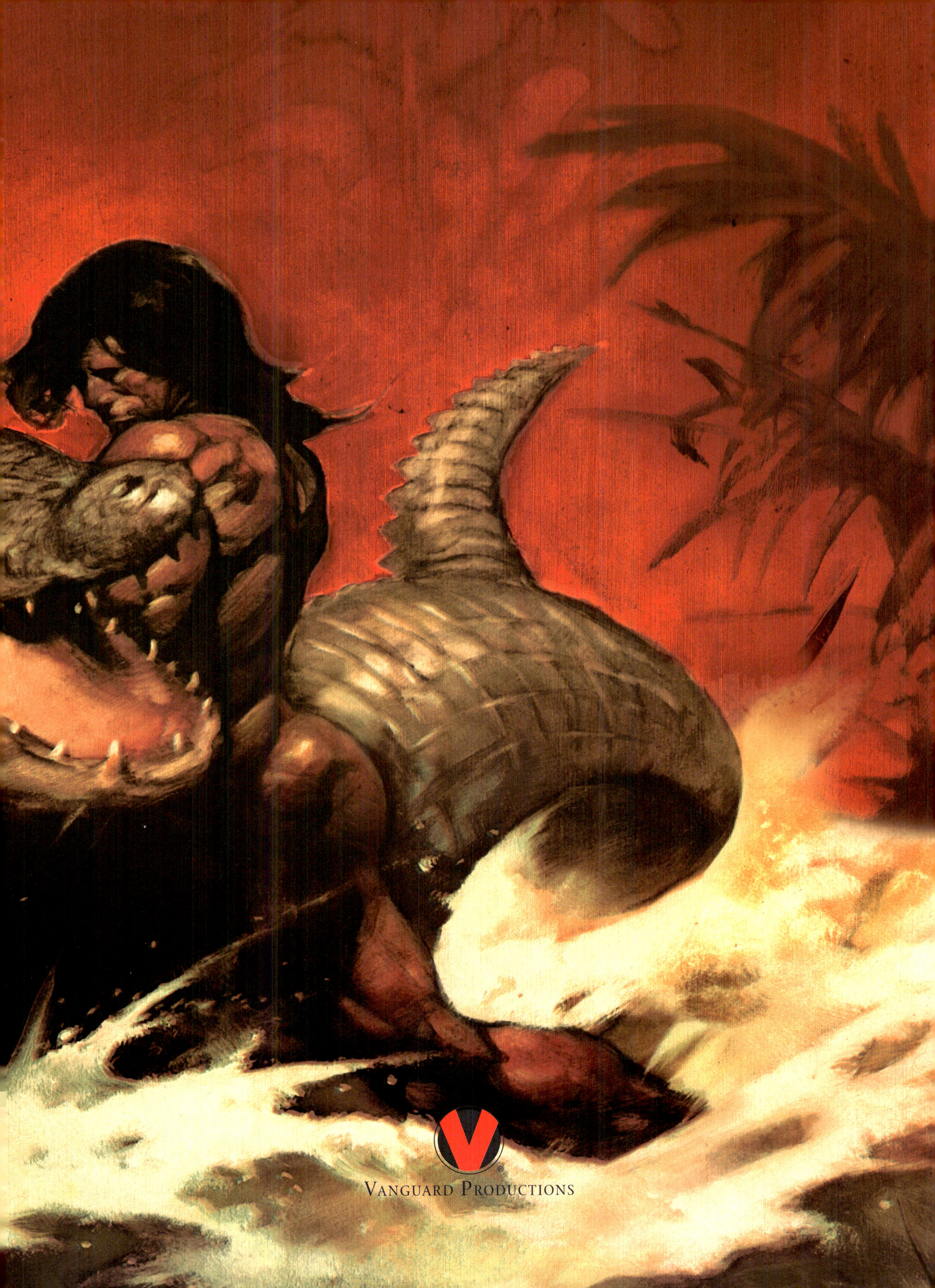

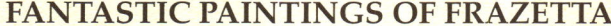

FANTASTIC PAINTINGS OF FRAZETTA
Written, Edited & Art Directed by J. David Spurlock
Afterword by Frank Frazetta, Jr.
Designer & Associate Editor: Patrick K. Hill

Special thanks to:
The Frazetta family, Michael Whelan, Leigh McMillan,
Patrick K. Hill, Dr. Dave Winiewicz, Jim Halperin,
Claudia Almaraz, Topper Helmers, Jeanne Quintile, Brent
Frankenhoff, Joe Maddalena, Adrian Olivera, Greg Obaugh,
and Robert Barrett.

Published by Vanguard. ISBN: 9781934331811
Hardcover ISBN: 978-1-934331-81-1 $39.95
Deluxe ISBN: 978-1-934331-82-8 $69.95

www.**VANGUARDPUBLISHING**.com
www.**FRAZETTAMUSEUM**.com

First Printing July 17, 2020
Second Printing November 18, 2020
Third Printing Halloween 2021
Fourth Printing Halloween 2022
Fifth Printing June, 2023
Sixth Printing July, 2024

Printed in China

TABLE OF CONTENTS

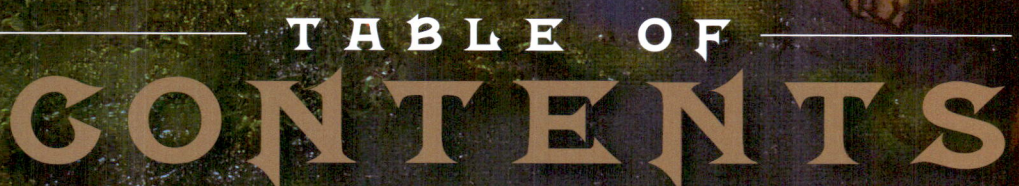

A Few Words about Frazetta
by Michael Whelan **7**

The Fantastic Art of Frank Frazetta
by J. David Spurlock **8**

Gallery of Paintings **22**

Afterword
by Frank Frazetta, Jr. **106**

Bonus Folio
(Deluxe Limited Edition Only) **113**

A FEW WORDS FROM MICHAEL WHELAN

MICHAEL WHELAN *is one of the world's premier painters of imaginative realism. He has created book and album covers for authors and musicians like Isaac Asimov, Stephen King, Ray Bradbury, Brandon Sanderson, the Jacksons and Meat Loaf. His clients have included every major U.S. book publisher, the National Geographic Society, CBS Records, and the Franklin Mint.*

Michael has won an unprecedented 15 Hugo Awards (SF's Oscar), 3 World Fantasy Awards, 13 Chesleys, Locus Magazine's Best Professional Artist 30 times and the Spectrum Annual of Fantastic Art *named him a Grand Master in 2004. Other awards include a Gold Medal from the Society of Illustrators, a Vargas Award, a Grumbacher Gold Medal, and the Solstice Award from the Science Fiction Writers of America. In 2009, he was inducted into the Science Fiction Hall of Fame in Seattle.*

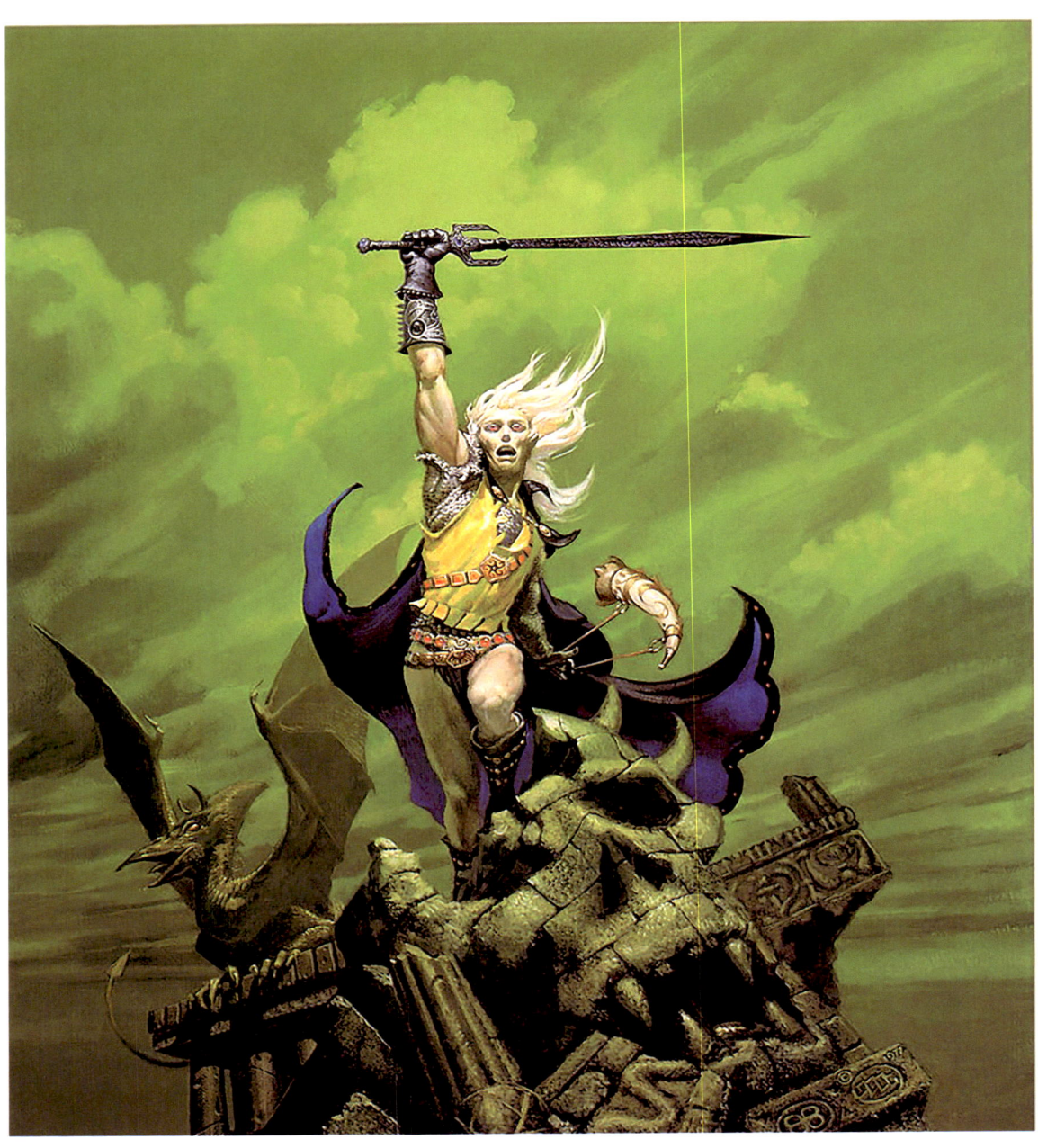

STORMBRINGER *by Michael Whelan*
Acrylic on masonite, 20" x 30" (1977)
Published as the cover to Stormbringer
written by Michael Moorcock
(Daw, 1977)

My first encounter with Frazetta artwork was the same year I saw my first tornado. This sticks in my mind because I regard them both as forces of nature — arresting and wonderful occurrences quickly engraved in my memory. I'm extremely fortunate to have been at a young and impressionable age when his work became part of our popular culture.

Every so often there are watershed artistic experiences that seem to come at just the right time, which occur as if people had been waiting for them without knowing it. Hearing the Beatles or Jimi Hendrix felt that way; making me think "This is just the music I've been waiting to hear!" So it was when Frazetta's artwork erupted into the world: it was art we had been wanting to see without knowing it, realized by one of the most singular talents of our time.

— MICHAEL WHELAN

THE FANTASTIC ART OF
FRANK FRAZETTA

J. DAVID SPURLOCK

J. DAVID SPURLOCK is an award-winning author, historian, advocate for creator rights, filmmaker and associate to Frazetta, Basil Gogos, Steranko, Joe Kubert, Carmine Infantino, Frank Brunner and many more. Launching in the 1990s, Spurlock created the comics artist sketchbook boom via Vanguard with tomes produced with Al Williamson, Neal Adams, Jeffrey Jones, John Buscema, John Romita, Alex Horley and multiple volumes on Frazetta. Spurlock's How to Draw Chiller Monsters, *for Random House, rose as high as #18 on the Bookspan best-seller list. Spurlock's award-winning* Alluring Art of Margaret Brundage *has been universally lauded including by MTV and the* Village Voice *who proclaimed it one of The Best of 2013. In 2012, Spurlock was appointed Director of the Estate of Hall of Fame MAD, Mars Attacks, Daredevil and Weird Science co-creator Wallace Wood. Spurlock's speaking engagements include: 2015 San Diego Comic-Con Jack Kirby panel; 2013 WorldCon panels on Robert E. Howard, Copyright Law, and Margaret Brundage; with Stan Lee for Dragon Con TV and a live audience of 4,600; Rutgers School of Law; University of the Arts in Philadelphia, the InkWell Awards and multiple Frank Frazetta tribute events at the San Diego Comic-Con. Film and TV credits include: "Frazetta Painting with Fire," STARZ network's "Comic Books Unbound," the PBS documentary, "Superheroes: A Never-Ending Battle" and, the Frazetta episode of "Strange Inheritance."*

FRAZETTA! A unique name that conjures in the minds of generations of fans from bikers and tattoo aficionados to Fine Art connoisseurs, a unique artistic vision which juxtaposes the classical with radical departures from reality as we know it — somehow made surprisingly palpable via Frazetta's masterful hand. *The New York Times* said, "Frazetta helped define fantasy heroes like Conan, Tarzan and John Carter of Mars with signature images of strikingly fierce, hard-bodied heroes and bosomy, callipygian damsels." Frazetta took the sex and violence of the pulp fiction of his youth and added even more action, fantasy and potency, but rendered his works with a panache seldom seen outside of Fine Art.

Despite his sword-and-sorcery, science-fiction and fantasy subject matter, the quality of the work has not only drawn comparisons to the most brilliant of illustrators, Maxfield Parrish, Frederic Remington, Norman Rockwell, N.C. Wyeth, J. Allen St. John, and Joseph Clement Coll, but even to the most brilliant of fine artists including Rembrandt and Michelangelo. And major Frazetta works now sell for millions of dollars. Many of today's Frazetta fans were yet to be born when Frazetta first grew beyond his 1950s and '60s work to explode into the American pop-culture collective consciousness in the 1970s. Others will recall faux-Frazetta mural paintings appearing across America throughout the custom van craze of the '70s and '80s. But here in the 21st century, the Master of Beasts, Beauties and Barbarians' original paintings keep breaking original art sales records, going from $1 million to $2 million and now $5.4 million.

Opposite: **THE MAMMOTH** (detail)

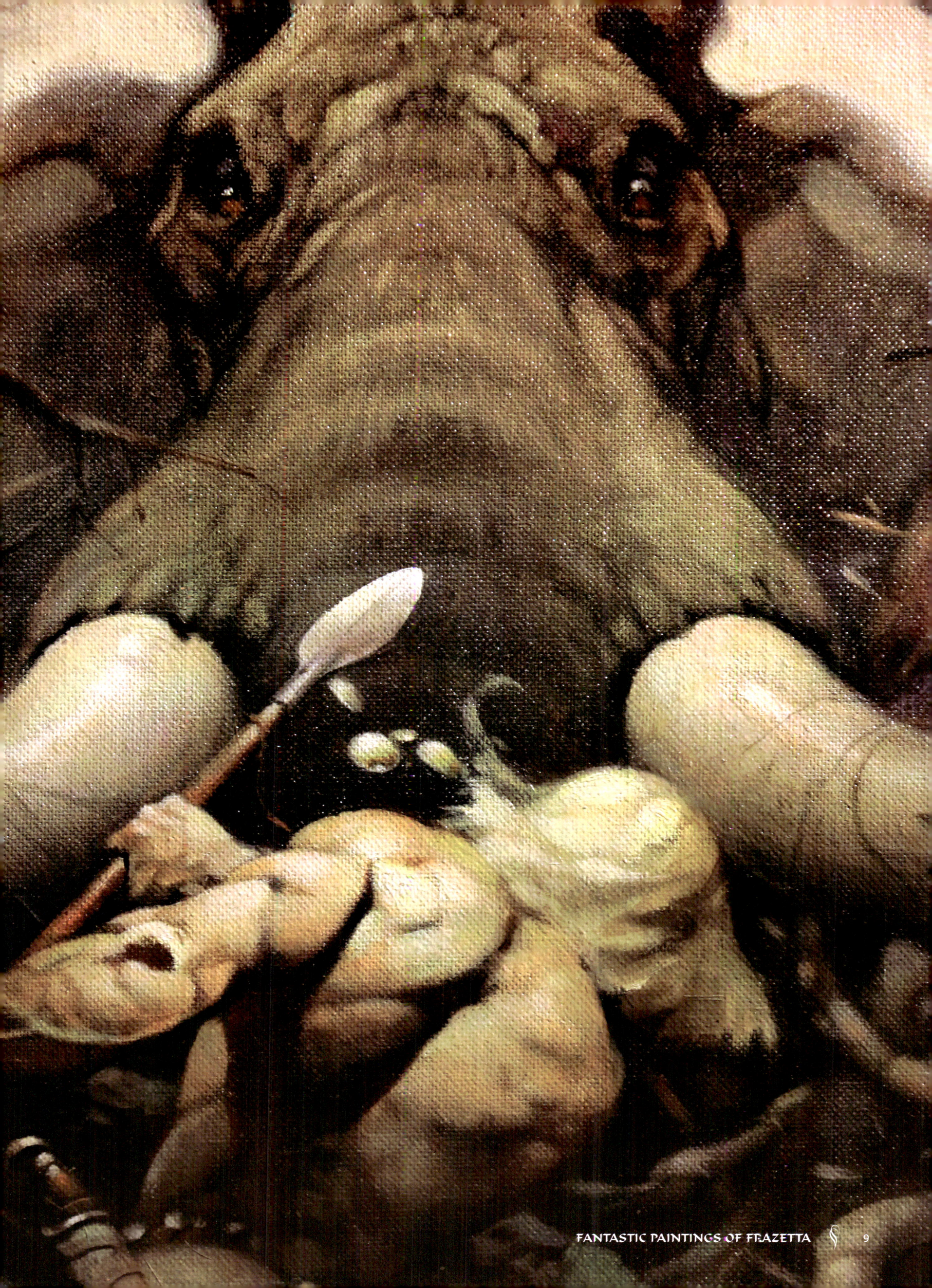

Frazetta is, quite rightfully, the world's most influential heroic fantasy artist —the big-bang father of them all — the Grand Master of Fantastic Art.

Once he left comics to paint book covers in the 1960s, the artist's nearly unprecedented work provoked an explosion of "sword and sorcery" material in books, comicbooks, magazines and eventually movies including "Conan," Frazetta's own "Fire and Ice" film, and the Death Dealer franchise of projects, as well as unexpected references by playful Americana films like 1983's "National Lampoon's Vacation" and the 1979 Steve Martin film, "The Jerk." Just a few of the noted artists to rise to acclaim while under Frazetta's influence, and in his wake, are Jeffrey Jones, Boris Vallejo, Ken Kelly, Sanjulián, John Buscema, Frank Brunner, Brom, Earl Norem, Justin Sweet, Mark Schultz, Simon Bisley, Mike Hoffman, Bernie Wrightson, Frank Cho, Angelo Torres, William Stout, Dave Stevens, Joe Jusko, Alex Horley, Arthur Suydam, Tom Grindberg and more. Frazetta is so identified with creating the look of the sword and sorcery genre that many know him solely for that. This innovator's work has not only inspired generations of artists, but also movies and directors including the Conan films, "John Carter of Mars," the sensationally successful "Lord of the Rings" trilogy, Robert Rodriguez' films including "From Dusk Till Dawn," Ralph Bakshi films, the epic, award-winning "Game of Thrones" series, Tim Burton's "Sleepy Hollow," Disney's animated Tarzan films, Francis Ford Coppola's "Apocalypse Now" and George Lucas' "Star Wars" series.

John Milius, the screenwriter whose credits include "Apocalypse Now," "Clear and Present Danger" and "Red Dawn," was the director and co-writer of "Conan the Barbarian," the 1982 film starring Arnold Schwarzenegger. Milius said to the *LA Times* upon Frazetta's passing that Frazetta's muscular paintings of Conan defined the character for him. Milius: "Not that I could ever redo Frazetta on film — he created a world and a mood that are impossible to simulate — but my goal in 'Conan the Barbarian' was to tell a story that was shaped by Frazetta and Wagner."

This author has long maintained that Schwarzenegger owes more than his acting career to Frazetta as, without the success of the Frazetta-covered Conan books, there would have been no Conan movies, and it was while Schwarzenegger was in America in connection with the Conan film that he met Kennedy family member Maria Shriver. Her family's deep roots in American politics opened doors for Schwarzenegger who ultimately won the governorship of California. In November of 2003, *Forbes* magazine echoed these sentiments with Christopher Helman's article, "Schwarzenegger's Sargent: Which artist helped make Arnold governor? Frank Frazetta, the Rembrandt of barbarians."

In 2019, Schwarzenegger recalled studying Frazetta's paintings in the 1970s as preparation for the lead role in the film, "Conan The Barbarian" saying, "I have not been intimidated that often in my life. But when I looked at Frazetta's paintings, I tell you, it was intimidating. How could I ever come close to looking like this kind of drama and magic that Frazetta created? It was intimidating!" Actors' appreciation of Frazetta didn't end with Schwarzenegger. Upon meeting this author in Tampa, Florida, the star of the 2013 "Conan The Barbarian" film, Jason Momoa — who also starred in "Game of Thrones" and in the title role for the box office smash "Aquaman" — said, "I accepted the Conan role because I am a big Frazetta fan."

Momoa told the DenOfGeek website, "I'm a huge admirer of Frank Frazetta and when he died during our filming, it was so sad because I wanted him to see it and say 'Wow, that's my Conan!' Just looking at his paintings, I wanted to put that up on the screen. I absolutely remember seeing that one where Conan's standing on a pile of skulls and it's seared into your memory." "Game of Thrones" creator George R. R. Martin said, "Though he bears only a passing resemblance to the Cimmerian as

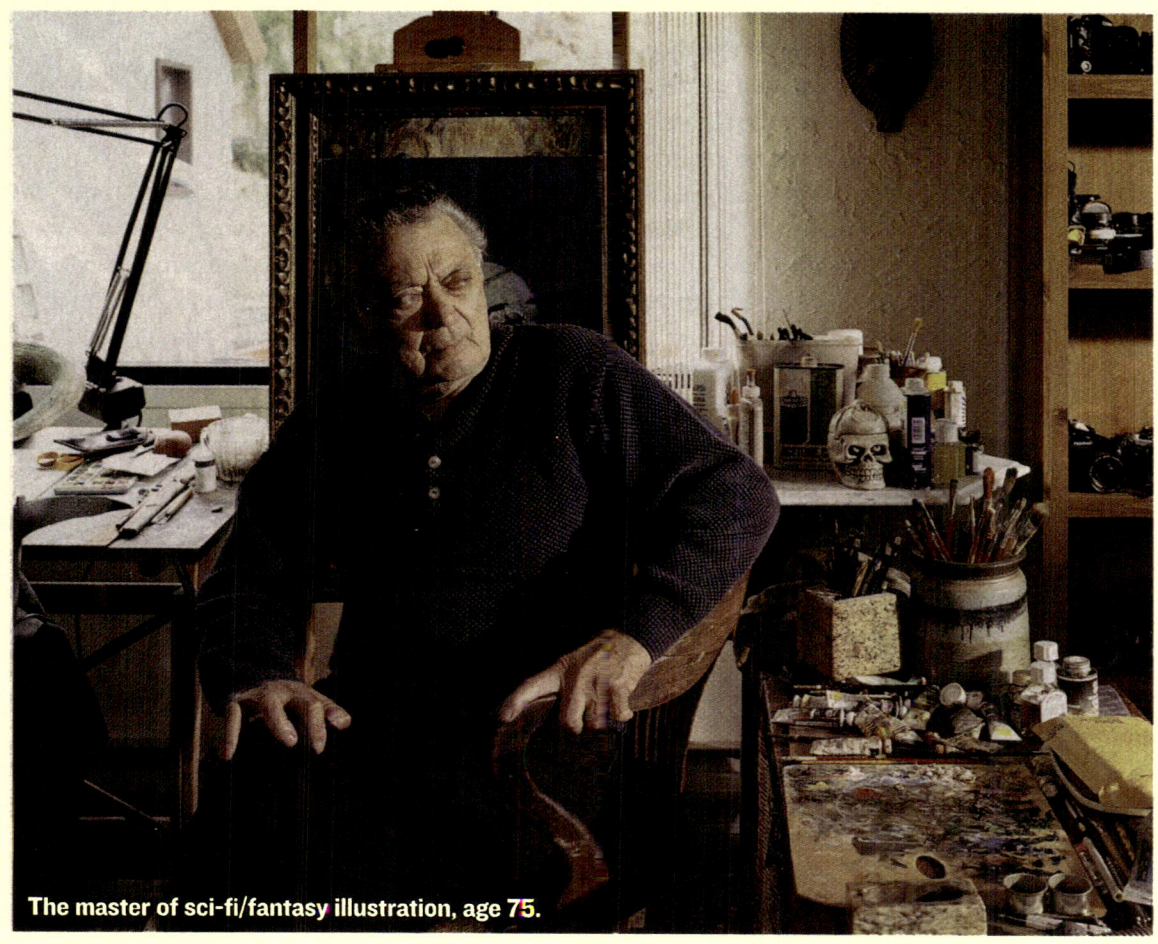

The master of sci-fi/fantasy illustration, age 75.

Take that, y

Schwarzenegger's Sargent

Which artist helped make Arnold governor? Frank Frazetta, the Rembrandt of barbarians.

BY CHRISTOPHER HELMAN

PUT ASIDE THE DEFT POLITICAL MACHINERY, THE KENNEDY FAMILY MISSUS AND THE seething masses' discontent. Californians today might not have Arnold if Arnold had not had Conan. The role of a virile, axe-wielding, fur-bearing, cranium-smashing barbarian suited Schwarzenegger to a tee. It made him first a star, then a public figure, now a politician. But who created Conan?

Pulp writer Robert E. Howard dreamed up the character in the 1930s. It was not until the 1970s, though, that the barbarian's popularity took off. That was when illustrator Frank Frazetta gave Conan his present form. Frazetta's wild cover art—fantastic, sensuous, a bit tawdry—moved paperbacks that previously had languished.

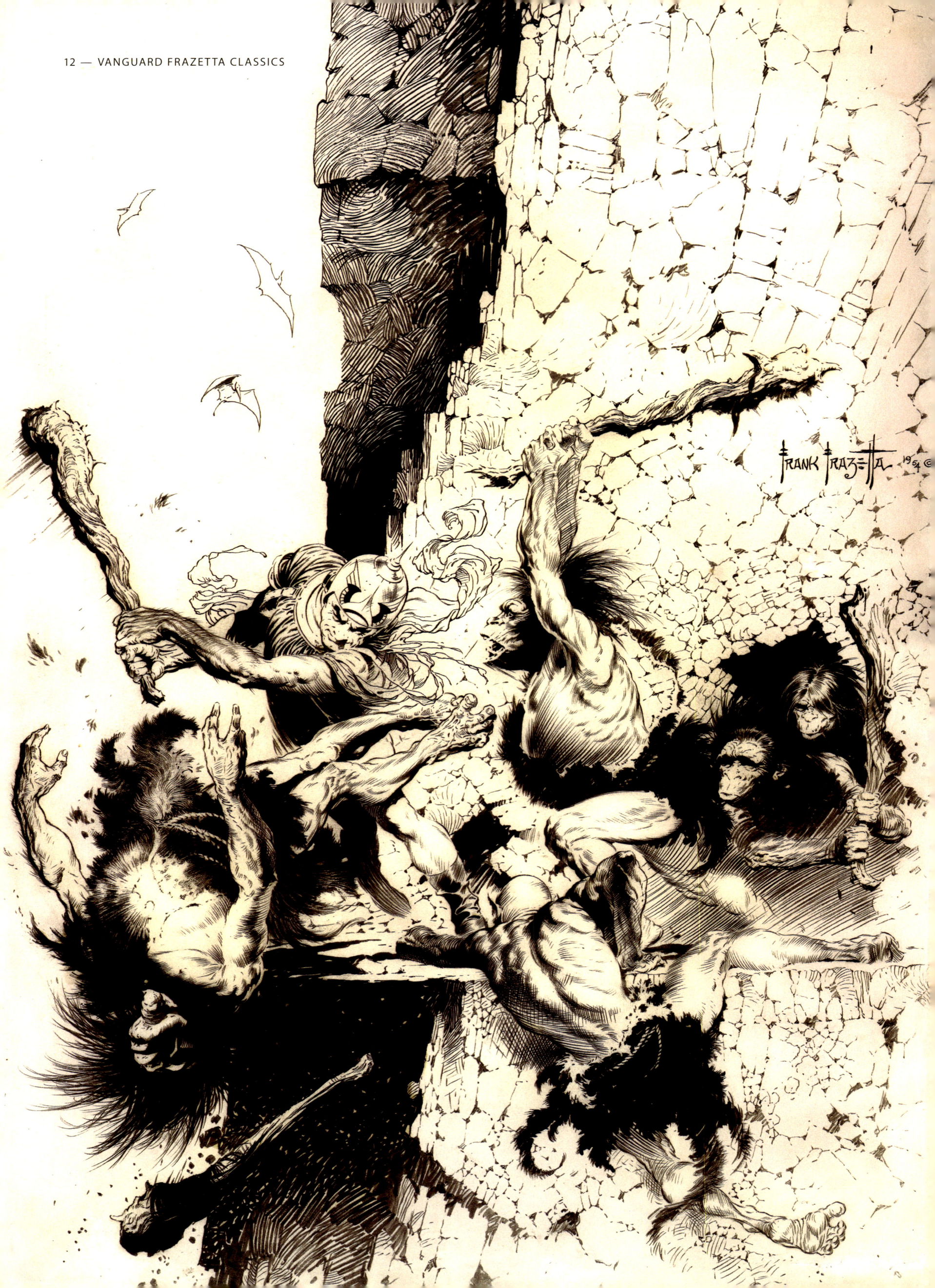

Robert E. Howard described him, Frazetta's covers of the Conan paperback collections of the '60s and '70s became the definitive picture of the character… still is."

The growing Frazetta-mania of the 1970s inspired a major art book series from Bantam running for over a decade from 1975 through the mid-'80s. Bantam Books is a major American publishing house owned by parent company Random House, which is one of the largest and most successful publishers in history. Bantam's 1945 list of founders included Ian and Betty Ballantine. Betty Ballantine knew how key Frazetta was to both Lancer's Conan paperbacks and to Doubleday's early-1970s line of Edgar Rice Burroughs hardcover books.

Circa late-1974, Ballantine negotiated a deal with Frazetta to publish his art prominently in mass market art books via Bantam and their Peacock line. *The New York Times*, on May 29, 2014, confirmed that not only was Bantam a top player in the paperback book field, but by 1980 Bantam was actually the single largest publisher of paperbacks in America with over 15% of the total market share, exceeding $100 million in sales. *The Fantastic Art of Frank Frazetta* was released in August of 1975 to great success. The highly respected Charles Scribner's Sons released a hardcover edition weeks later in September. The 1975 book, copyright by Frank Frazetta, also promoted Frazetta's own art print line, Frazetta Prints. The artist's wife Ellie said the family made their first million dollars on print sales.

Opposite: **CAVEMAN**
Originally deemed too violent for comics,
Famous Funnies *Buck Rogers artwork was later revised for* Weird Science-Fantasy #29 *cover, 1954*

The Frazetta family sold this piece in June 2010 to Jim Halperin, for $380,000, a record sale at that time for comic work.

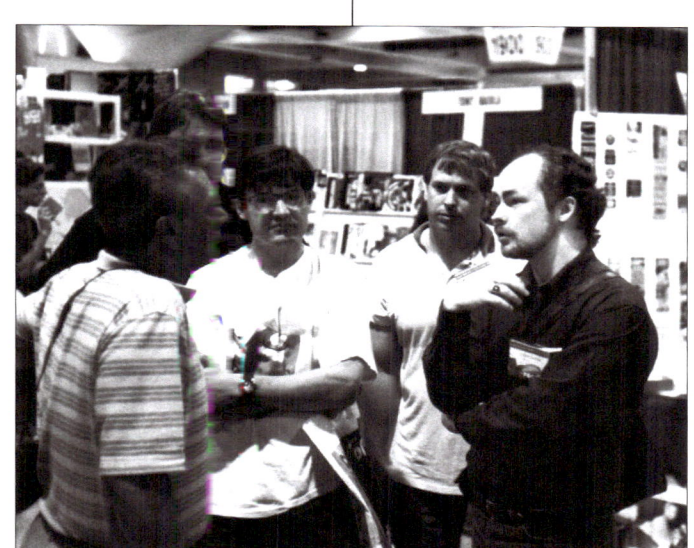

Frazetta discusses art with J. David Spurlock during Frank's surprise San Diego Comic Con appearance in 1995. Photo by Doc Dave Winiewicz.

In her Introduction to the book, Betty Ballantine wrote of Frazetta's segue from Fine Art child prodigy to being a young comicbook illustrator, saying, "Brooklyn-born Frank Frazetta started drawing practically as soon as he could walk. At the tender age of three he was selling his work (true, to relatives, but he quickly expanded his activities to the denizens of his block). By the time he was eight he was wedded to a career in art. His teachers persuaded his parents to enter him in the Brooklyn Academy of Fine Arts, a small but exclusive school with students ranging from eight to eighty. Here, Frazetta was fortunate enough to encounter Michele Falanga. Under the tutelage of this fine Italian classicist for the next eight years of his life, the young artist's eye was put firmly on the path of reality — but never at the cost of the bouncing, ebullient life which is a hallmark of Frazetta's work."

Ballantine continued, "When Frazetta was sixteen, his beloved mentor died and the young man was forced to think of ways to earn a living. He immediately entered the world of commercial art as an assistant to John Giunta, doing fill-in work on comicbooks. He did succeed in persuading Giunta to produce a comic which Frazetta himself had originated many years before as a child. It was actually published, under the title "Snowman" in *Tally-ho Comics* of December 1944. This was the start of a long career in the comicbook and comic strip field, a career which lasted more than twenty years, during which Frazetta produced an astonishing quantity and variety of work, everything from the "funny-animal" comic to the Western, from adventure of all kinds to mystery and creepies, from fantasy to historical, all for various comicbooks. By 1949 he was working for three different comicbook publishers. In 1952 he added yet another of his own contributions, *Thun'da*, the first issue of which has become a classic (it was the only one done by Frazetta). And he added yet another comicbook publisher, Entertaining Comics [EC], to his list."

Ballantine continued, "He was, of course, doing covers for the comics and, in the early 1950's he created his famous *Buck Rogers* series. Not too long after that he worked on newspaper strips, and ended up for nine years working on *Li'l Abner*. It was an effort to break loose from the safety of a steady paycheck but eventually, at the insistence of his friend Roy Krenkel, he did. It never occurred to him to do anything but go back to the comicbook field but the going was tough. Styles had changed. Frazetta was told his work looked old-fashioned. He did odd jobs for men's magazines, eventually ending up with *Playboy* doing "Li'l Annie Fanny" along with Harvey Kurtzman, Will Elder and Jack Davis, the grand old gang that had done the early, vintage *Mad* comics. Frazetta worked exclusively on the women in this *Playboy* parody of the strips."

1975's *Fantastic Art of Frank Frazetta* book was such a hit that it totaled six printings in its first year of publication and launched a major series that continued for a decade, including *Frank Frazetta Book Two* in 1977, *Frank Frazetta Book Three* in early 1978, *Frank Frazetta Book Four* in 1980, and *Frank Frazetta Book Five* in 1985.

The first three Frazetta art books were reported by editor Betty Ballantine to have sold a third of a million copies each within two years of publication. Collectively, one million books sold by the time Book Four was being prepared for release. As Frazetta was running out of his backlist of paintings, there was a delay in the release of Book Five for Frazetta to produce more paintings.

Ballantine had said, "It was not until 1964 that Frazetta began to hit his stride with paperbound book covers. There was a big Edgar Rice Burroughs boom and his rendition of Tarzan began to be compared with the early J. Allen St. John art. Soon Frazetta covers began to appear on the publications of several paperback houses. From the beginning, the quality of his work stood out from all the

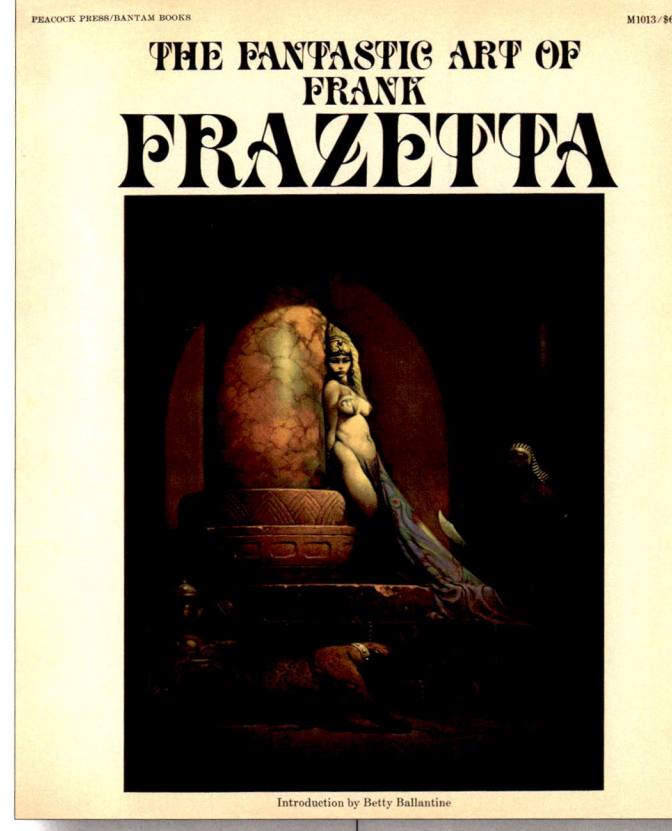

PEACOCK PRESS/BANTAM BOOKS

THE FANTASTIC ART OF FRANK

FRAZETTA

M1013/$6.95

Introduction by Betty Ballantine

rest, to the point where readers frequently bought books not for their contents but for the cover art!" Frazetta's sensuous, untamed art proved even more popular than the savage heroes whose adventures filled the books his cover paintings so effectively sold. The Frazetta art books, from 1975 to 1985, generated OVER TEN TIMES the income of any one of the various series of savage/barbarian character books for which Frazetta had come to acclaim with his cover paintings — including Conan, Tarzan, Brak the Barbarian, Jongor of the Lost Lands, and John Carter of Mars. Bantam also produced very successful mass market Frazetta Calendars every year from 1976-1982. There were likely at least a million sold in all, widely distributed in all the major book stores over several years.

Ballantine, in 1975, on how Frazetta's early years in comicbooks and strips helped advise and influence the subjects of the sumptuous oil paintings for which he became so famous:

In the establishment world, and even in the popular marketplace, cartoon strips and comicbooks are not regarded as fine art. Peanuts *may be universally beloved,* Li'l Abner *a national institution,* Pogo *everyman's philosopher and their creators highly respected. But few think of spending thousands of dollars in a gallery to buy an original Milt Caniff or Al Capp. Fewer still regard the strips as an acceptable training ground for fine art. Yet the strips, and particularly the comicbooks, have produced many a fine artist precisely because drawing for such a restrictive medium is a demanding discipline. The space in which an artist must work is clearly defined and very limited. The inescapable box must accommodate not only a*

Opposite: **CINDY IS SAVED**
Heroic Comics #94, 1954

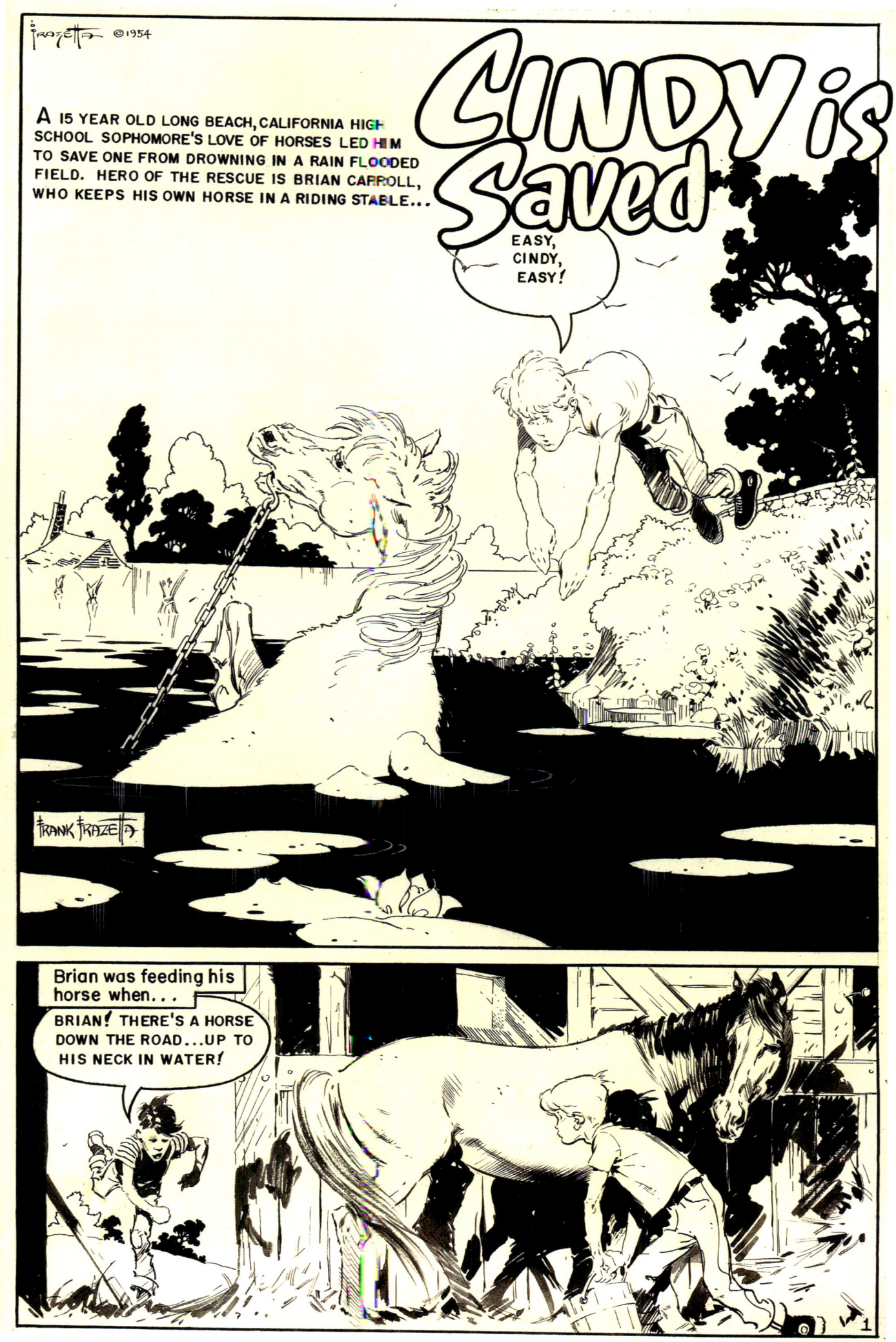

storyline but an incredible amount of active, lively, appealing, striking action which itself tells a story. And the deadlines must be met, day after day. The profusion of work required demands ingenuity to avoid repetitive imagery. Perspectives are manipulated and slewed for dramatic effect, exaggeration is mercilessly used to create freshness and difference. And beneath it all, any talented artist must be concerned with the stamp of his own individuality in a medium where, most often, he is called upon to imitate an already well established style. So the artists who do emerge from the maelstrom of the comics must, above all, have talent.

And this Frank Frazetta has in abundance. He also has drive, energy, power and a will to survive. All these qualities emerge in his paintings. He is, in toto, the perfect product of the school of comicbook art, for his work, while powerfully individual, shows the influence of its background in its heavily muscled hero figures and particularly in its intense composition which invariably directs the eye to the most important element of any painting. His background is implicit also in the quality of humor he has managed to inject into the cover paintings, for instance, the Flashman series. The Frazetta female, however, is uniquely his own. In contrast to the generally Vargas-like comicbook ladies, the Frazetta female is small of stature but lushly rounded and curved. She is recognizable just about anywhere, whether over the withers of a horse, or the shoulder of a large human male, or sometimes contesting with gigantic creatures from Paleolithic times or imperiously commanding a swamp monster or controlling some fantastic creature of the deep. She is a sorceress, a child, a woman; she is erotic, she is improbable and lovely and very much alive.

As indeed are all the creatures of Frazetta's imagination. His painting is intensely alive, vibrant, even when the figures are in repose. It is perhaps this quality of life, of energy, which most signally sets Frazetta's work apart from all others in comparable fields. Anything that has movement captures his attention — his great cats, reptiles, horses, animals of all kinds, and of course his fiercely battling male figures of Vikings, stonemen, primitives of one kind or another; the writhing roots and branches of trees, the ebb and flow and swirl of water — nothing in the typical Frazetta painting is really still. His work is all sinuosity and movement. Yet the trappings that surround all this vivid life are well done too, the textures of stone and bone and leather, of heavily wrought metals, of armor. What is often overlooked in a Frazetta painting because of his own strong tendency to emphasize its dominant element, is the subtle work that occurs in the background, the half-hidden figures, the glimpsed detail of some portion of a creature hinting at gigantic size, the shadowy suggestions of hosts unbidden to prominence.

After a decade of great success with the Ballantine/Bantam/Peacock series, other Frazetta art books followed; first from Underwood Books and then Vanguard Publishing. The publishers have been fortunate in having had access to this original source material from which to obtain good reproductions as Frank and Ellie were forward thinkers in retaining Frank's originals. Since their passing in 2009 and 2010, the works retained by the family were divided amongst the four sibling heirs. While a number of pieces have been famously sold for record prices, Frank Frazetta, Jr. and his family are committed to keeping their collection together. That art is on exhibit at the Frazetta Art Museum in East Stoudsburg, PA which they curate.

Opposite: **CINDY IS SAVED**
Heroic Comics #94, 1954

Above: Peacock counter display for
Frank Frazetta Book Two, 1977

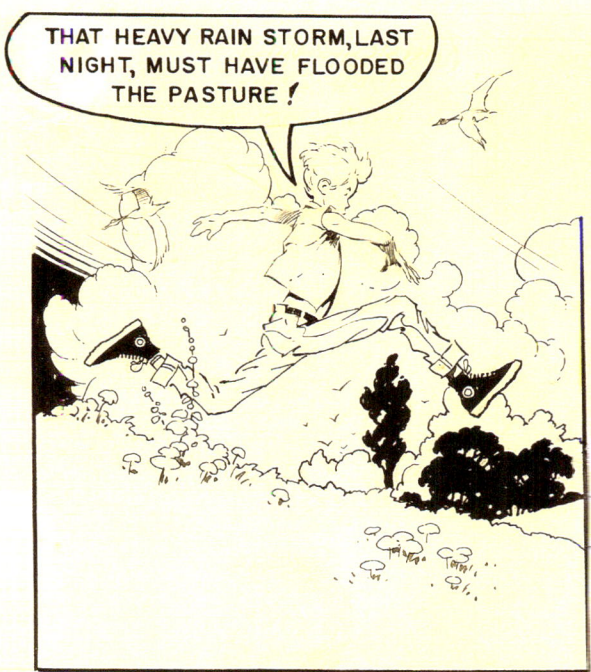

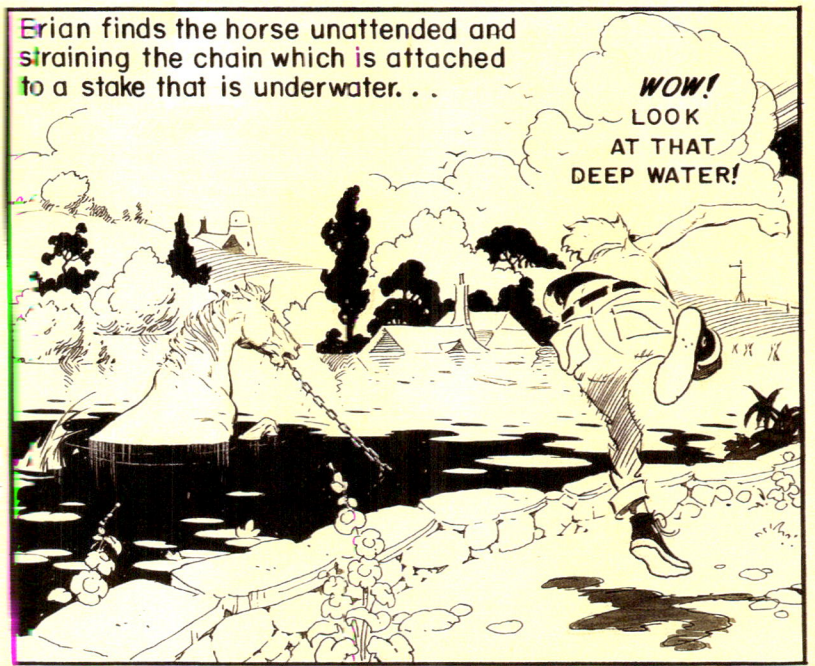

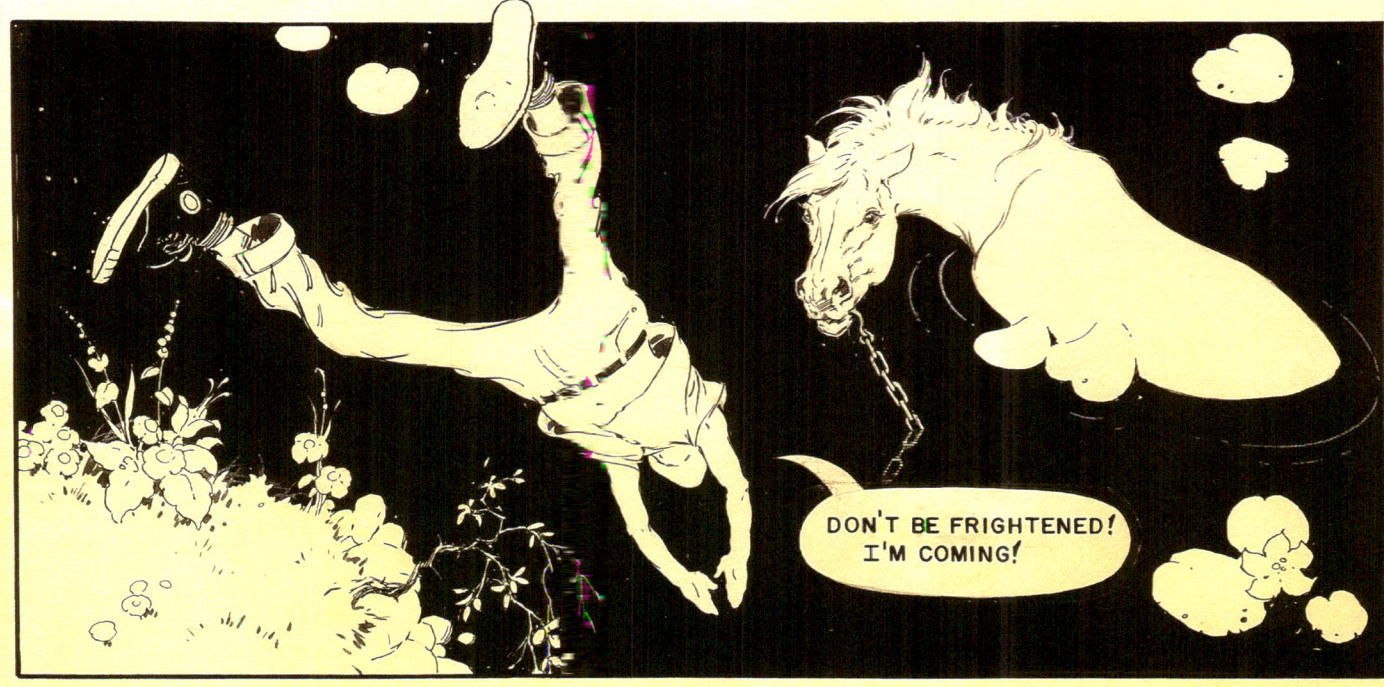

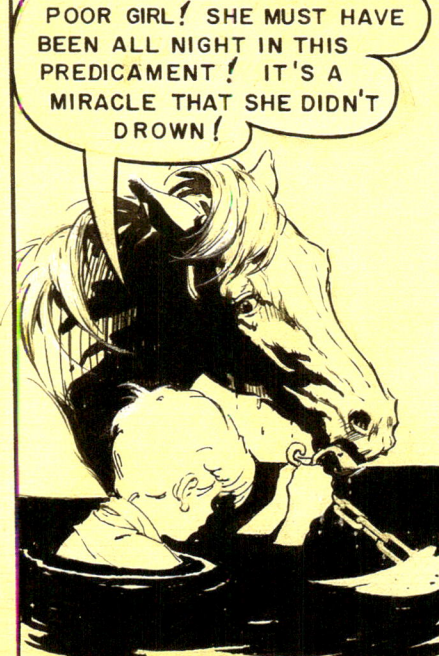

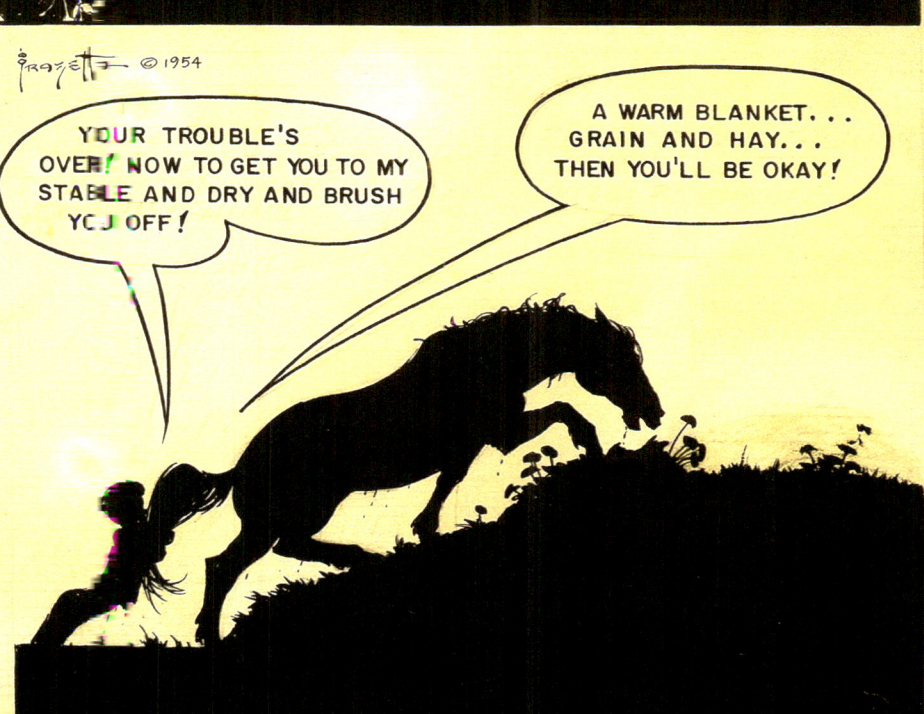

APEMAN
Cover and interior to
Tarzan and the
Castaways
Pen and ink,
1965

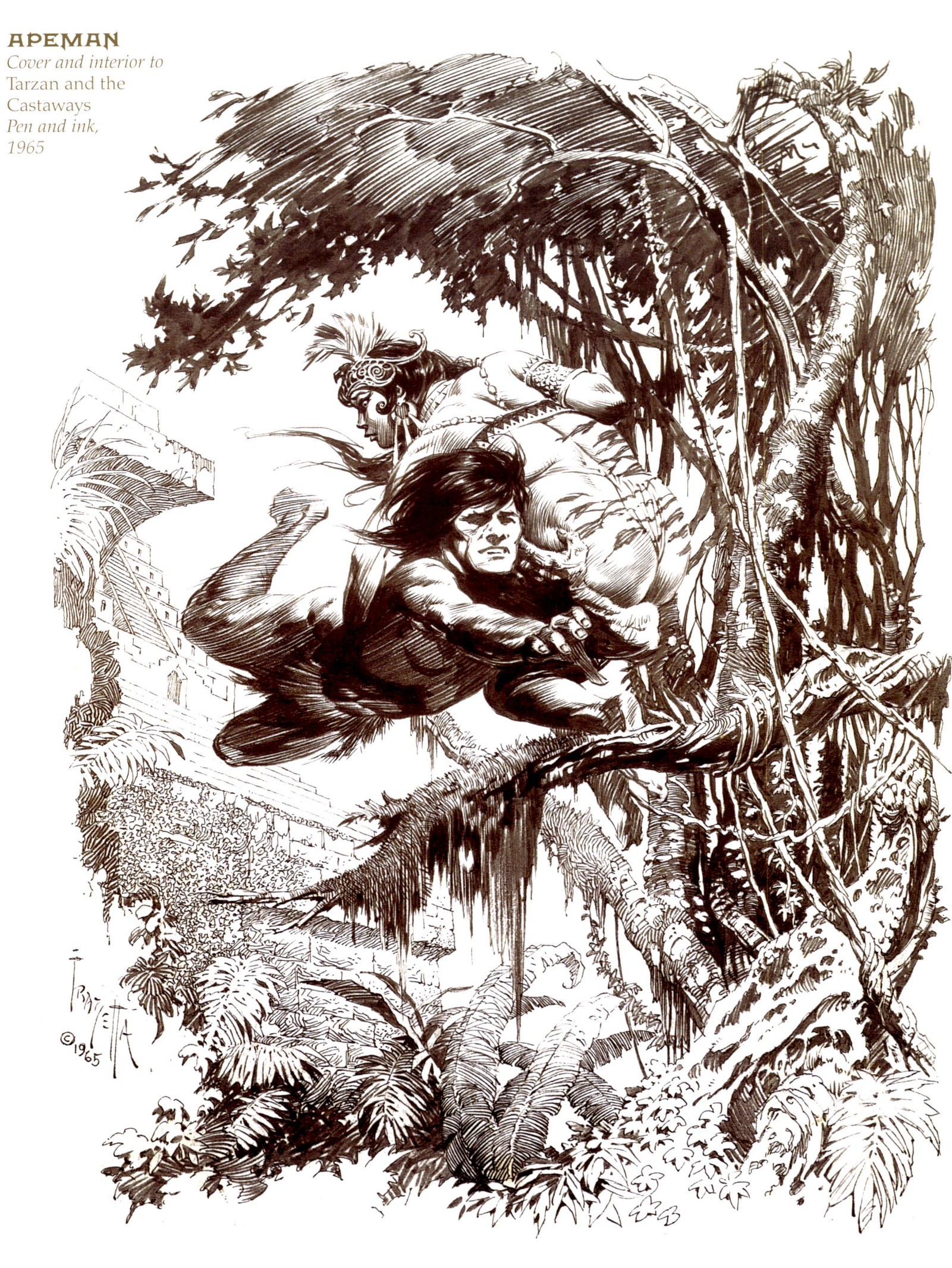

STONE AGE
Pen and ink, 1962
Cover and frontis to Tarzan at the Earth's Core
(Canaveral Press, 1962)

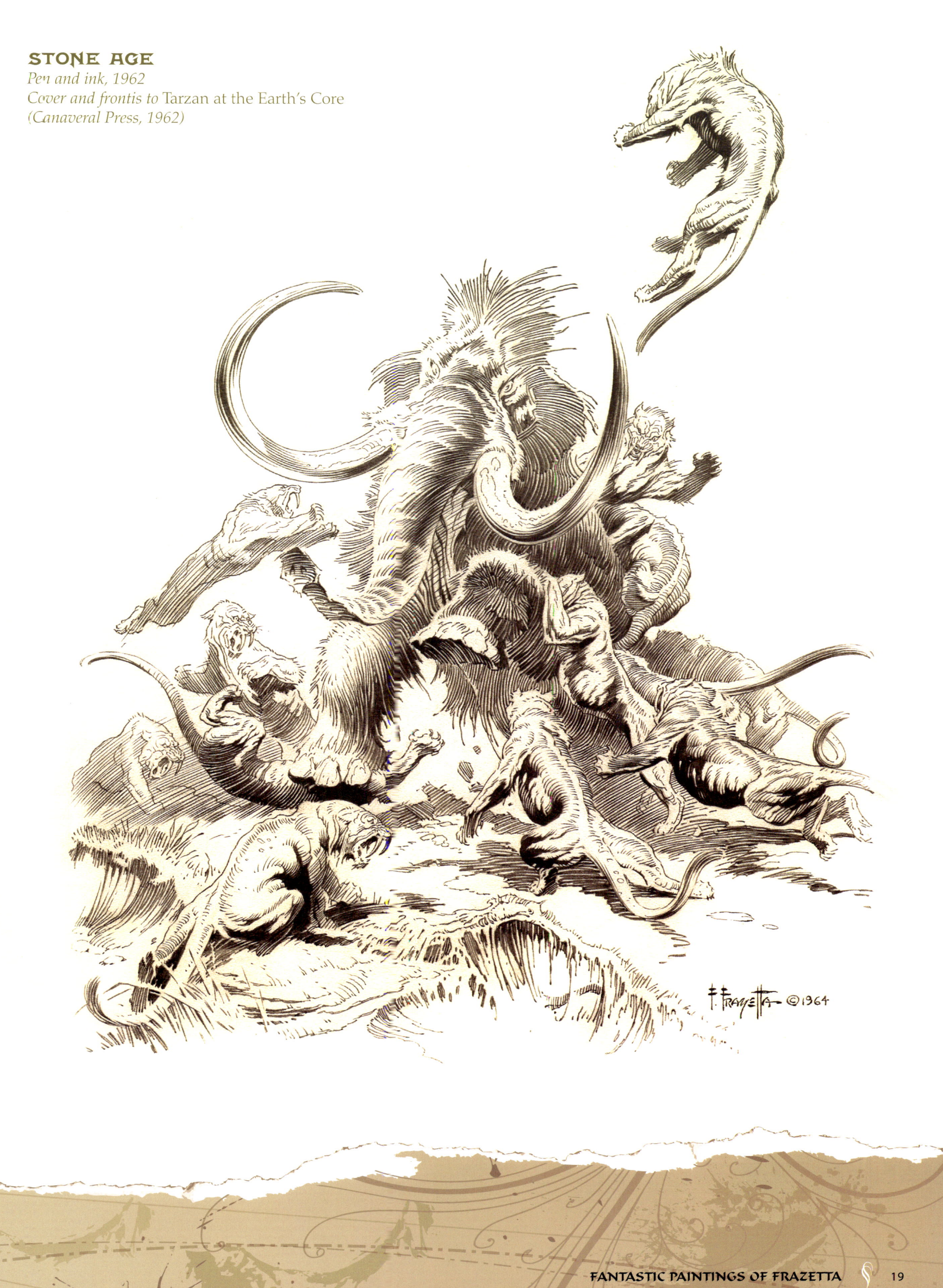

As the more recent books, including *Frazetta Sketchbook* volumes I and II as well as *The Sensuous Frazetta*, have focused on rare, often previously unpublished material, it has been some time since a major collection of prime, Frazetta oil paintings were readily available in print. In brainstorming this new collection, we have looked back to that original, groundbreaking collection, *The Fantastic Art of Frank Frazetta*, for inspiration. In some regards, this new book can be considered a revised edition of that grand bestseller from the golden, advent dawn of Frazetta popularity. But we have more than doubled the number of images, replaced just a few with newer and/or rarer items, incorporated more lavish graphic design and many newer production techniques. But while the 1975 book was only available at 9"x 11"and only available to the masses in paperback (the vintage hardcover was limited and few people were lucky enough to know about it, let alone acquire one), this grand new collection is readily available in hardcover and at the much more substantial 10.5"x 14.625"; the largest size ever for any Frazetta book available through major retail outlets.

This volume's cover image is particularly timely and notable. The EGYPTIAN QUEEN painting has also been called "Frazetta's Mona Lisa." In their May 17, 2019 article entitled, "Frank Frazetta's 'Egyptian Queen' Sets $5.4 Million World Record,"the venerable publication *Antiques and The Arts Weekly* (est 1963) said, "EGYPTIAN QUEEN, Frank Frazetta's original art painted for *Eerie* magazine #23, sold at $5.4 million, with premium, on Thursday,

George Lucas told me that my Famous Funnies covers were an influence on STAR WARS. Specifically, #213 on Chewbacca and #214 on the Death Star

FRANK FRAZETTA

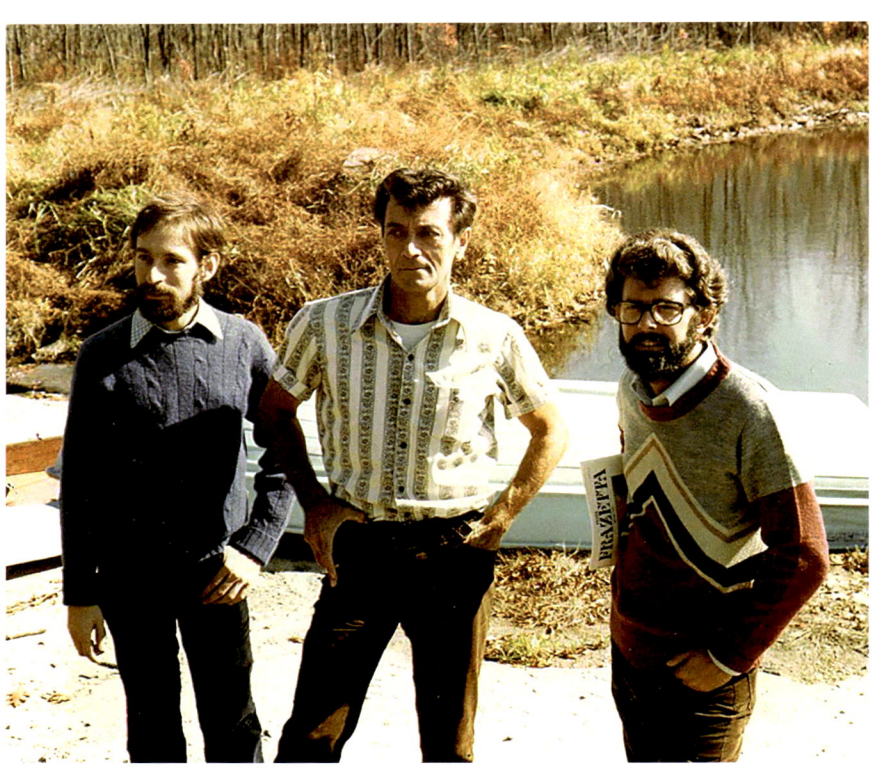

In 1979, Conan movie co-producer, Edward Summer took his friend George Lucas to meet Frank Frazetta.

May 16, setting a world record at Heritage Auctions; the genre-defining masterpiece of American fantasy art is now the most expensive piece of original comicbook art ever auctioned." They went on to say, "The 1969 fantasy painting … bests the previous record… $1.79 million paid for Frazetta's DEATH DEALER VI, 1990, which was set… May 2018." According to *Antiques and The Arts*, "The masterpiece is credited more than any other with revolutionizing fantasy illustration in American art." In addition to a world record, the painting also set a house record as the most expensive item ever sold by Heritage Auctions. Heritage Auctions vice president Todd Hignite said, "This result elevates Frank Frazetta's art into the stratosphere of visual narrative art on a par with the likes of Norman Rockwell, Maxfield Parrish and other luminaries."

Also of keen interest is that inspired by Frazetta's EGYPTIAN QUEEN,"Star Wars"costume designers Aggie Guerard Rodgers and Nilo Rodis-Jamero designed a related outfit which Princess Leia wore when she was enslaved by the villain, Jabba the Hutt, in the now-classic 1983 George Lucas film "Return of the Jedi." "Jedi" is reported to have grossed between $475 million and $572 million worldwide. The Box Office Mojo website estimates that the film sold over 80 million tickets in the US in its initial theatrical run.

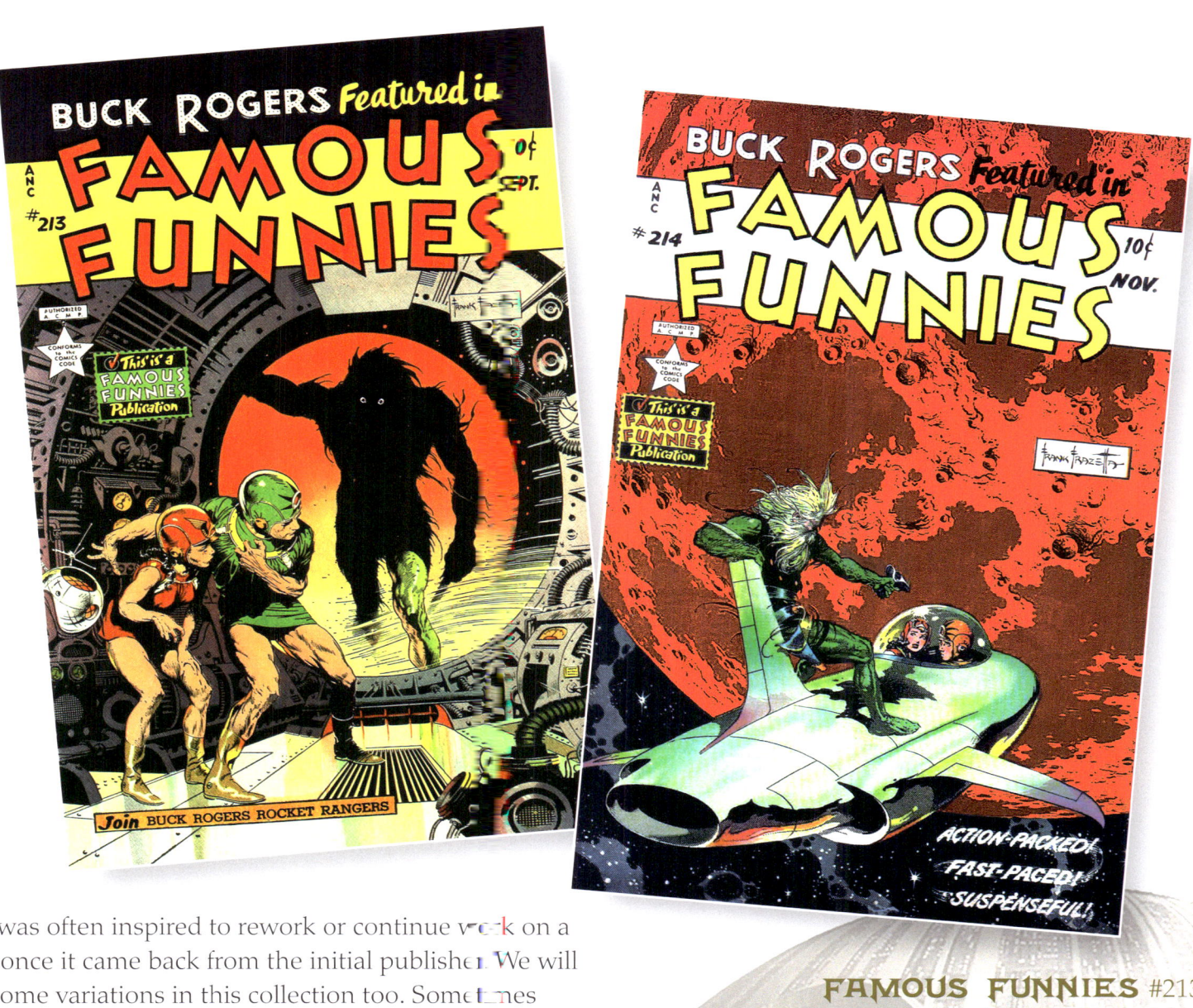

Frazetta was often inspired to rework or continue work on a painting once it came back from the initial publisher. We will explore some variations in this collection too. Sometimes presenting the work as it is today and sometimes with a rare early take that either hasn't been seen in decades, or possibly ever, in print. As with the original 1970s volumes, this is the launch of a series. To echo Betty Ballantine we persevere, in this book and in future volumes, to do justice to the remarkable qualities of this very extraordinary artist.

FAMOUS FUNNIES #213 & #214
original 1954 comicbook covers.
Frazetta said Lucas cited these as inspiration
for Chewbacca and the Death Star.

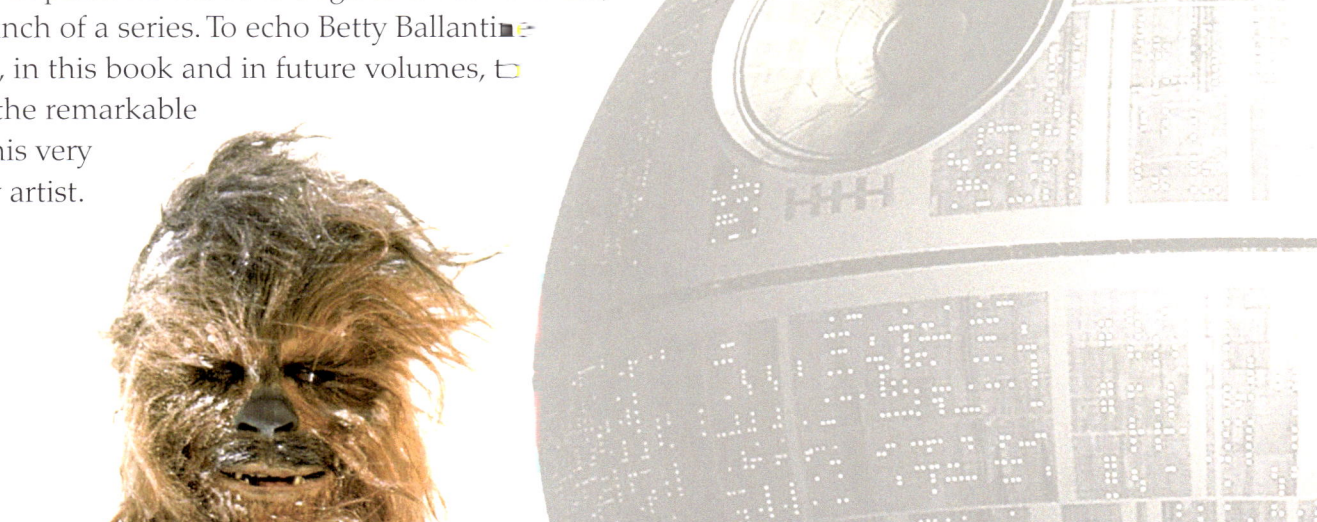

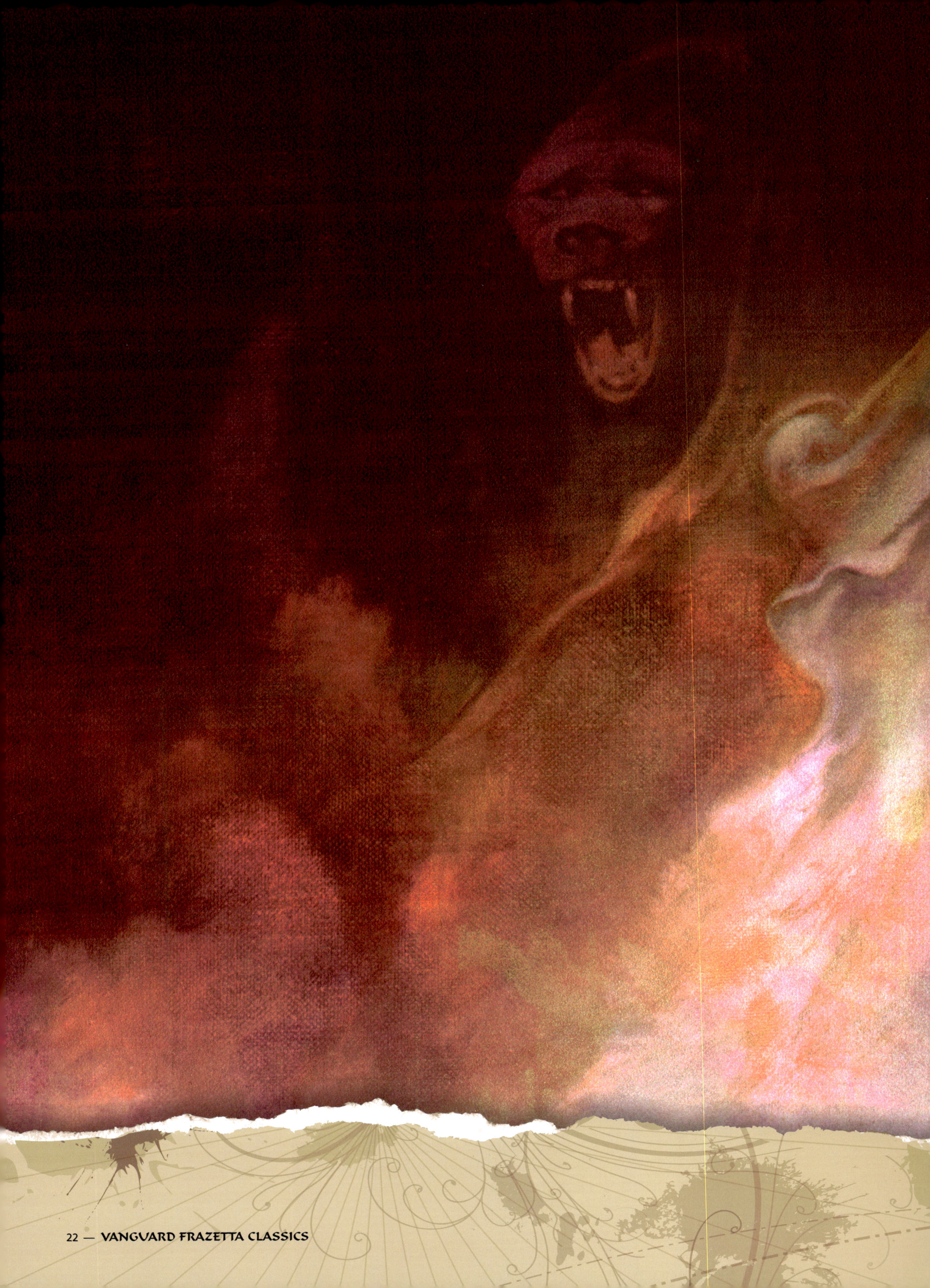

GALLERY OF PAINTINGS

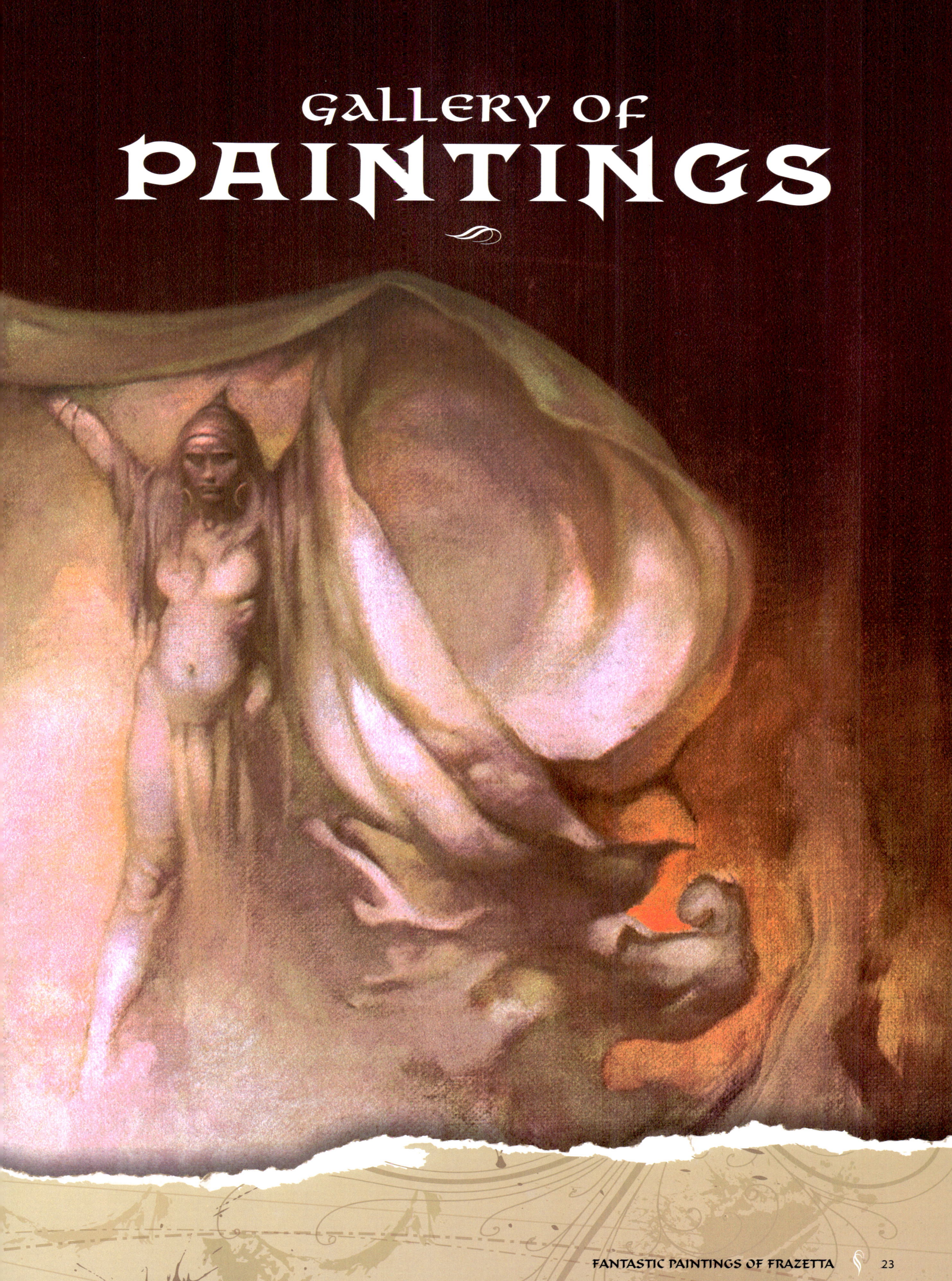

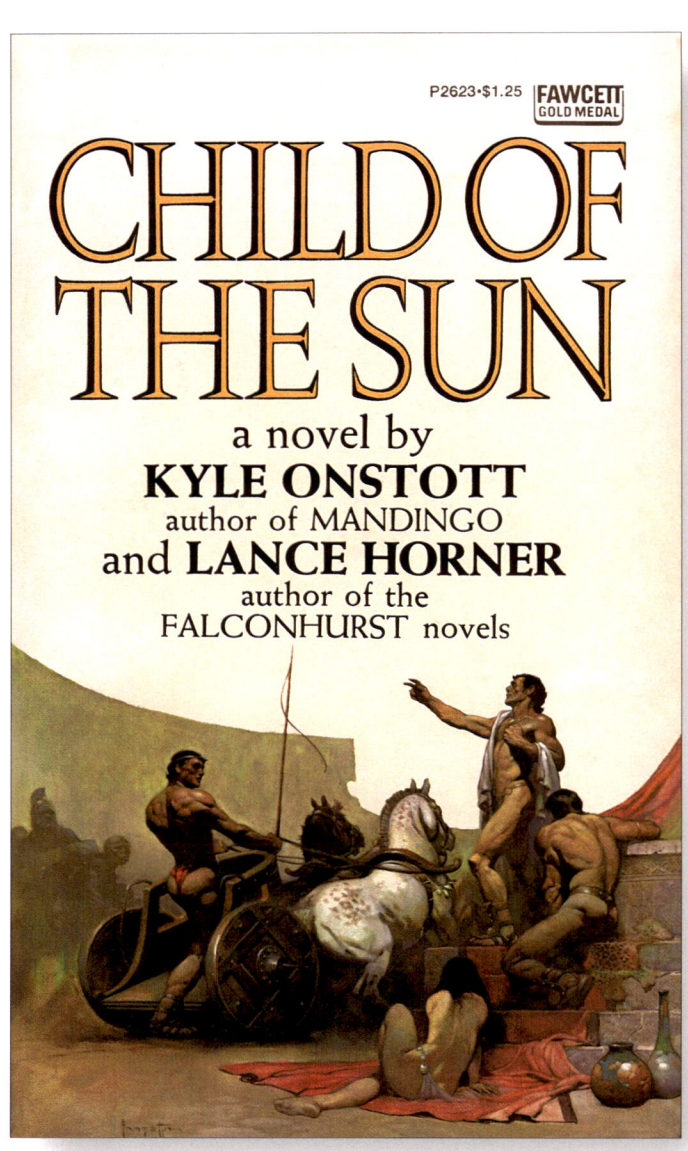

ROMAN CHARIOT

Oil on masonite, 1972
First printed as the cover to
Child of the Sun *(Fawcett, 1972)*

Sold for $495,000 at Heritage, October 2019
Imaged by Heritage Auctions (HA.com)

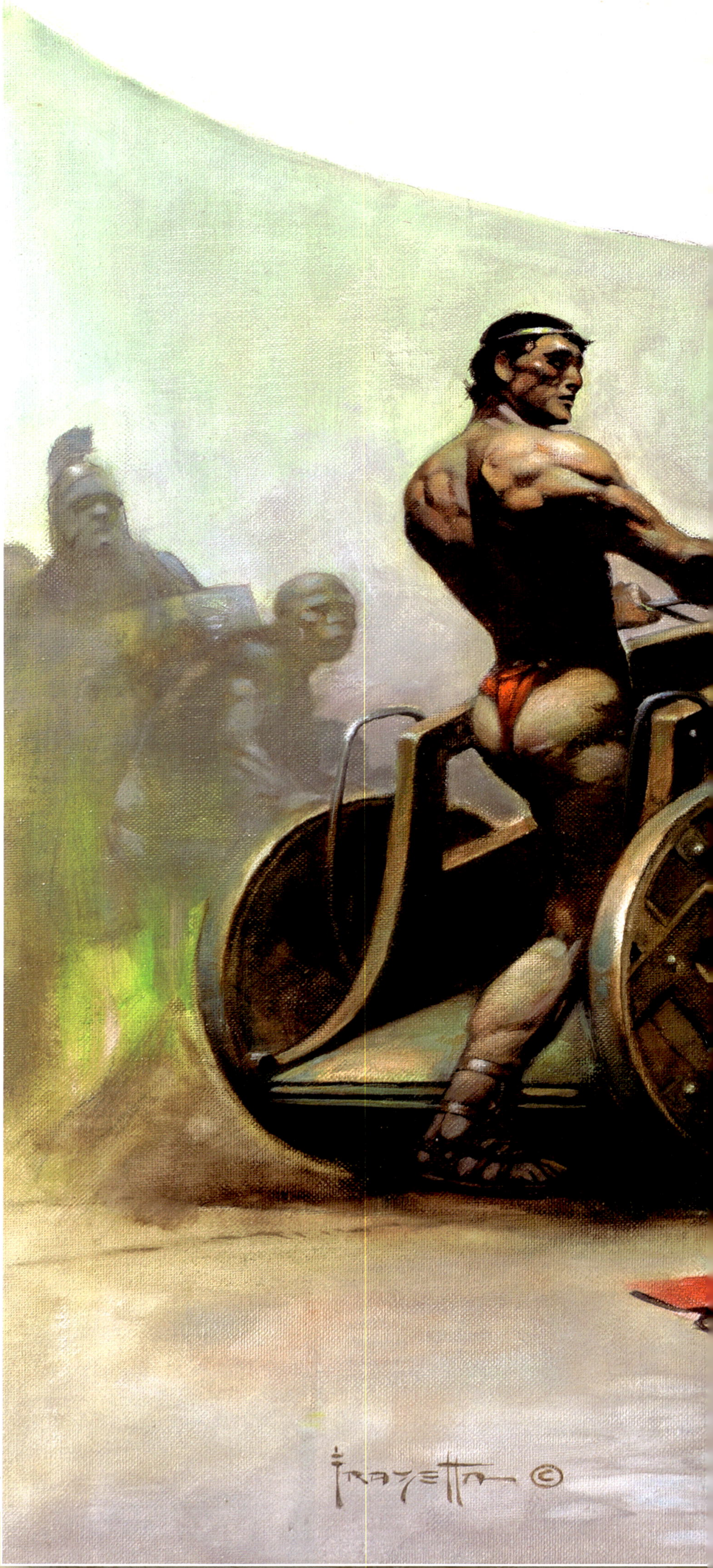

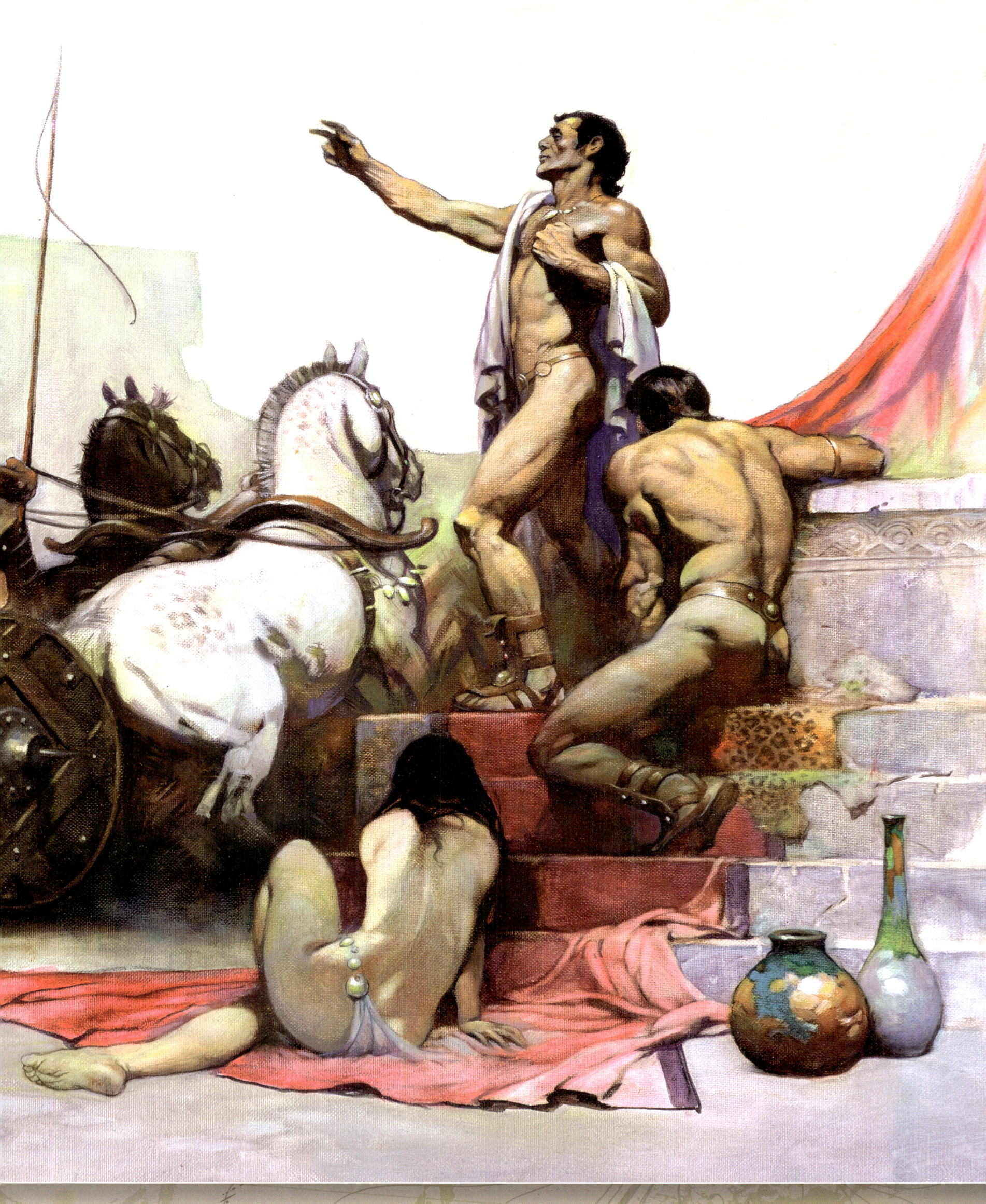

*This was an almost finished piece.
My grandfather realized he didn't have
enough room to do the reflection in the
water, so he had to repaint it. Luckily
my father gave him a new canvas so he
didn't paint over this original version.
This is really the best example of a work
in progress, and has some real
charm of its own.*

—— WILLIAM FRAZETTA

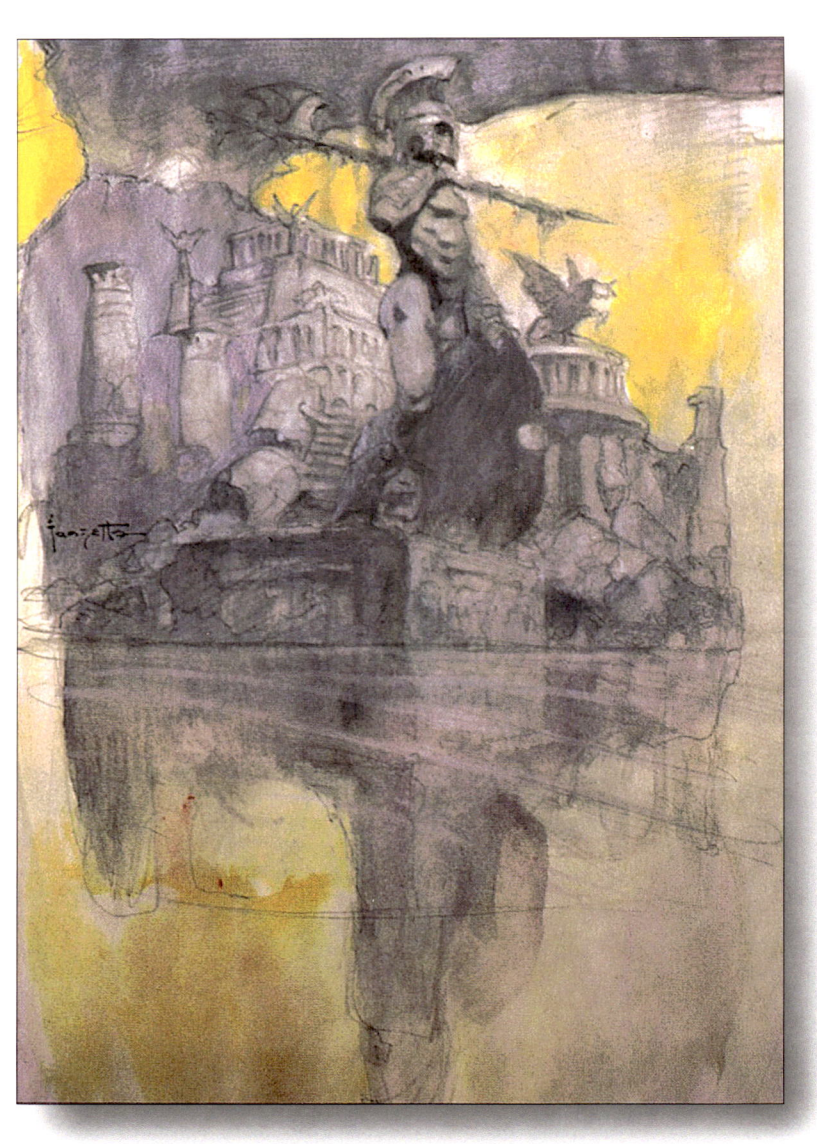

ATLANTIS *preliminary*
Watercolor, 5" x 7"
First printed as the cover to
Qua Brot *fanzine*
(Kyle Hailey, 1985)

ATLANTIS I
Oil on canvas, 1972
First printed as an interior,
2017 Frazetta Calendar
(Sellers Pub., 2016)

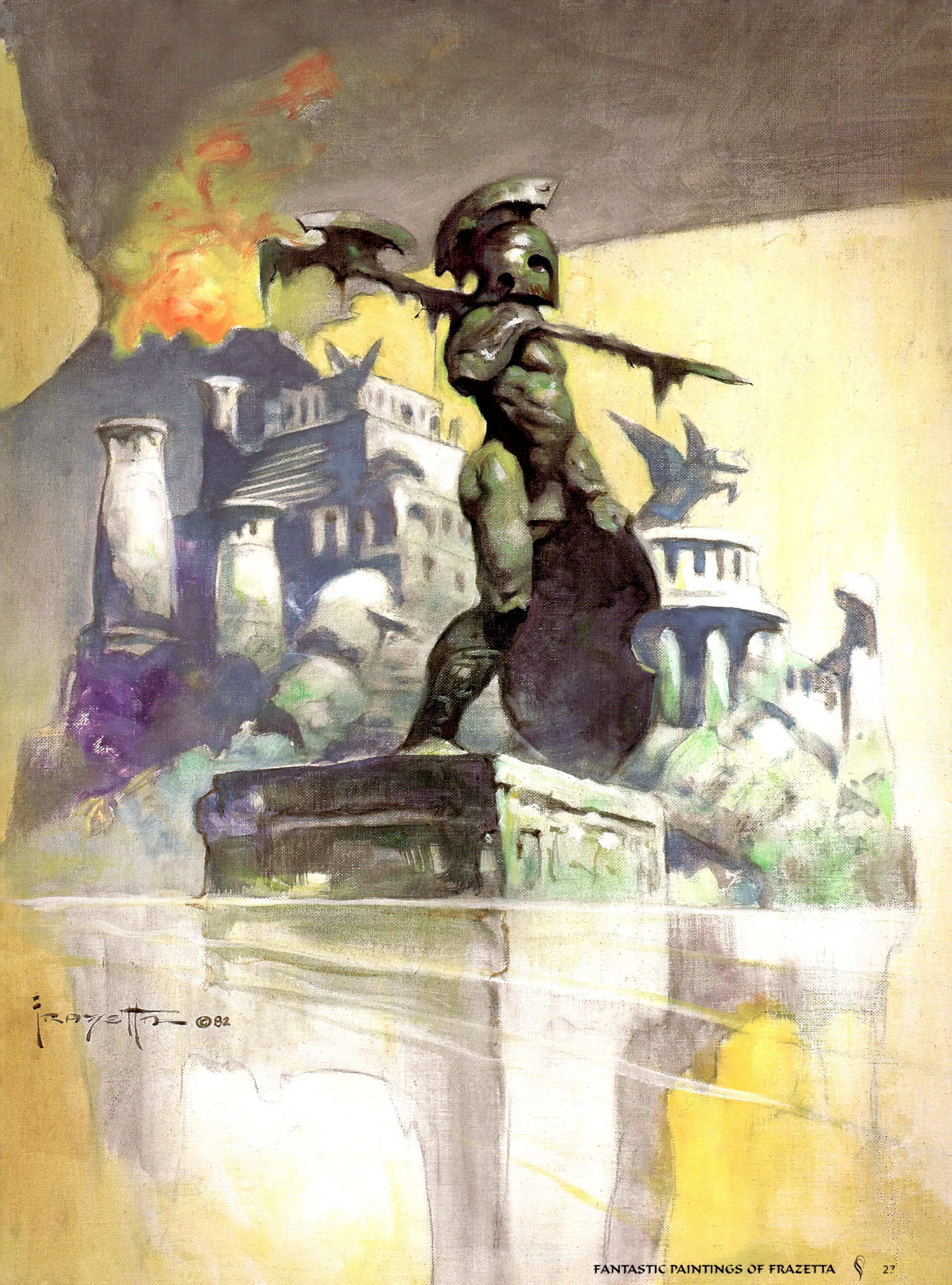

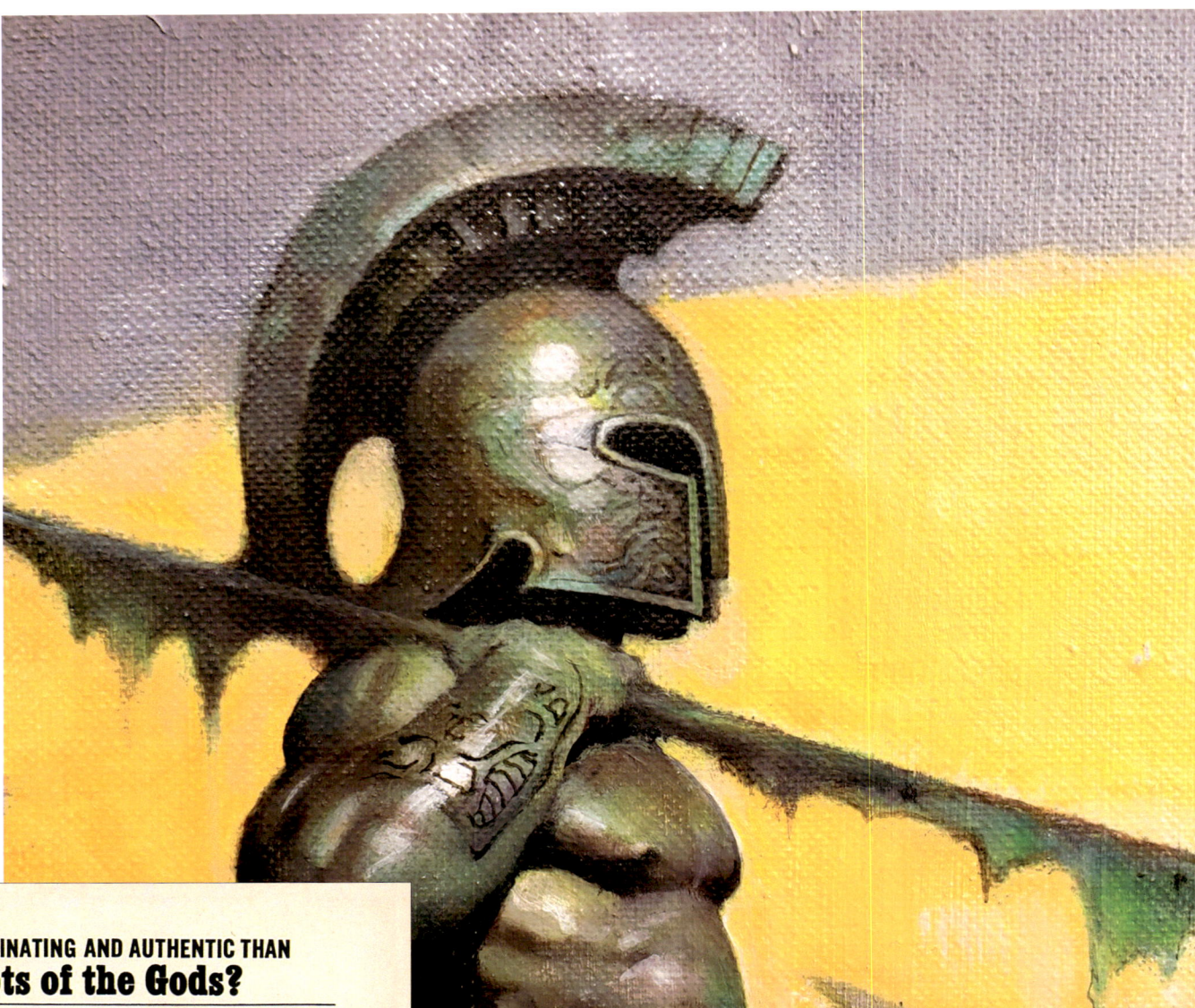

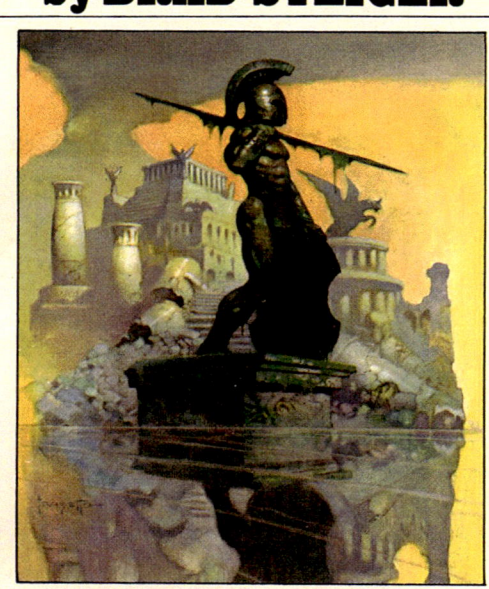

EVEN MORE FASCINATING AND AUTHENTIC THAN
Chariots of the Gods?
ATLANTIS RISING
by **BRAD STEIGER**

DELL · 1182 · 95c

THE AMAZING BOOK THAT GIVES PROOF OF:

A SUPER-RACE THAT CAME BEFORE MAN

A SUBTERRANEAN CIVILIZATION OF INNER EARTH
THAT STILL MAY EXIST

THE TRUTH ABOUT THE MIGHTY EMPIRE OF ATLANTIS AND
ITS IMPORTANT MEANING TO US TODAY

ATLANTIS II
Oil on academy board, 1972
First printed as the cover to Atlantis Rising
(Dell, 1974)

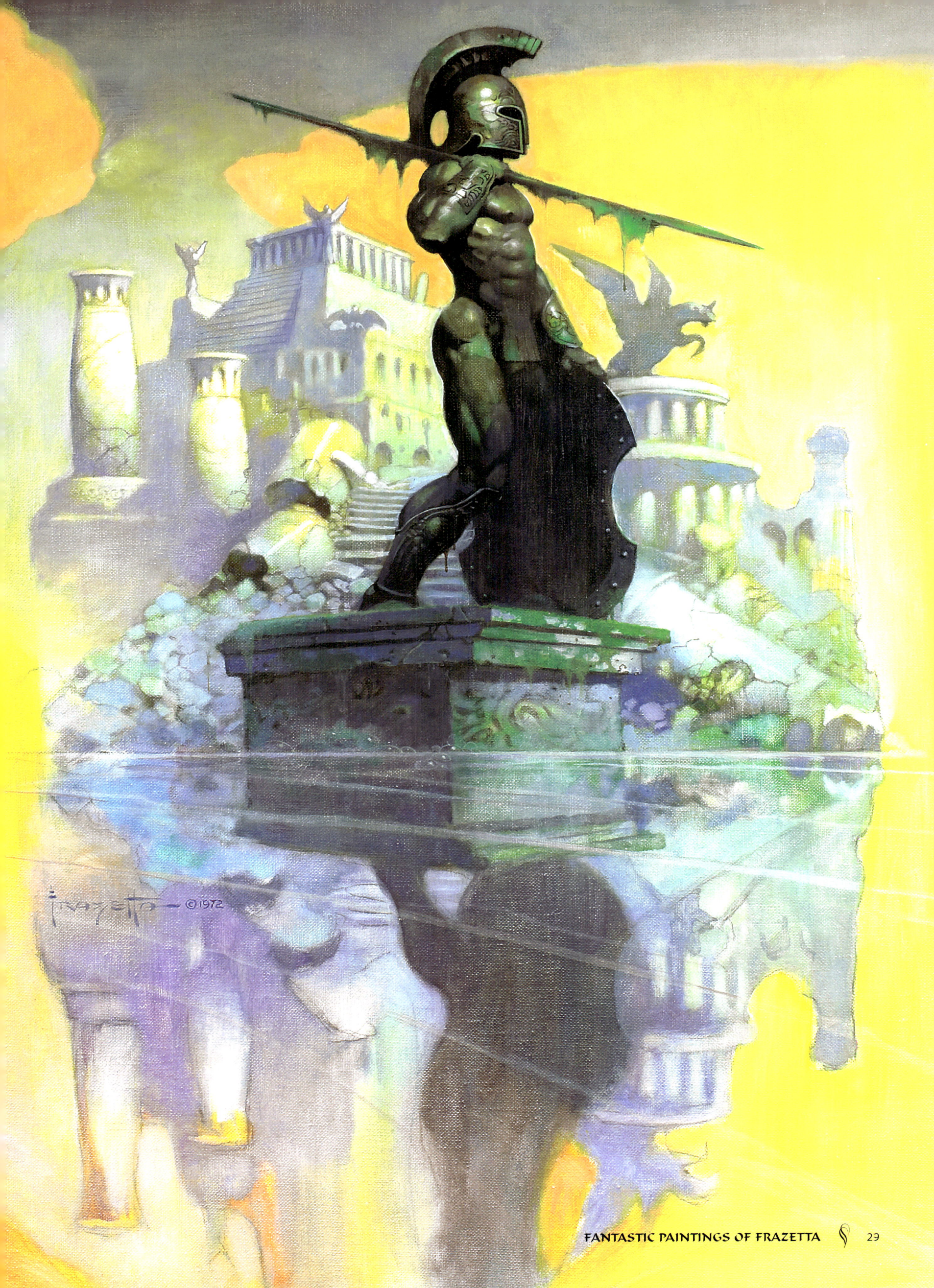

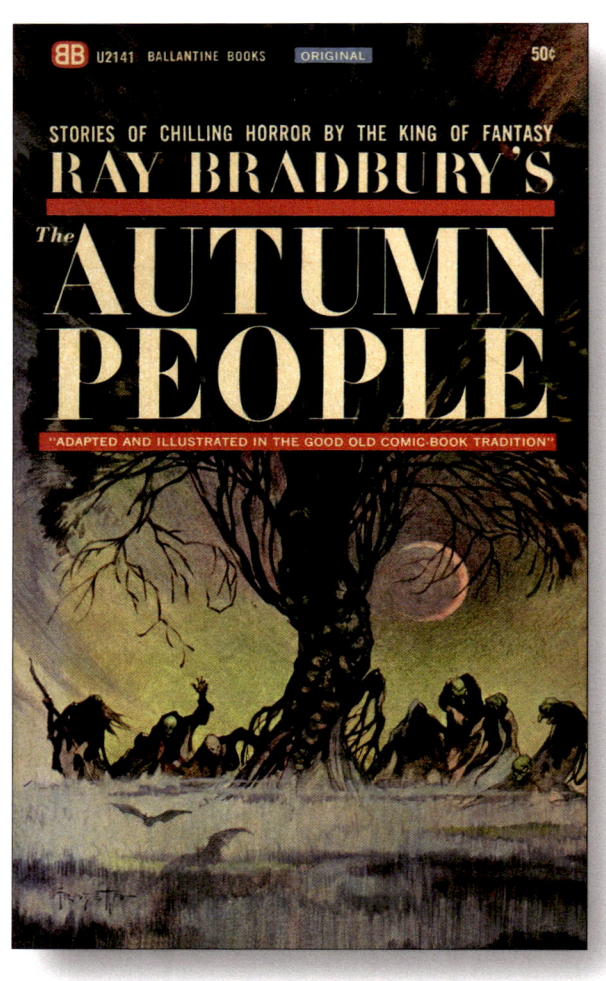

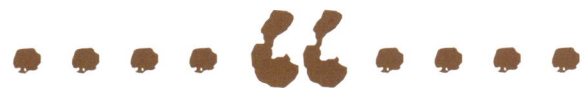

I've stated upon many occasions that the magic of Frank Frazetta parallels the magic of my stories."

RAY BRADBURY

from Jerry Weist's book Ray Bradbury: An Illustrated Life

From 1950 to 1954, 31 of Bradbury's stories were adapted by EC Comics. Sixteen of these were collected in the Ballantine paperbacks, The Autumn People *(1965) and* Tomorrow Midnight *(1966) with cover illustrations by Frazetta.*

Immediate Left: This original version of STRANDED, was painted in 1965 but remained unpublished in any book until Frank Frazetta Book Two, in 1977. Frazetta released it as a poster (#46) in the '70s and, as seen here, in its second rare book/magazine appearance, as a 1990 cover in Roger Broughton's revival of the ACG comics line, Adventures Into the Unknown #2.

Opposite:
STRANDED
(revised)
Oil on illustration board, 1966; First printed as the cover to Tomorrow Midnight *(Ballantine, 1966)*

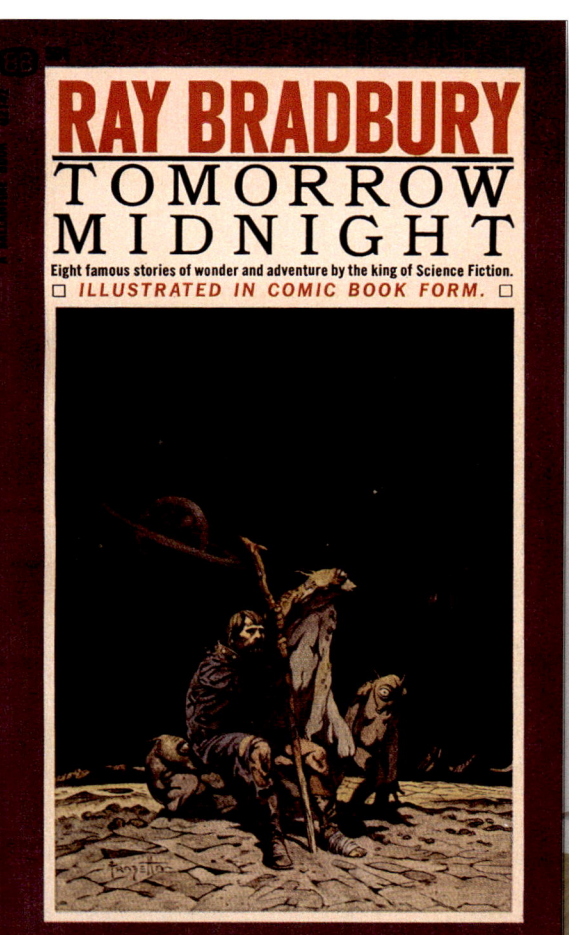

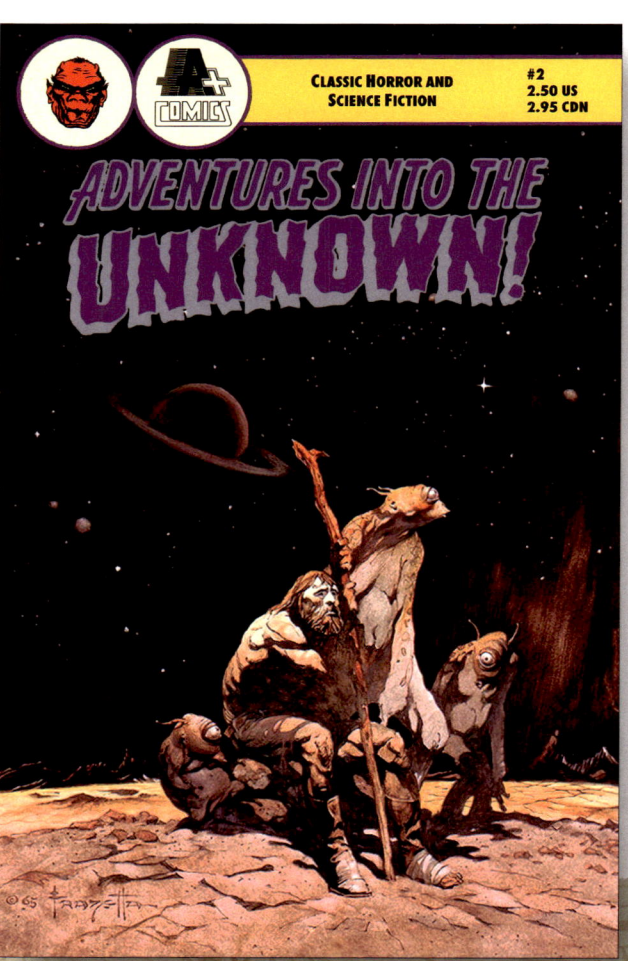

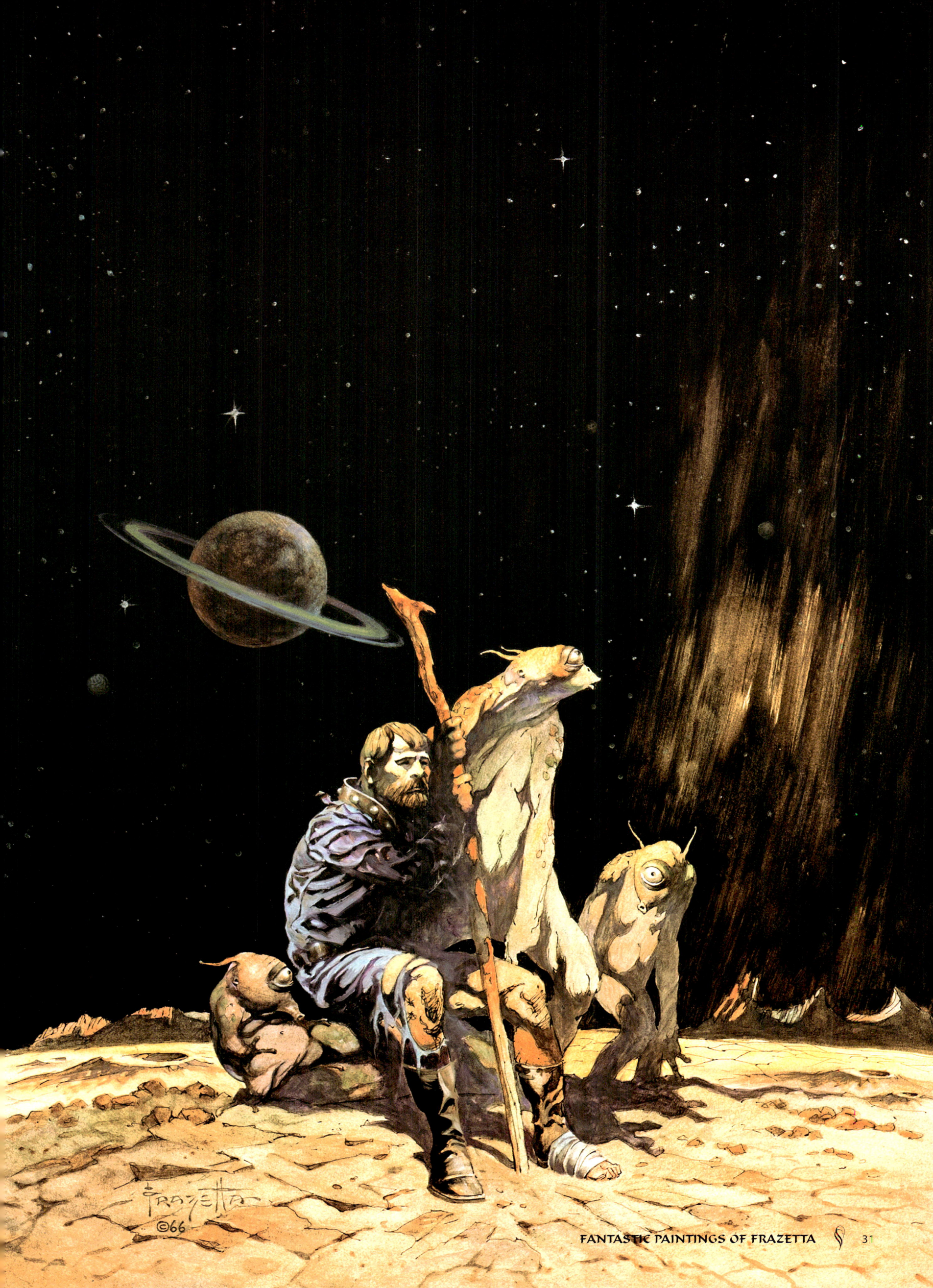

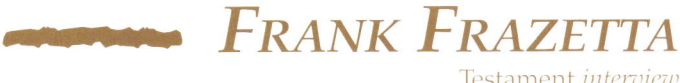

When we offered 'Spiderman' as a poster people went ape. They loved it. And I started getting letters from people asking about the green swirl: What was it? What did it mean? Was it an alien? They were reading all sorts of things into that patch of green. I didn't have the heart to tell them I just thought the painting needed a little green for interest. I wasn't trying to create a mystery.

FRANK FRAZETTA

Testament *interview*

SPIDERMAN
Oil on academy board, 1966
First printed as the cover to Nightwalk
(Banner, 1967)

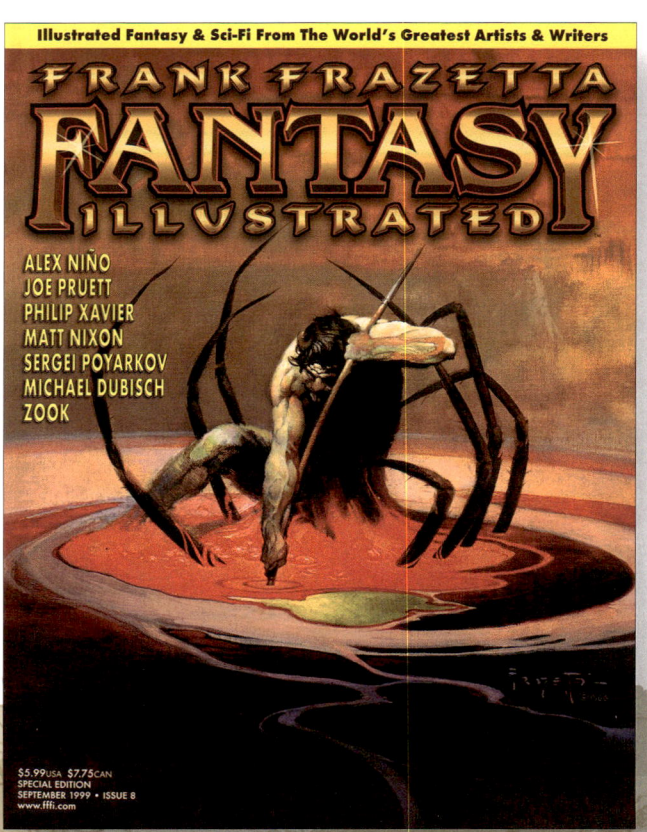

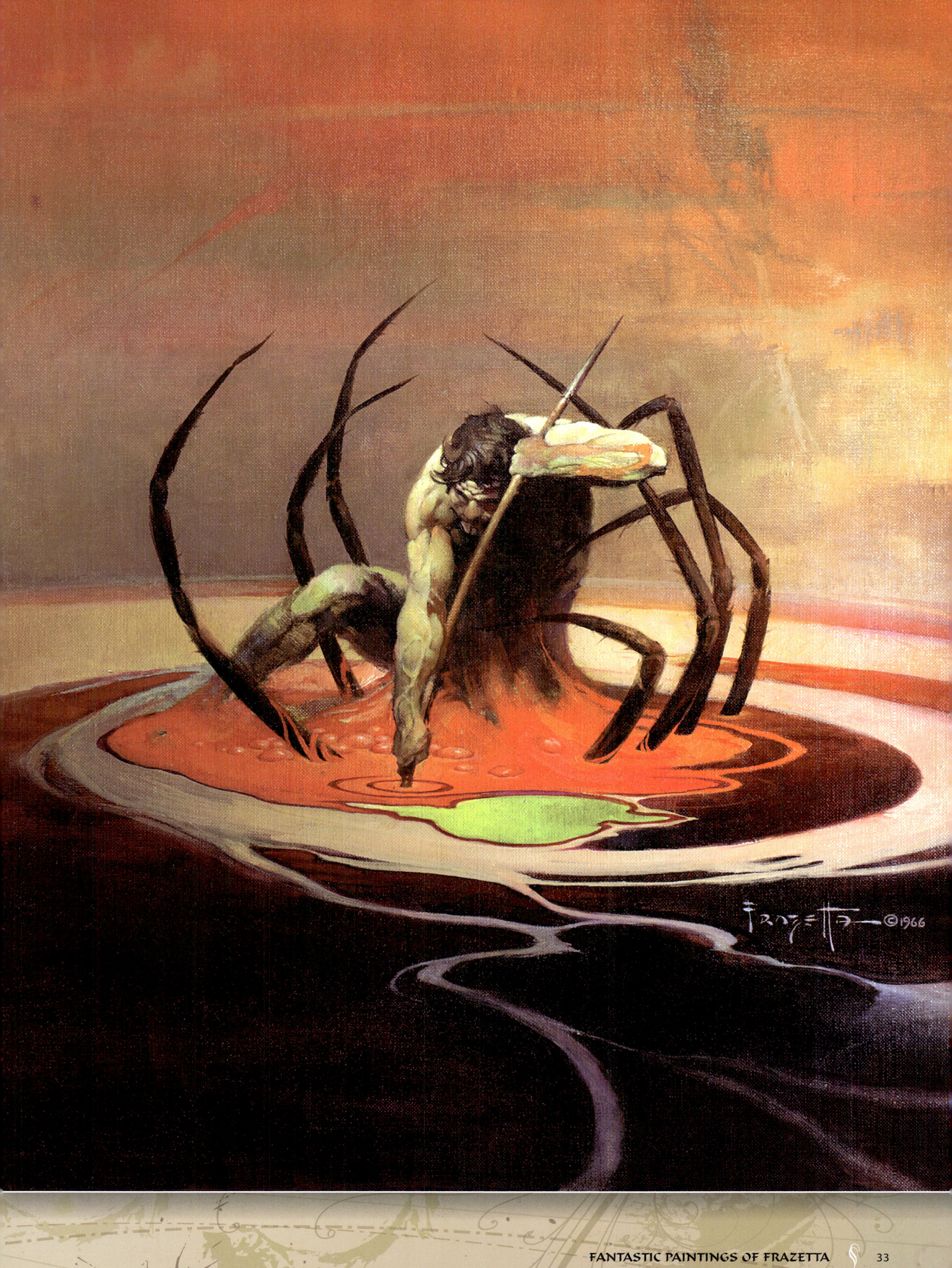

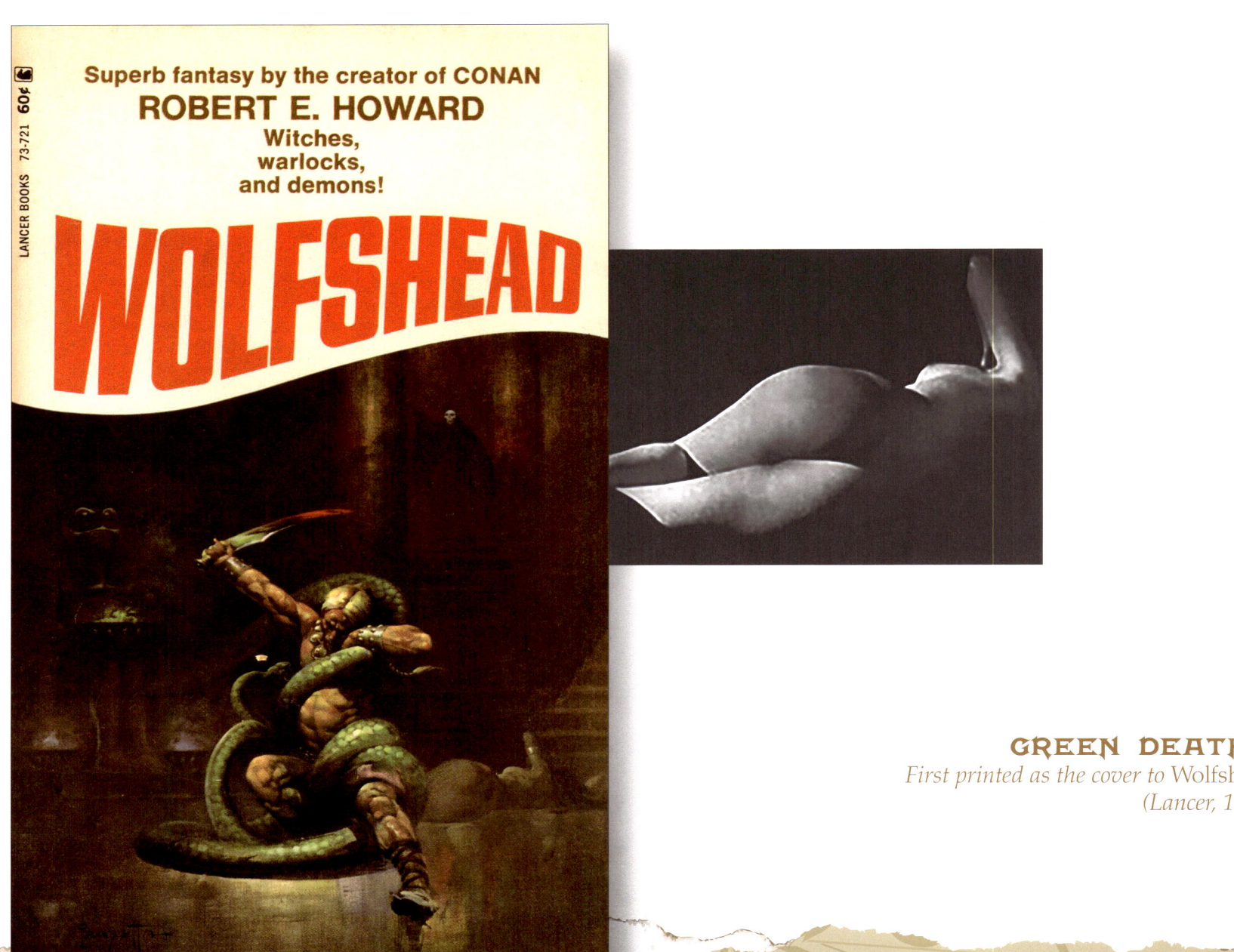

Unlike most illustrators who tend to regularly work from photo reference, Frazetta only occasionally used reference, and was possibly less dependent upon it than any other major realistic illustrator. Frazetta also had a near-photographic memory. He could see something once and if he liked it, it stayed with him. Besides being exposed to the work of Golden Age illustrators in his youth, as an adult, his friend Roy Krenkel would frequently show Frank works by great, old painters and illustrators. N.C. Wyeth, Willy Pogany, J. Allen St. John, Heinrich Kley, Howard Pyle, Hal Foster, Zdenek Burian, Josep Segrelles and Walt Disney are all ghosts of inspiration that might get conjured up into the strange brew of magic revealed through Frazetta's uniquely creative talents.

—— J. DAVID SPURLOCK

Superb fantasy by the creator of CONAN
ROBERT E. HOWARD
Witches,
warlocks,
and demons!

LANCER BOOKS 73-721 60¢

WOLFSHEAD

GREEN DEATH I
First printed as the cover to Wolfshead
(Lancer, 1967)

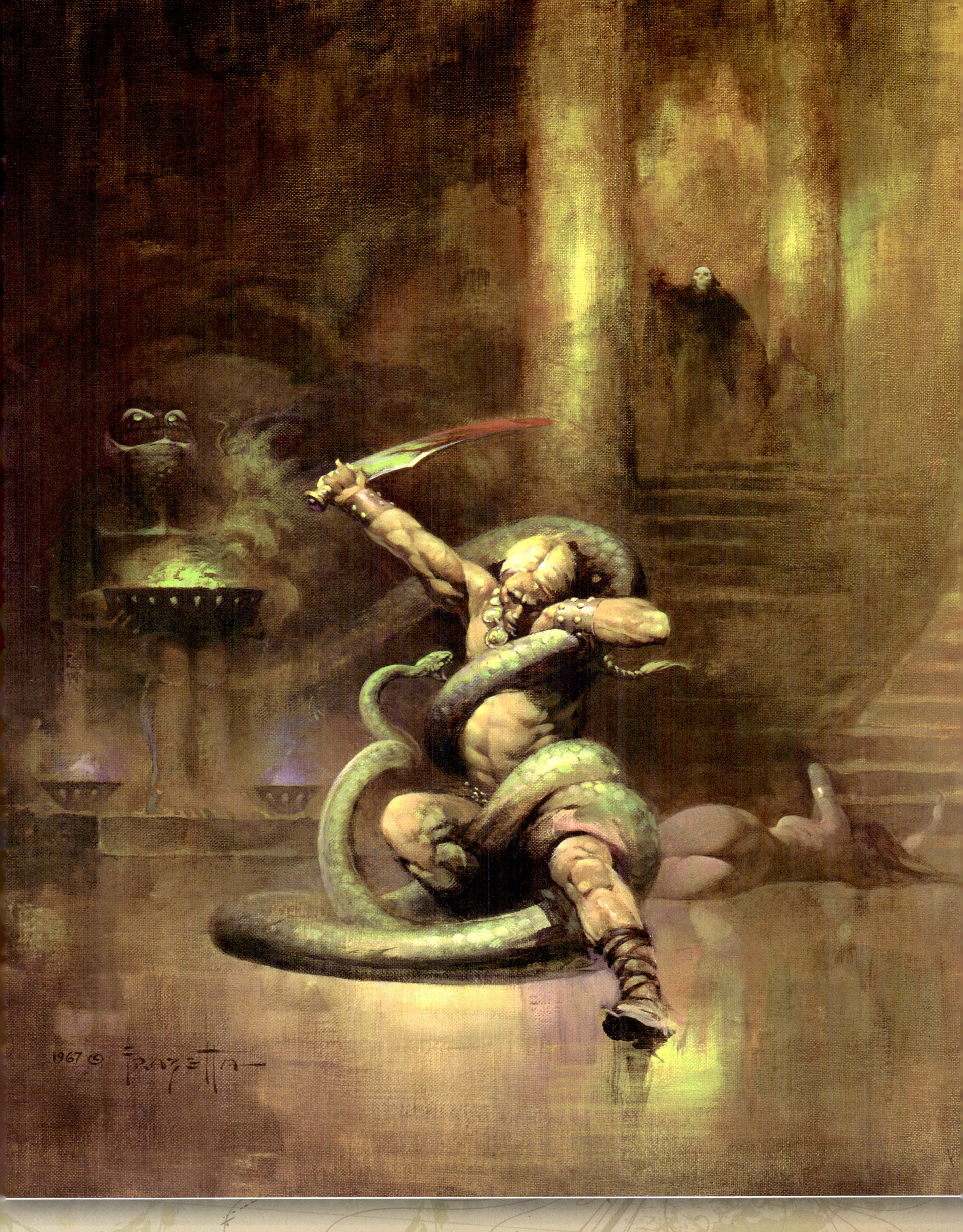

1967 © Frazetta

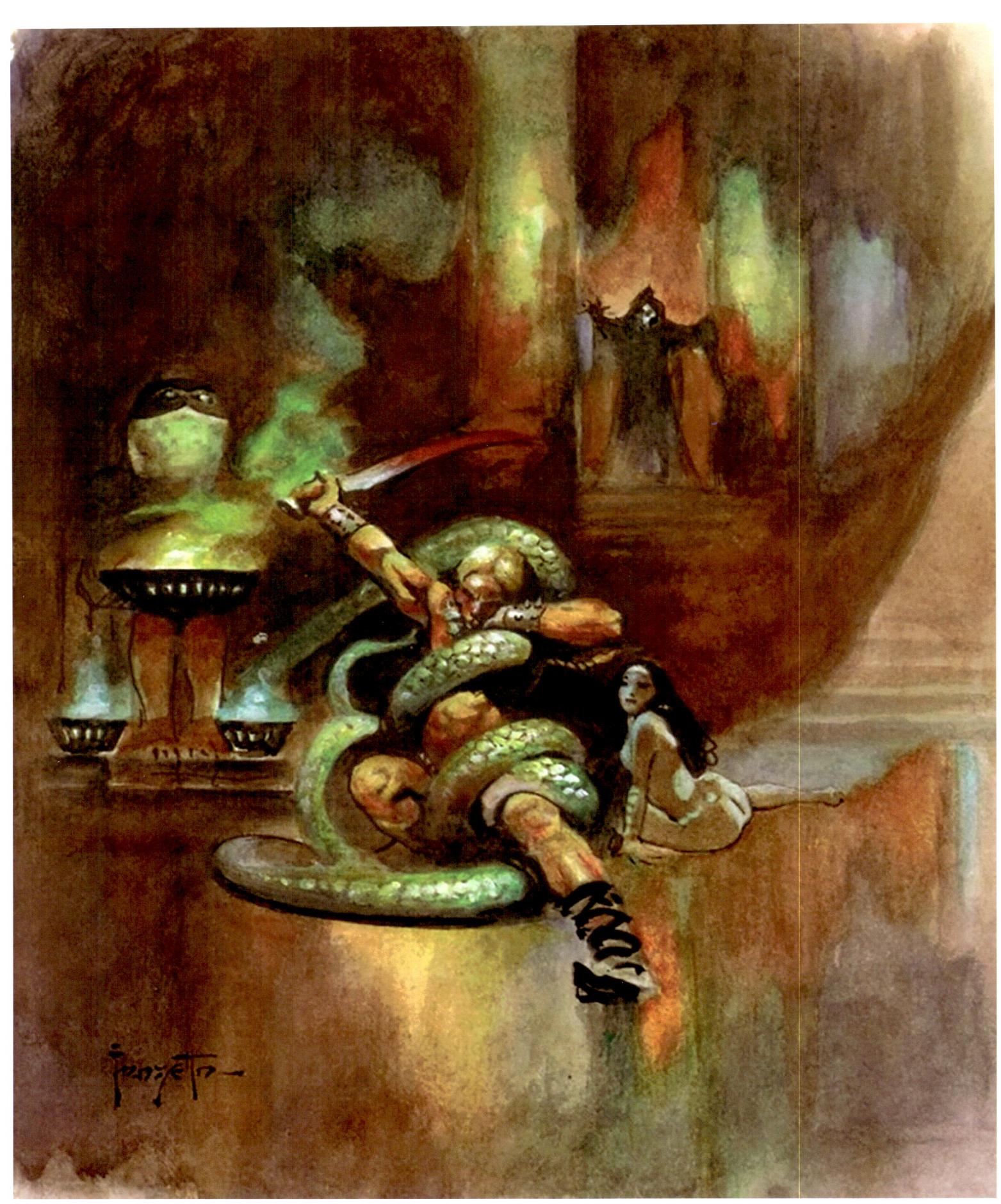

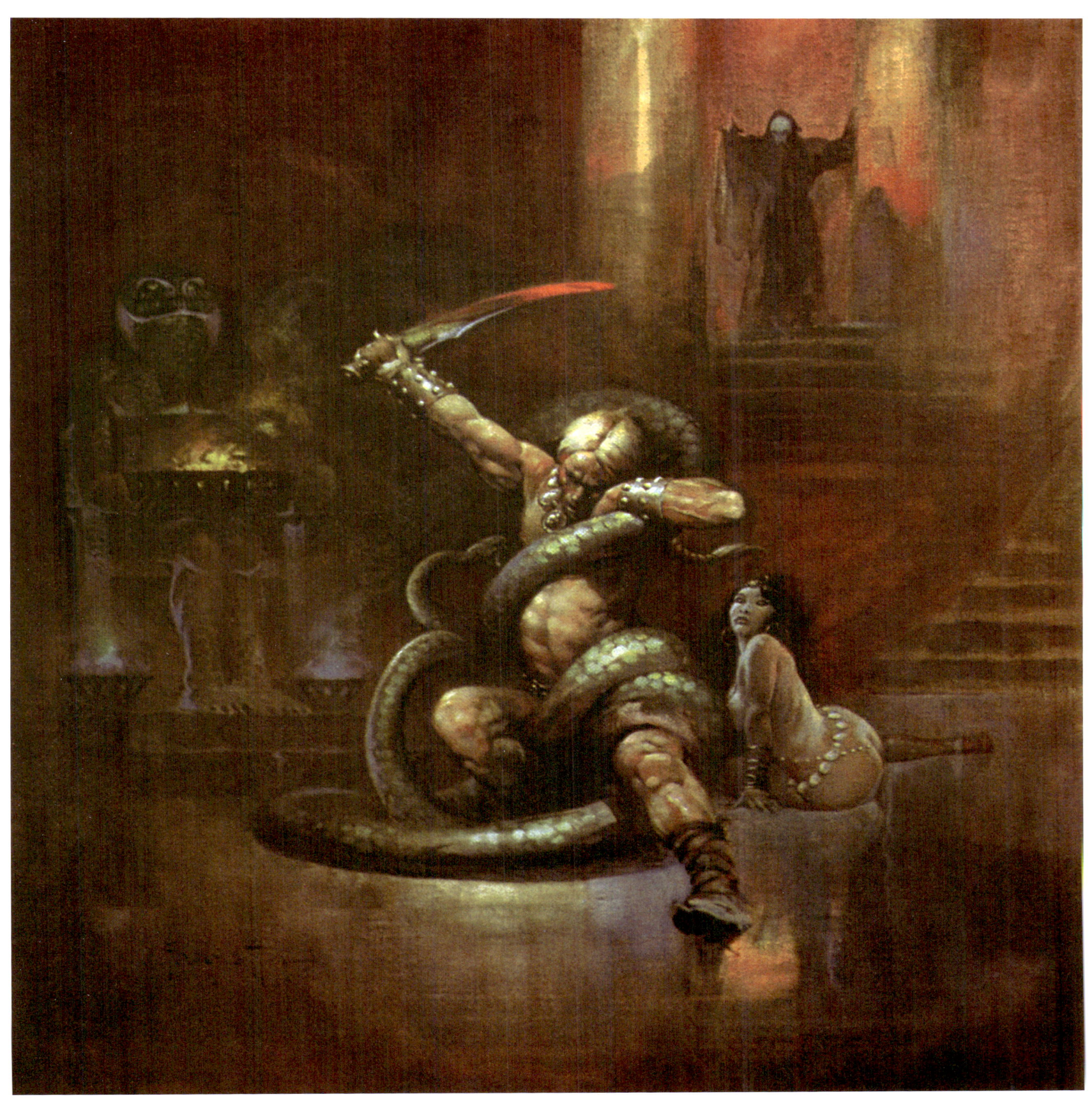

Opposite:
GREEN DEATH II *preliminary*
Previously unpublished, c. 1980

This page:
GREEN DEATH II
Frank Frazetta Book Four, *1980*

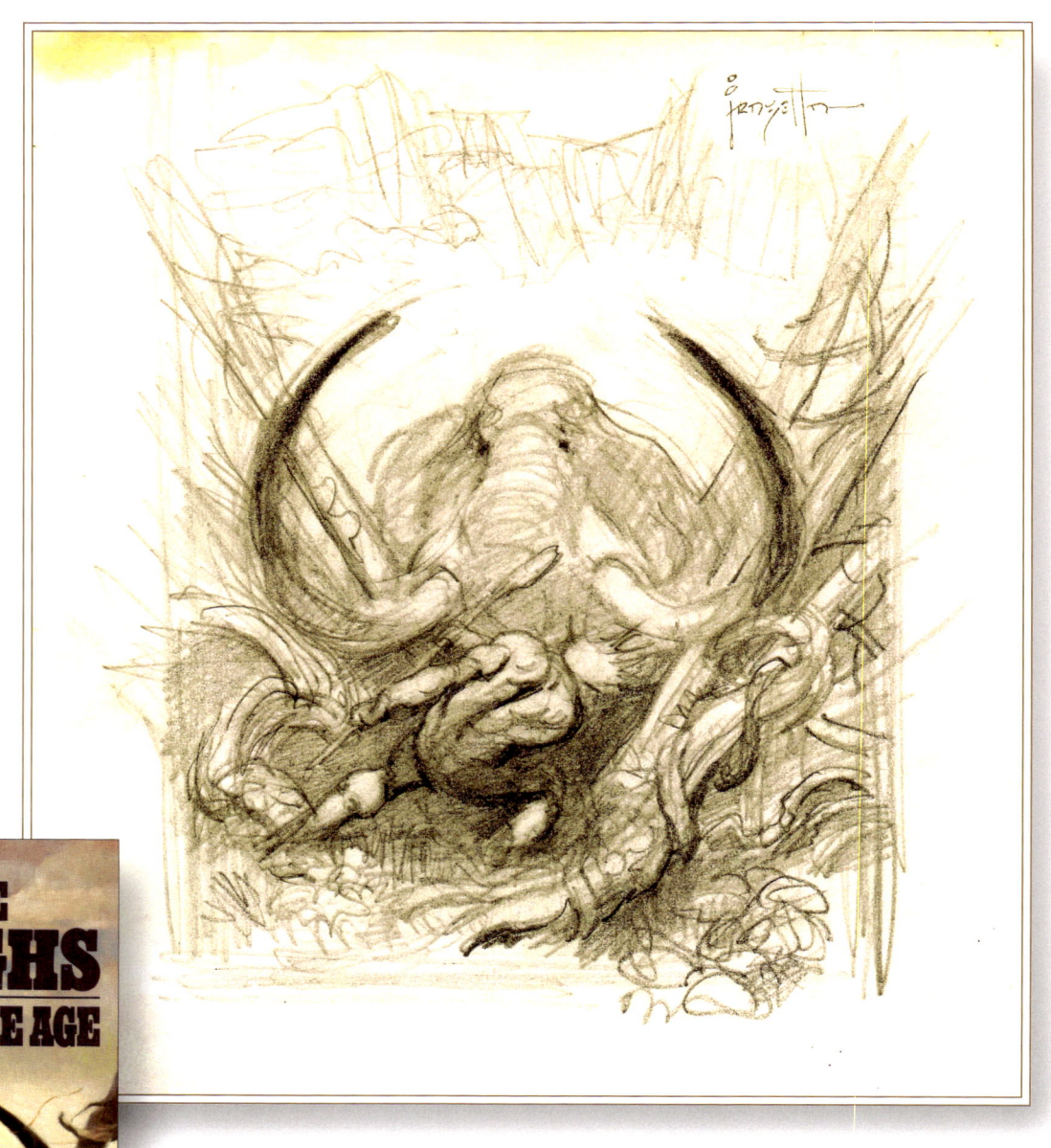

EDGAR RICE
BURROUGHS
BACK TO THE STONE AGE

THE MAMMOTH
Oil on canvas panel, 1972
First printed as the cover to Back to the Stone Age
Above: Preliminary sketch 7.25" x 9.75"

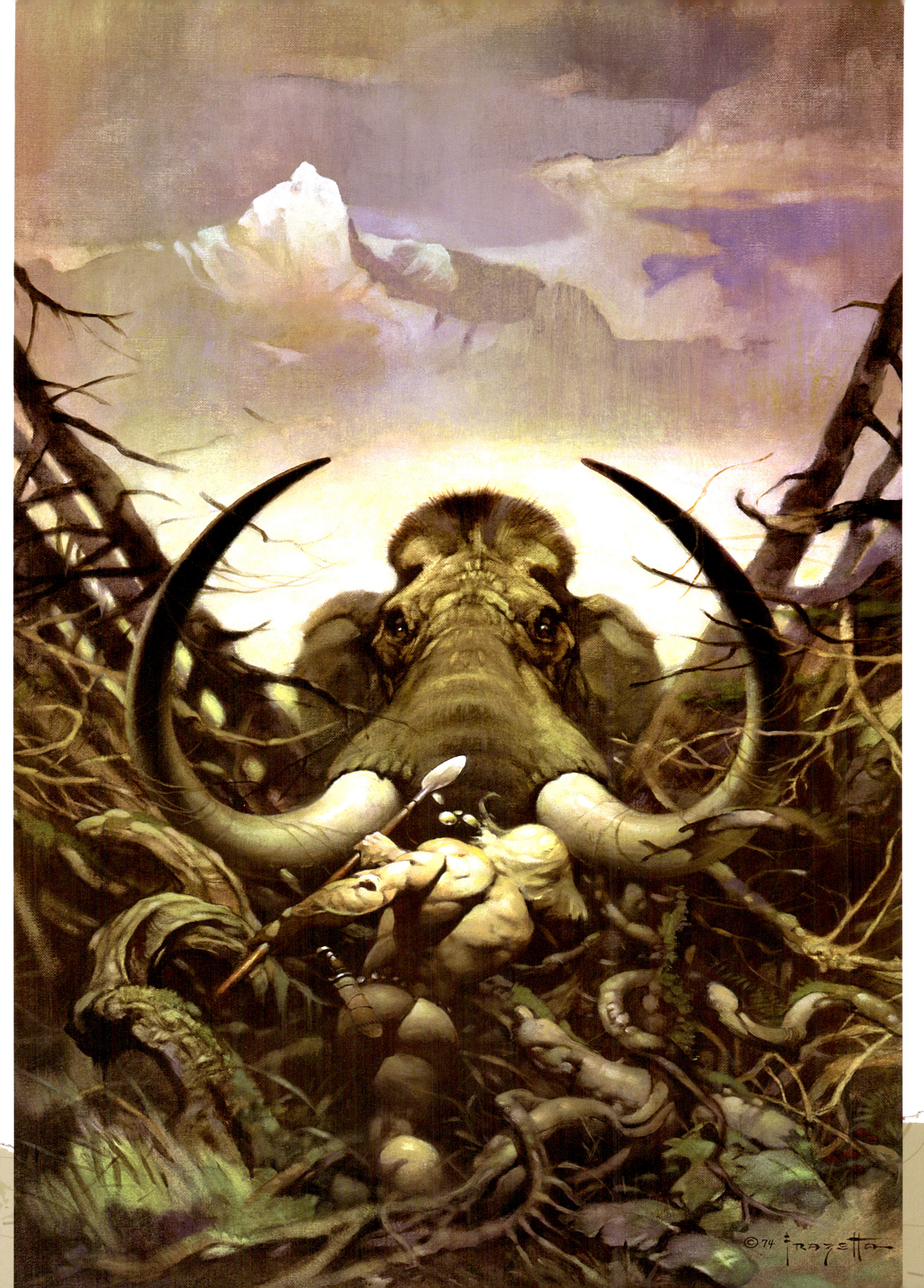

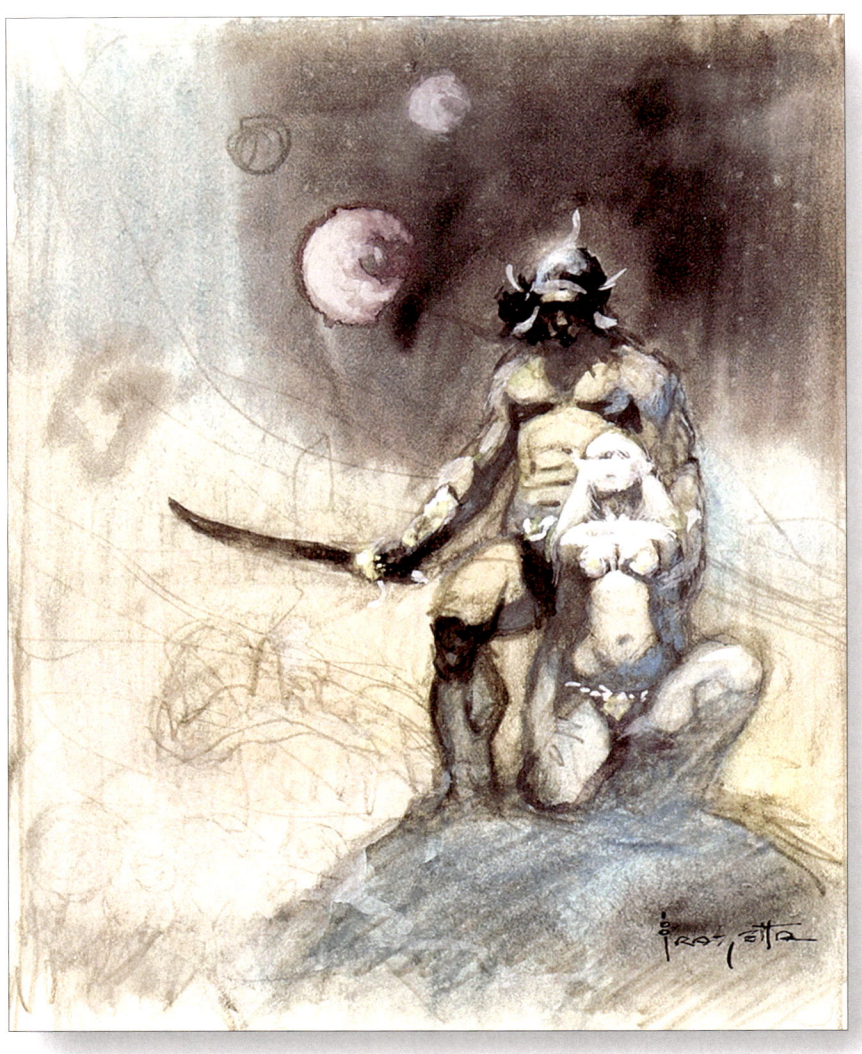

Preliminary artwork, 4.75" x 5.75"
Previously unpublished

A FIGHTING MAN OF MARS

Oil on masonite, 1973
First published as the cover to
A Fighting Man of Mars
(Doubleday, 1974)

Frazetta: The Definitive Reference, *second printing*

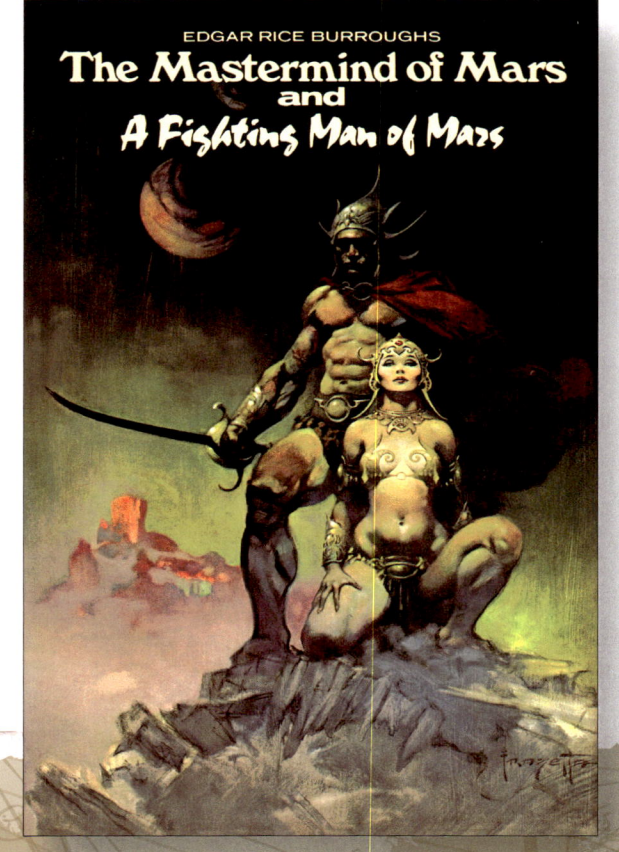

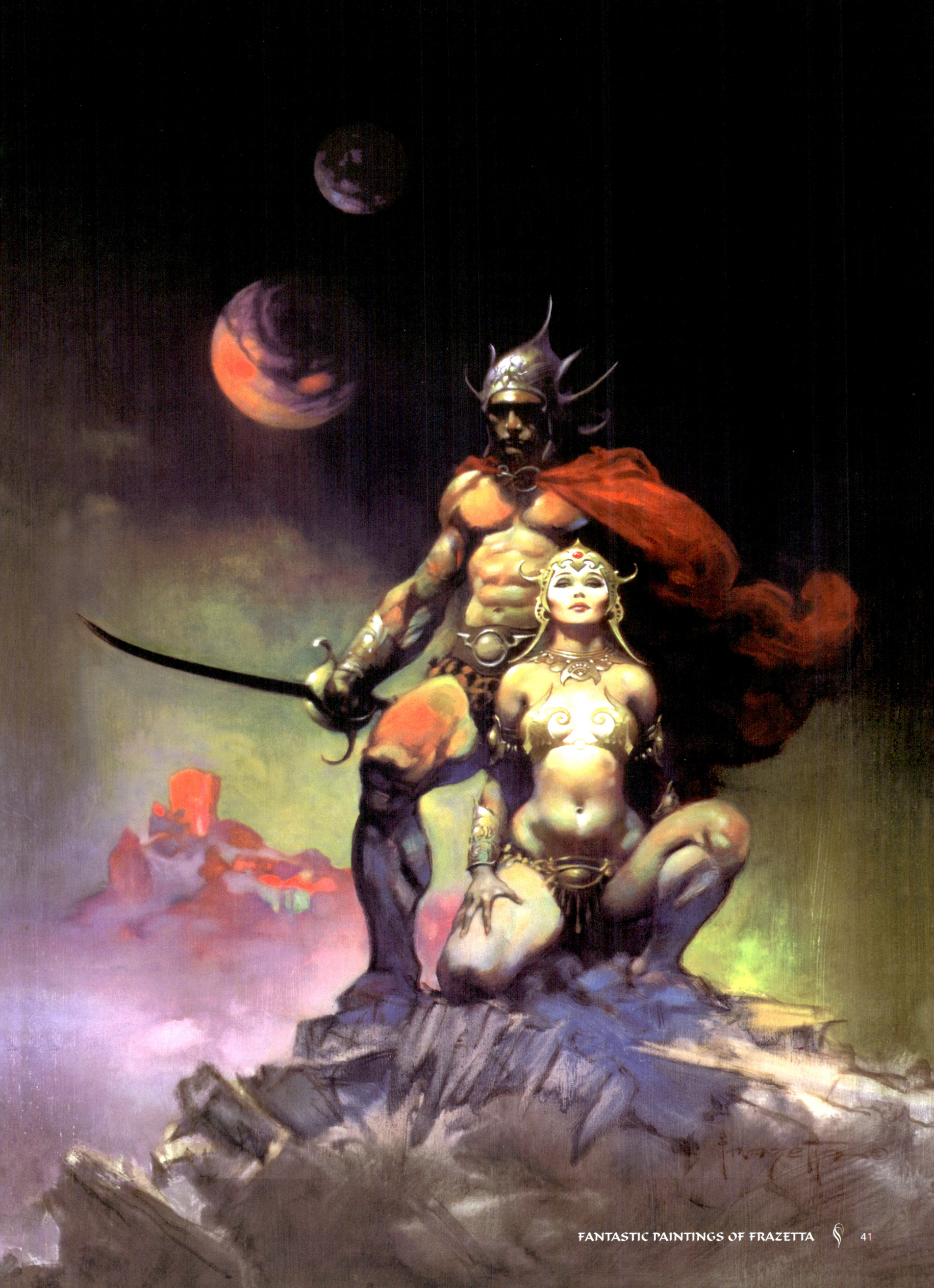

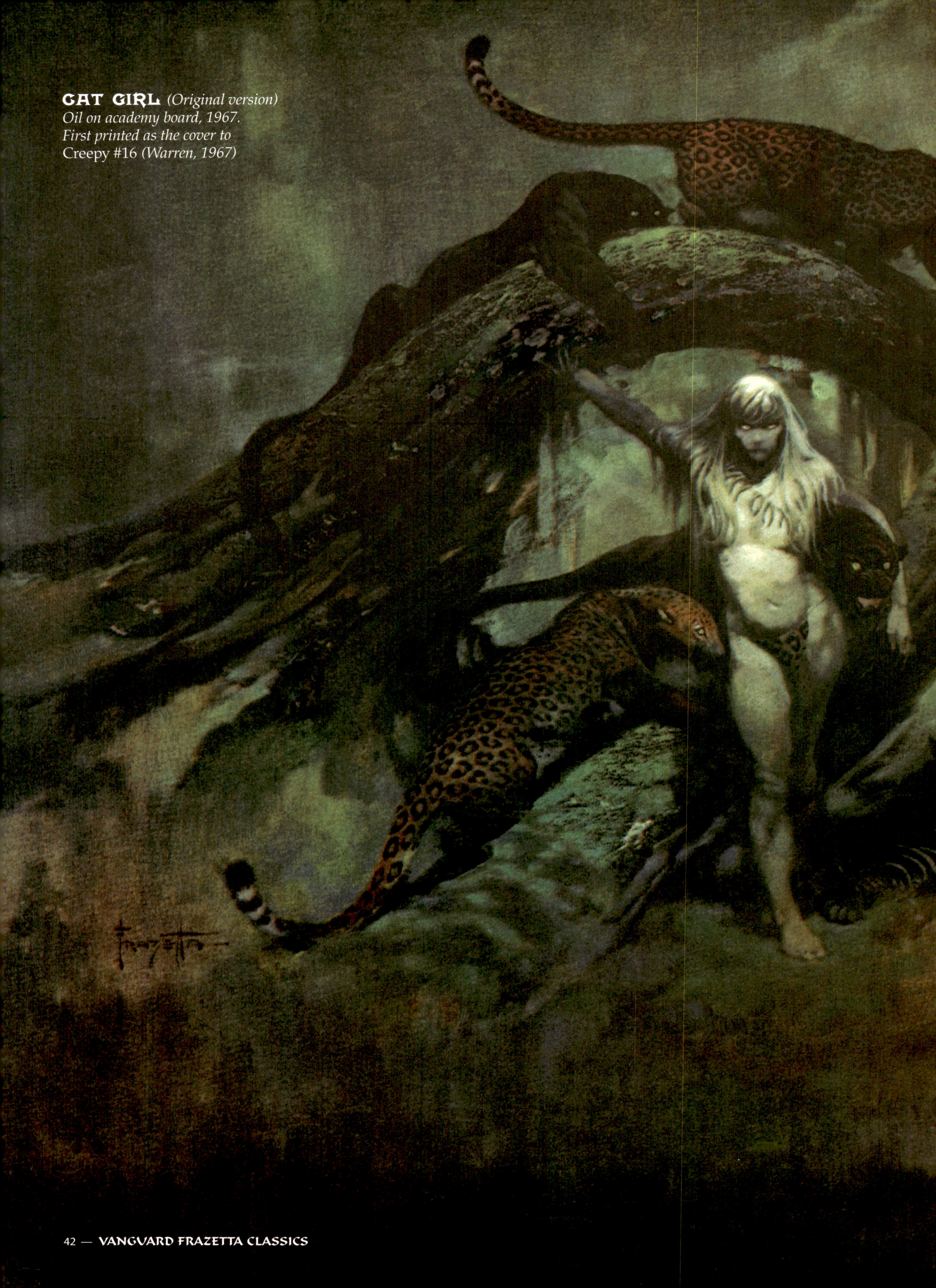

CAT GIRL *(Original version)*
Oil on academy board, 1967.
First printed as the cover to
Creepy #16 *(Warren, 1967)*

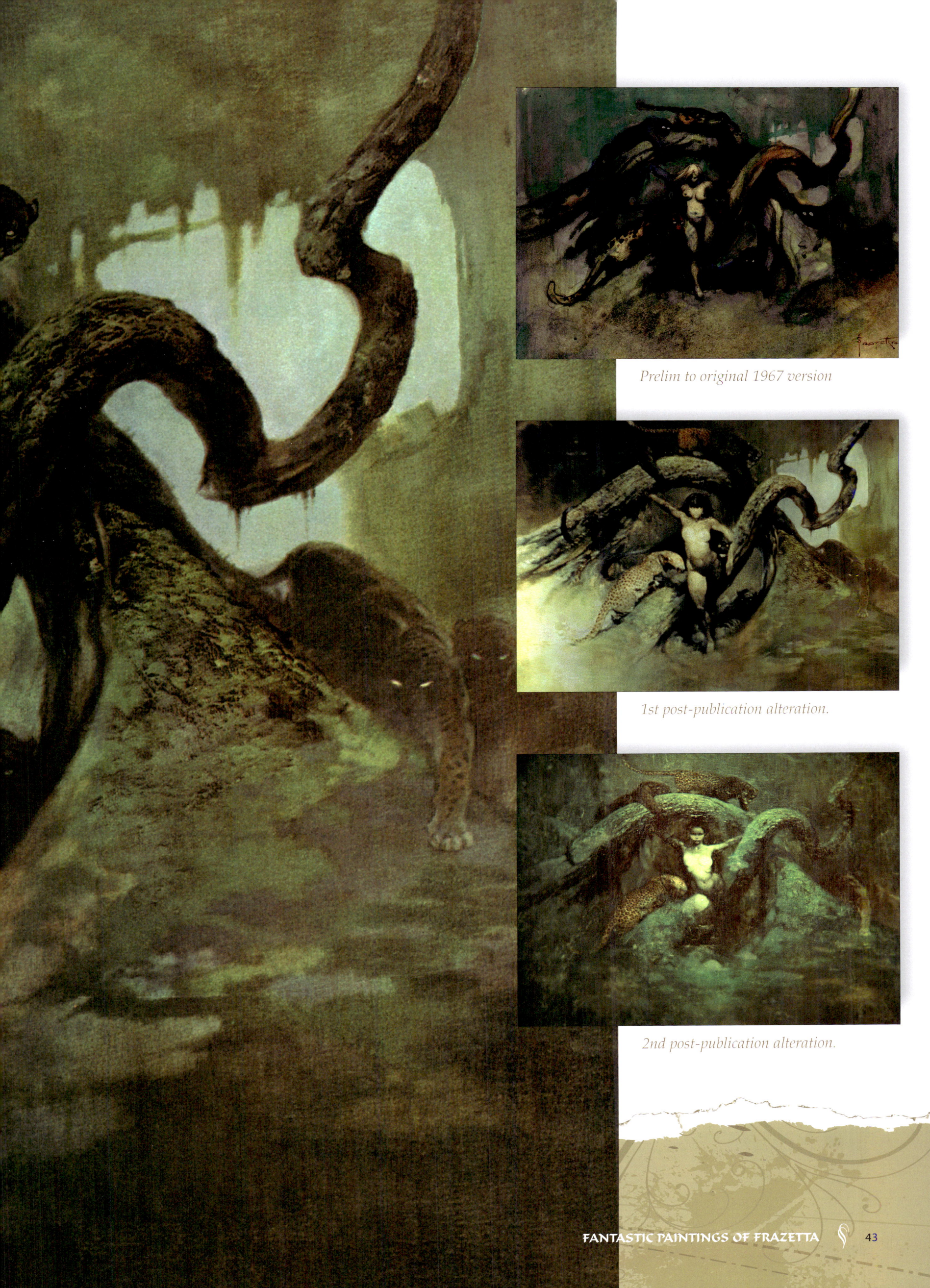

Prelim to original 1967 version

1st post-publication alteration.

2nd post-publication alteration.

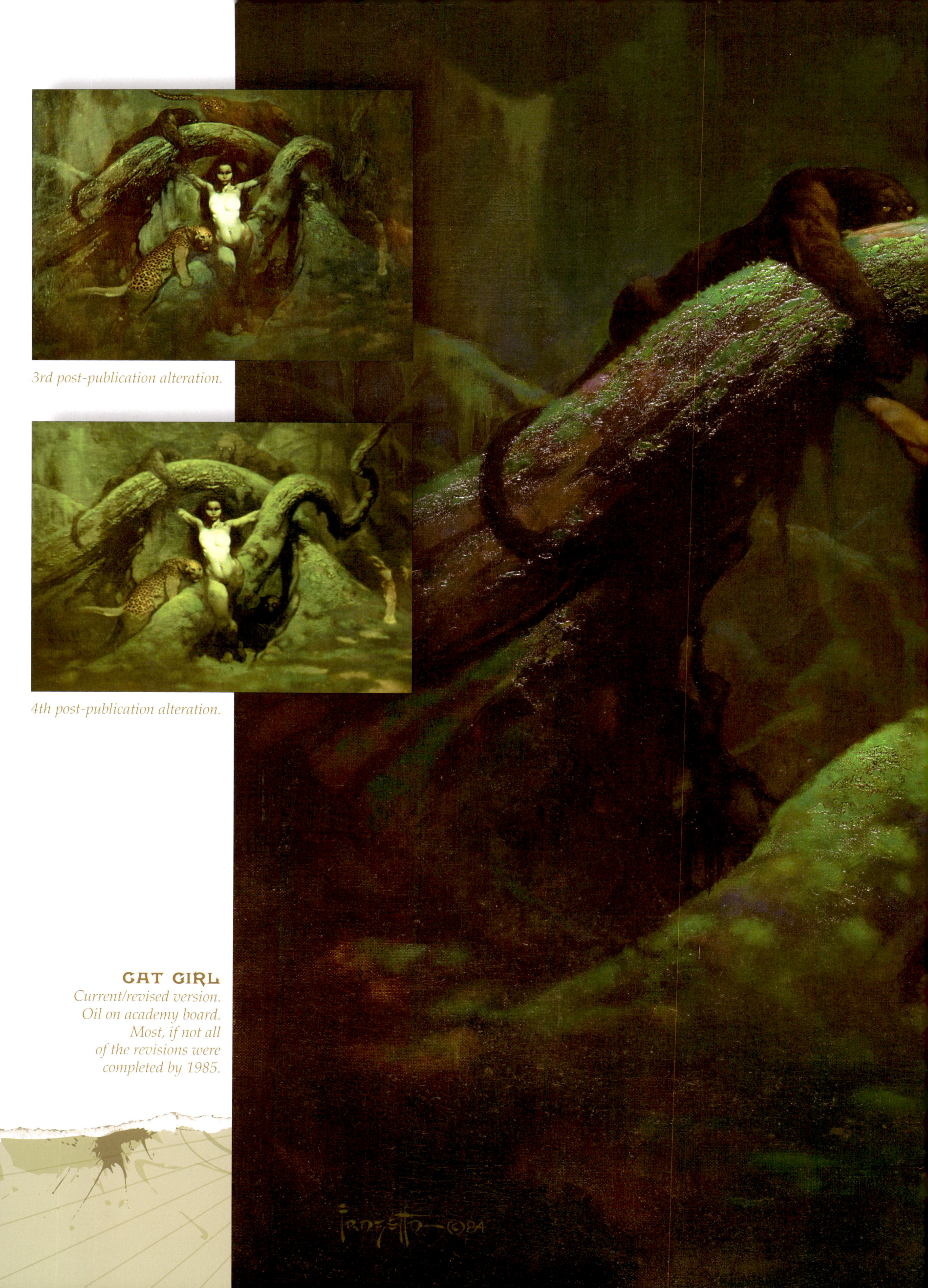

3rd post-publication alteration.

4th post-publication alteration.

CAT GIRL
Current/revised version.
Oil on academy board.
Most, if not all
of the revisions were
completed by 1985.

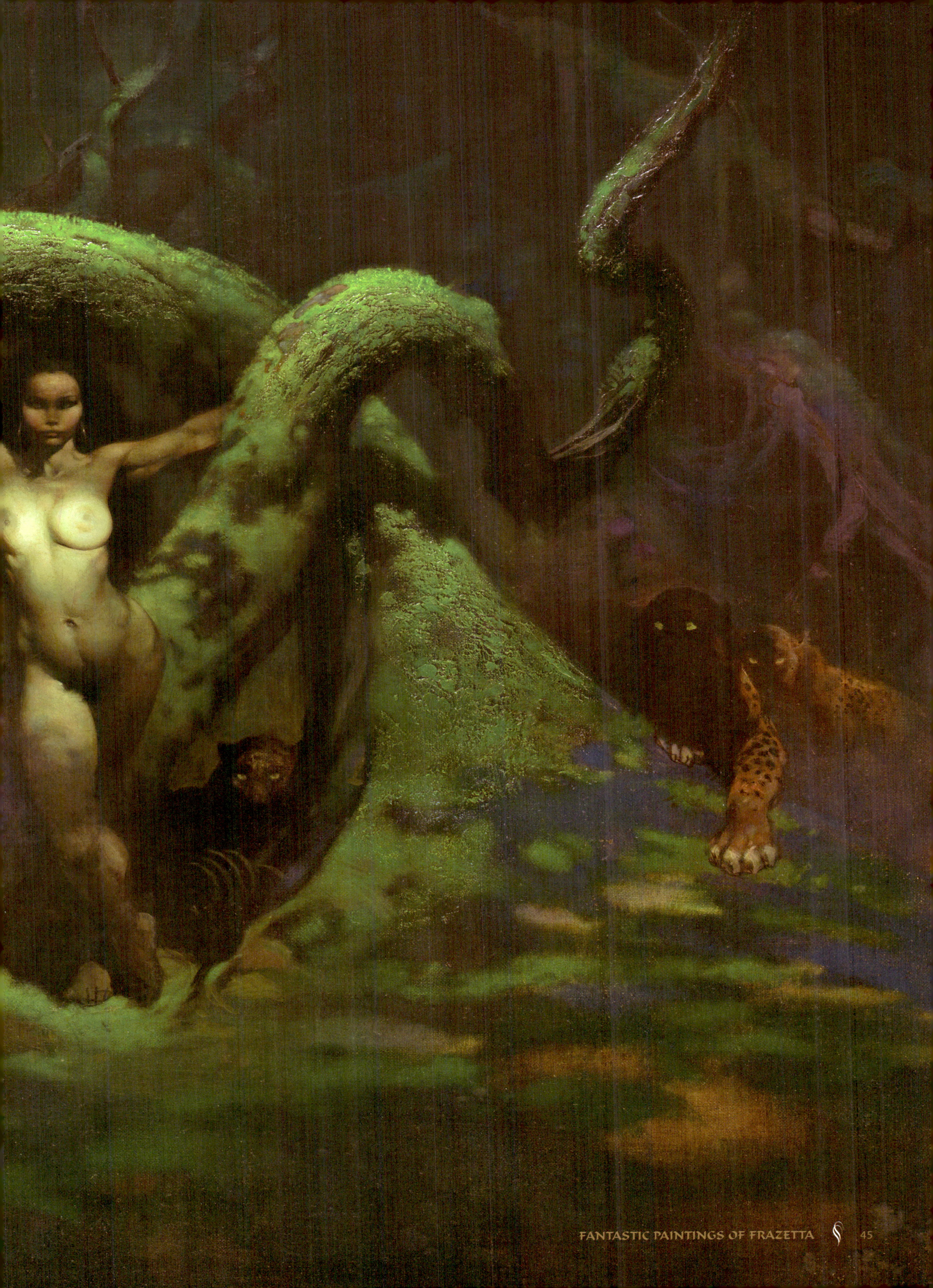

THE BRAIN *(slightly revised)*
Oil on academy board, 1966
First printed as the cover to
Eerie #8 (Warren, 1967)

A slightly revised version first appeared on the cover to
Eerie #84 (Warren, 1975) and the Nazareth LP,
Expect No Mercy (A&M Records, 1977).

Nazareth is a Scottish hard rock band with major hits including
Love Hurts and Hair of the Dog (with the familiar refrain "Now
your messing with a sonuvabitch"). In 1981, they contributed
the song Crazy (A Suitable Case for Treatment) to the soundtrack
to the film, Heavy Metal. Nazareth's use of THE BRAIN on
the Expect No Mercy album cover is one of the earliest usages
of Frazetta's barbaric art by a hard rock band. But the record
company censored the painting slightly by cropping out the
warrior's nude bottom.

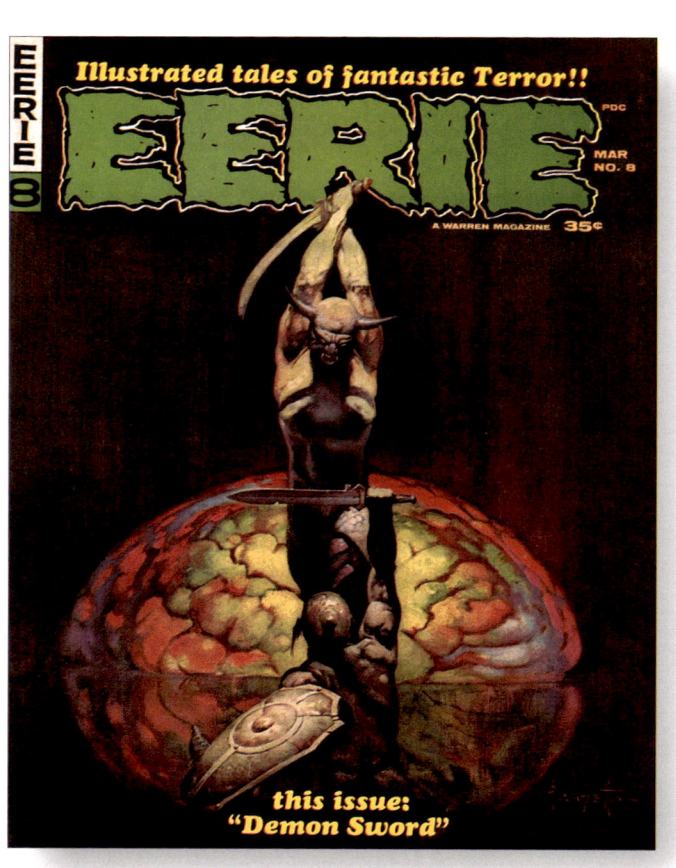

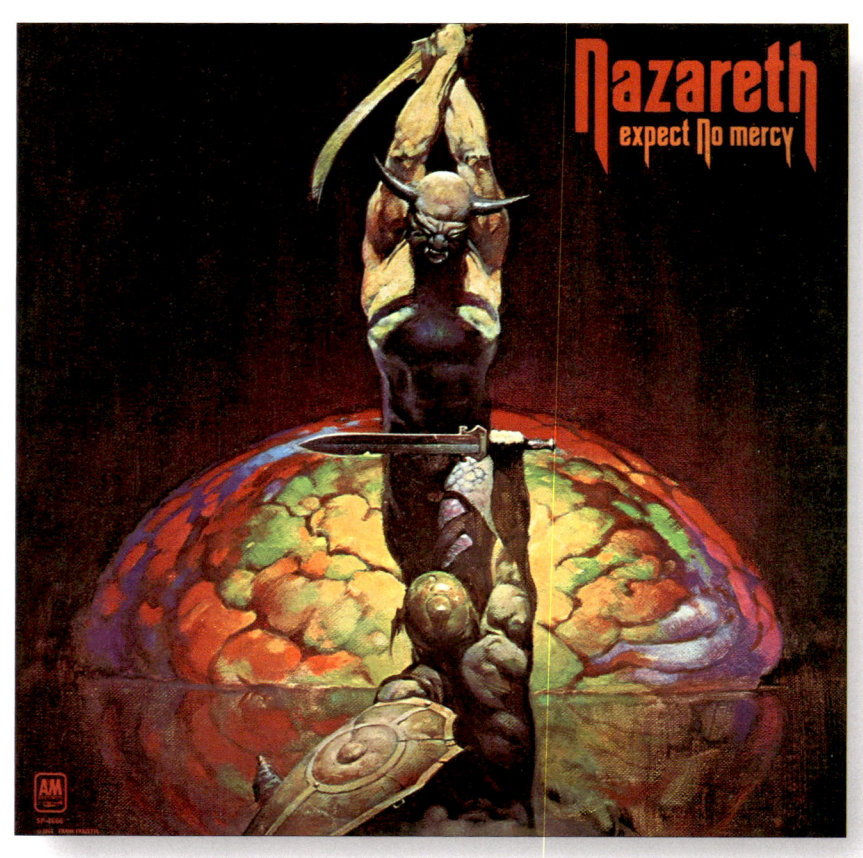

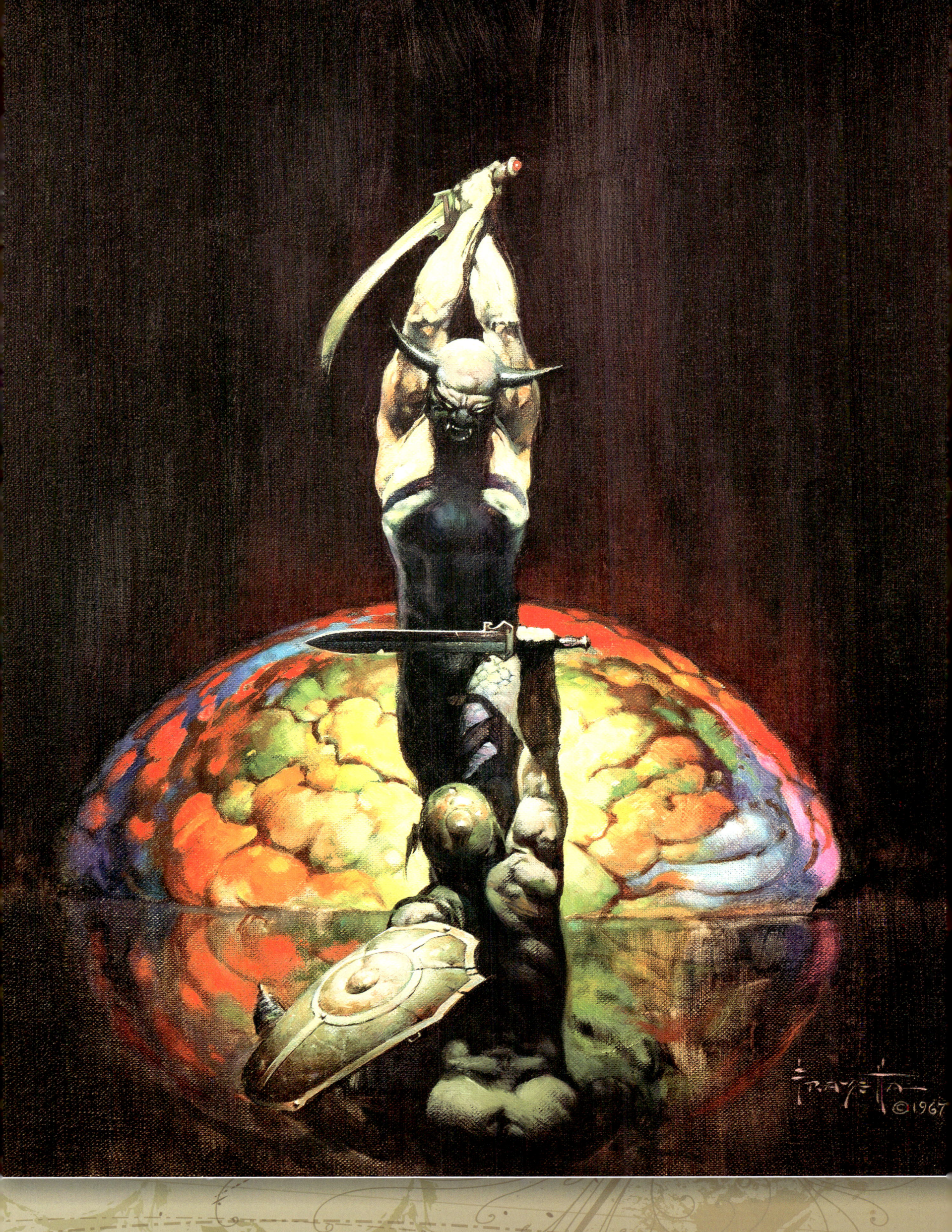

John Jakes (b. 1932), is one of America's most distinguished writers of historical fiction. Jakes's commitment to historical accuracy and evocative storytelling earned him the title of "the godfather of historical novelists" from the Los Angeles Times and led to a streak of sixteen consecutive New York Times bestsellers. But since his start as early as the 1950s, Jakes was drawn to writing science fiction and fantasy. He was a member of the Swordsmen and Sorcerers' Guild of America (SAGA), a loose-knit group of heroic fantasy authors founded in the 1960s and led by Lin Carter. They sought to promote the popularity and respectability of the "Sword and Sorcery" sub genre including Brak the Barbarian stories by Jakes. Jakes gained widespread popularity with the publication of his 1970s Kent Family Chronicles series which sold 55 million copies. His North and South trilogy about the U.S. Civil War, sold 10 million copies and was adapted as an ABC-TV miniseries. Jakes books with Frazetta covers include Brak the Barbarian, Witch of the Dark Gate and, Brak the Barbarian Versus the Sorceress.

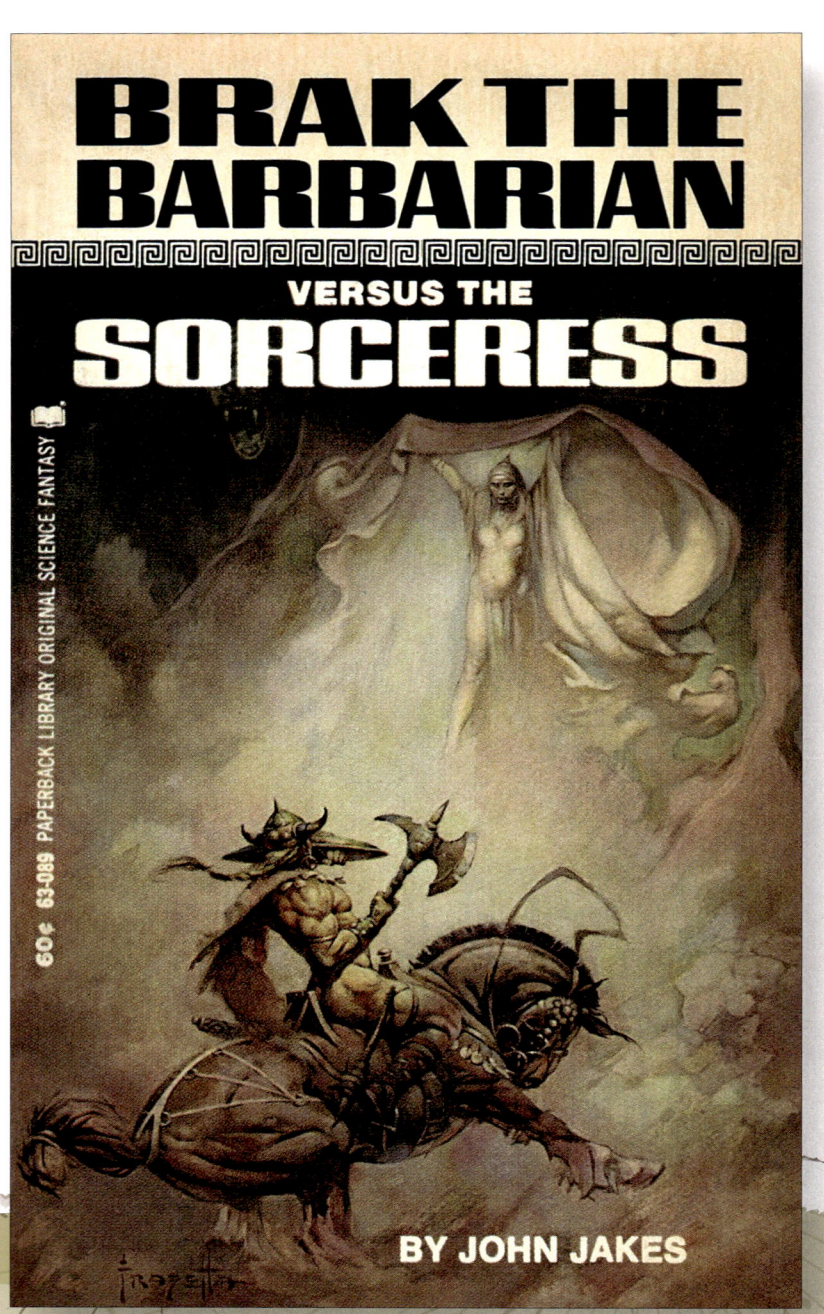

THE APPARITION
Oil on canvas, 1967
First printed as the cover to
Brak the Barbarian Versus the Sorceress
(Paperback Library, 1969)

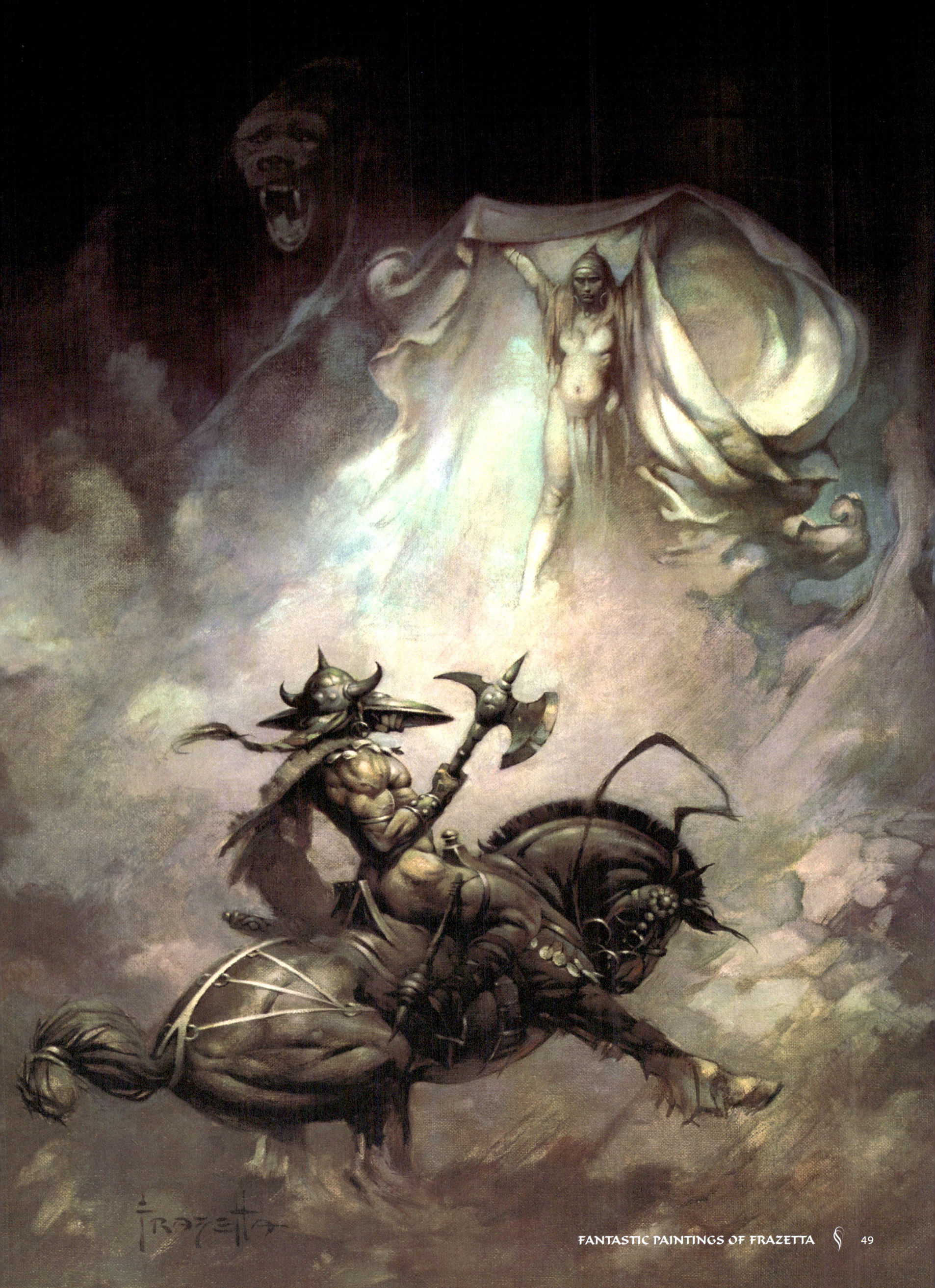

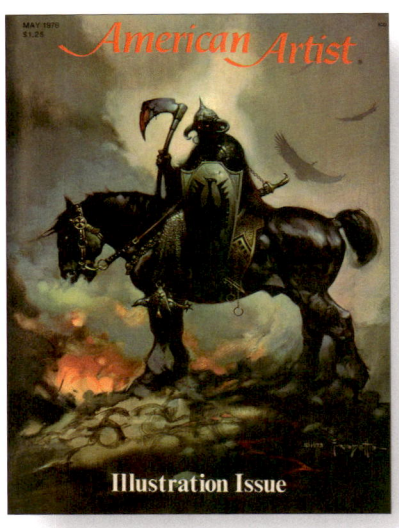

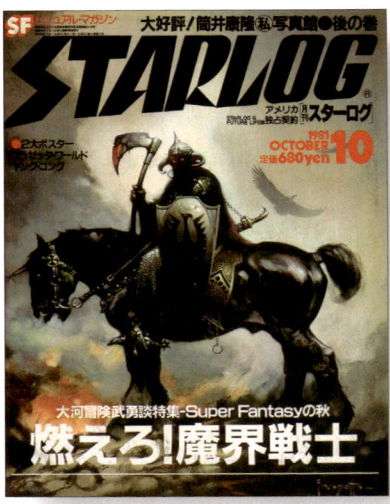

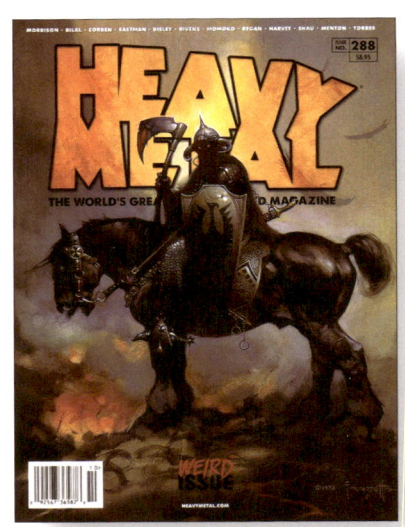

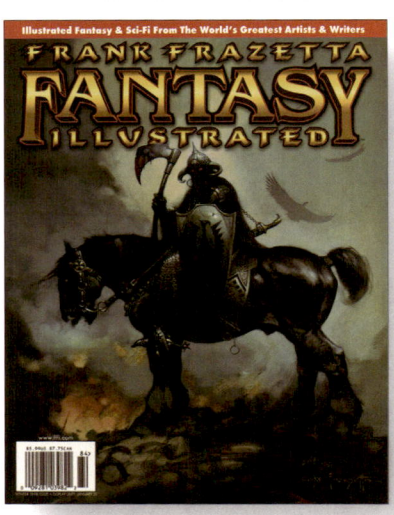

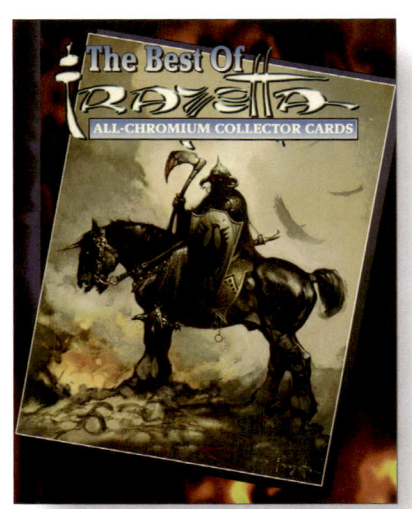

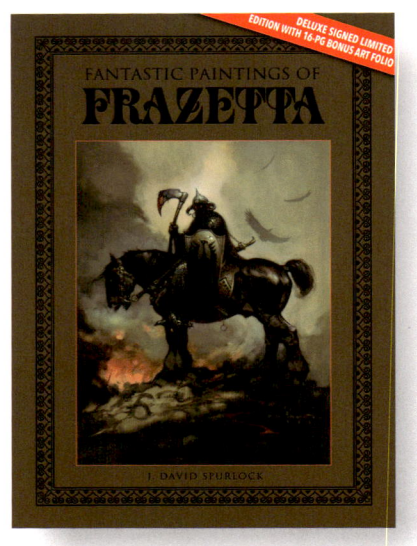

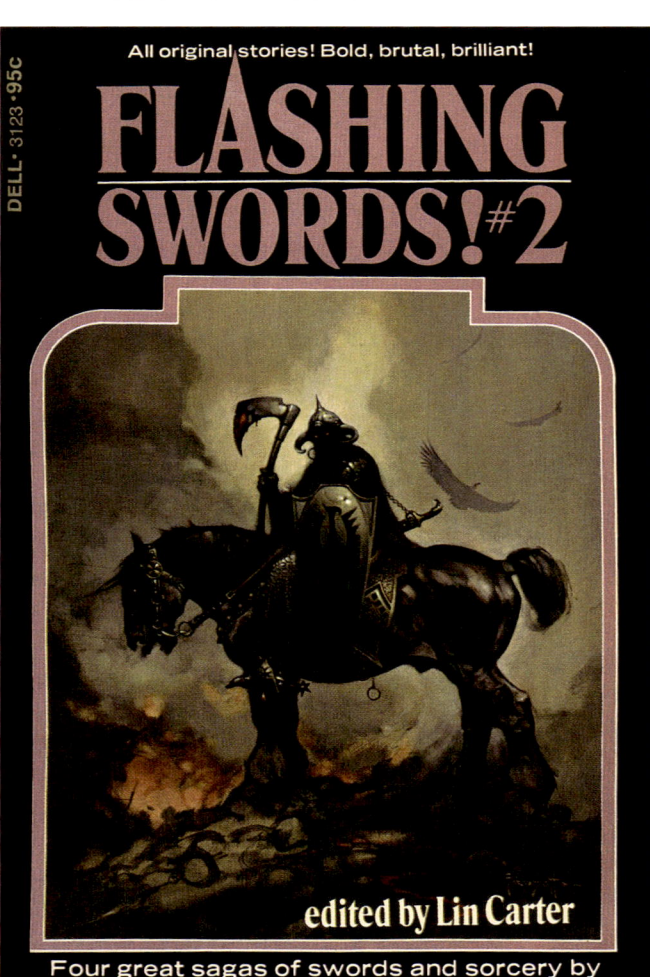

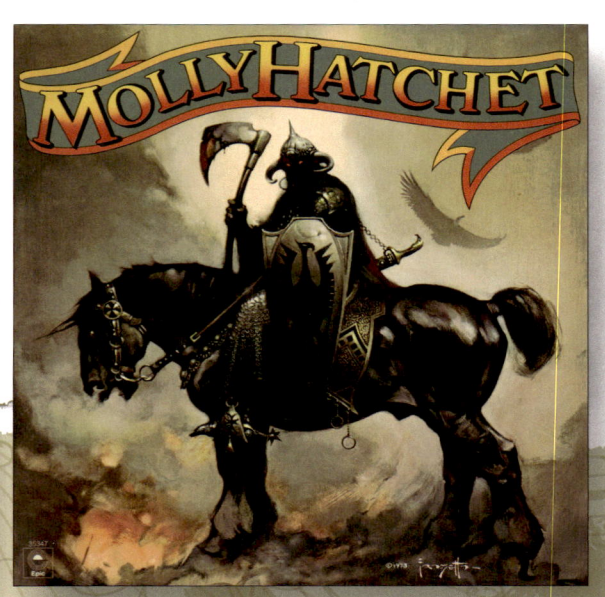

THE DEATH DEALER
Oil on academy board, 1973
First printed as the cover to Flashing Swords #2
(Dell, 1973)

Frazetta created one of his most famous characters, the Death Dealer, loosely inspired by a scene in a short story by Fritz Leiber, contained in the Flashing Swords anthology on which, the original painting first appeared as the cover and wherein, Fafhrd and the Gray Mouser are about to confront and defy Death.

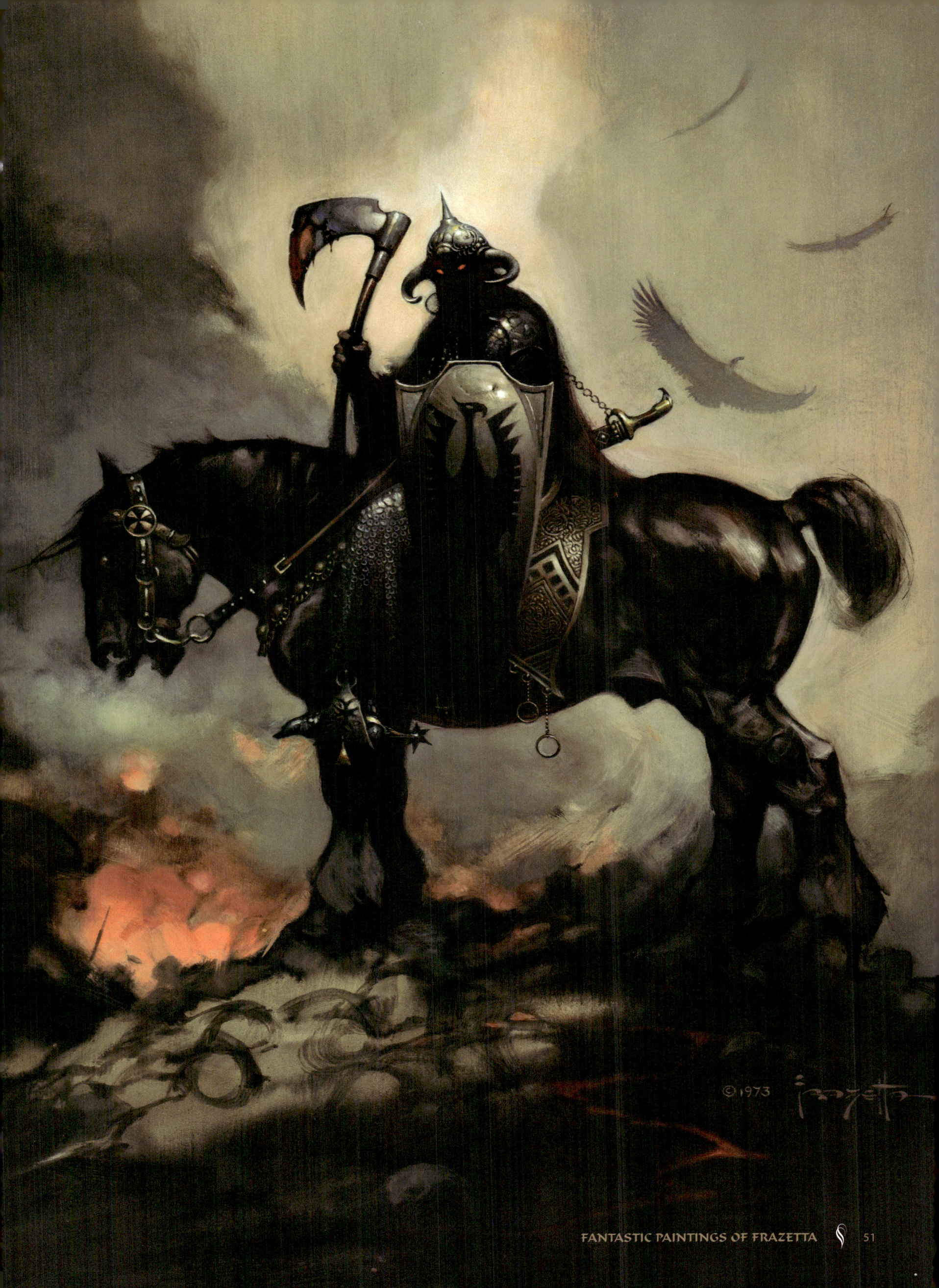

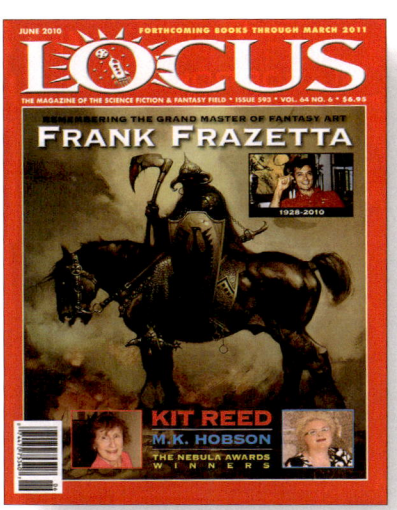

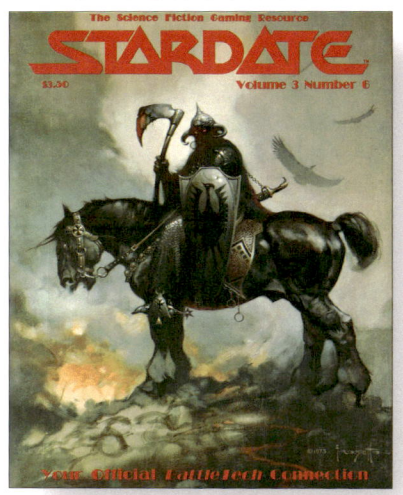

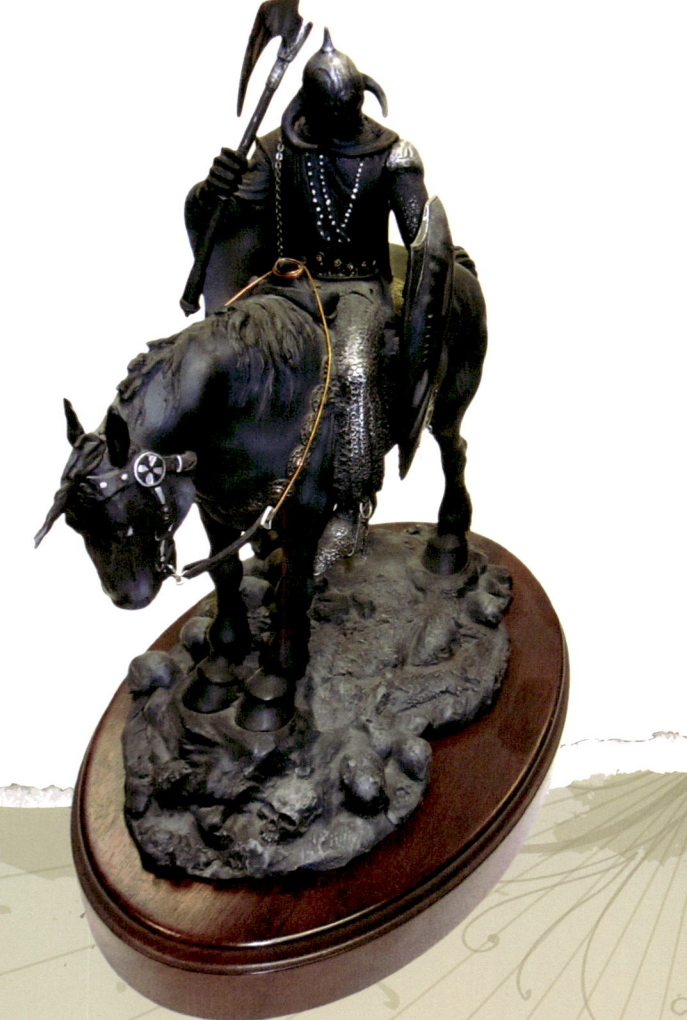

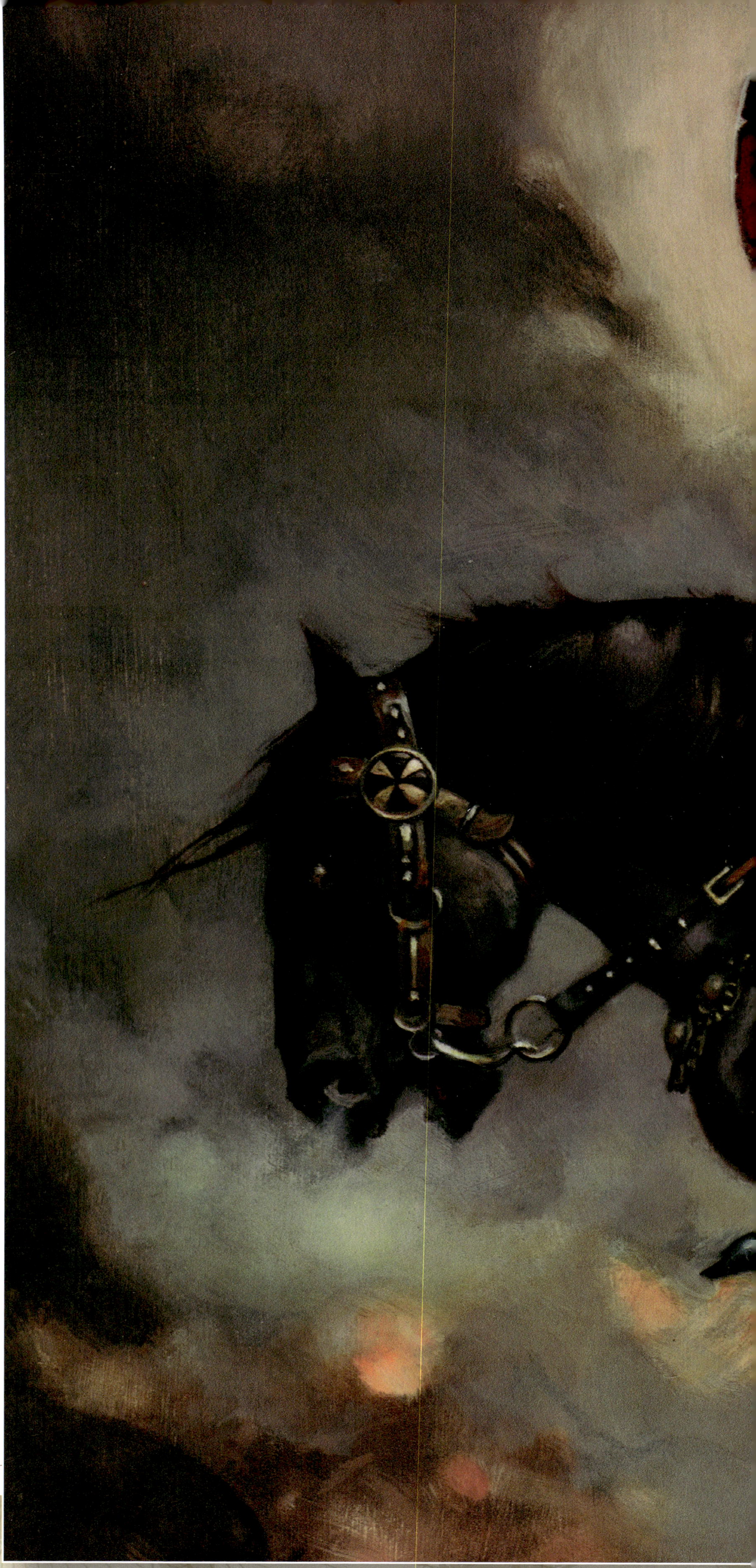

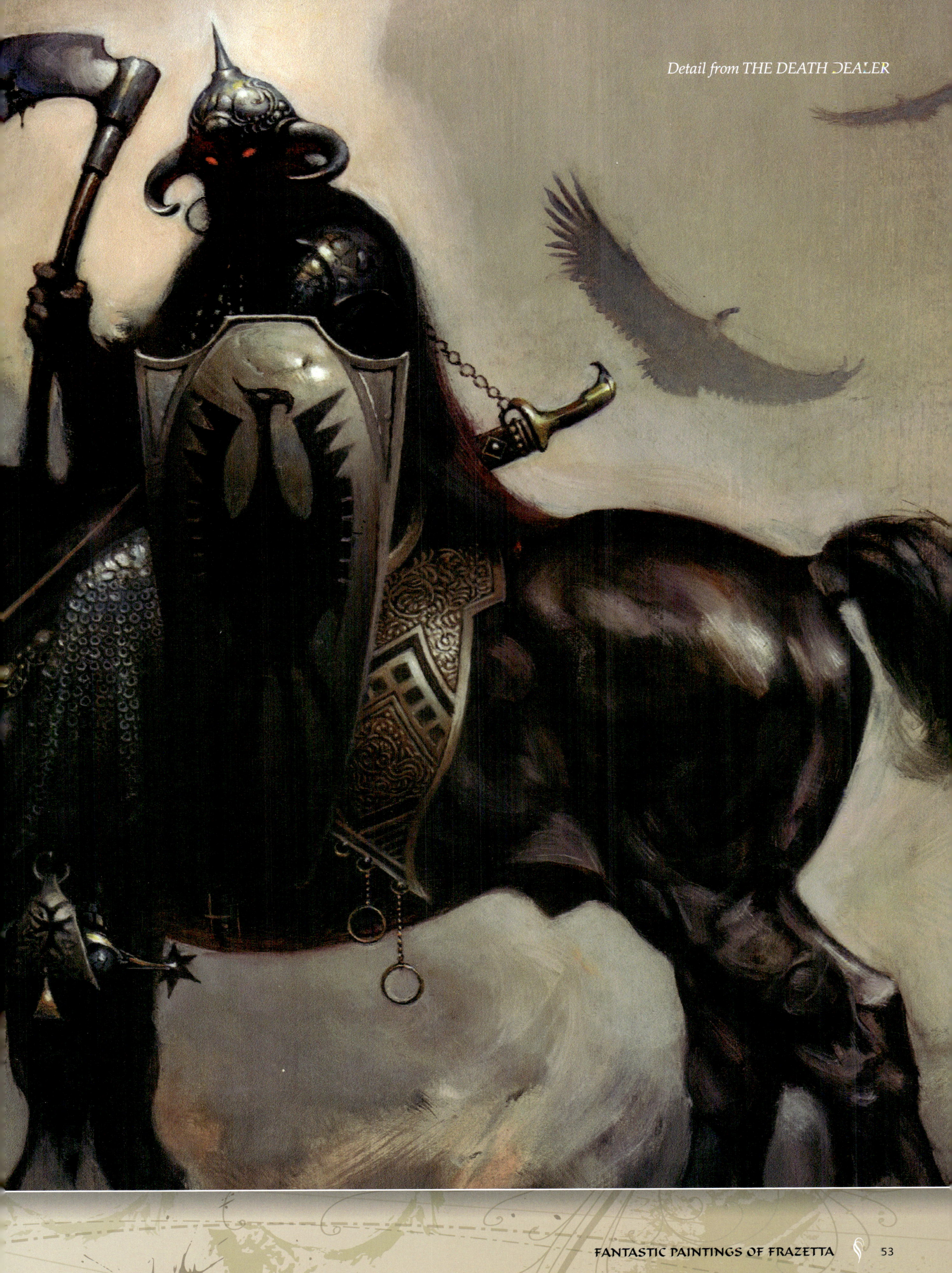

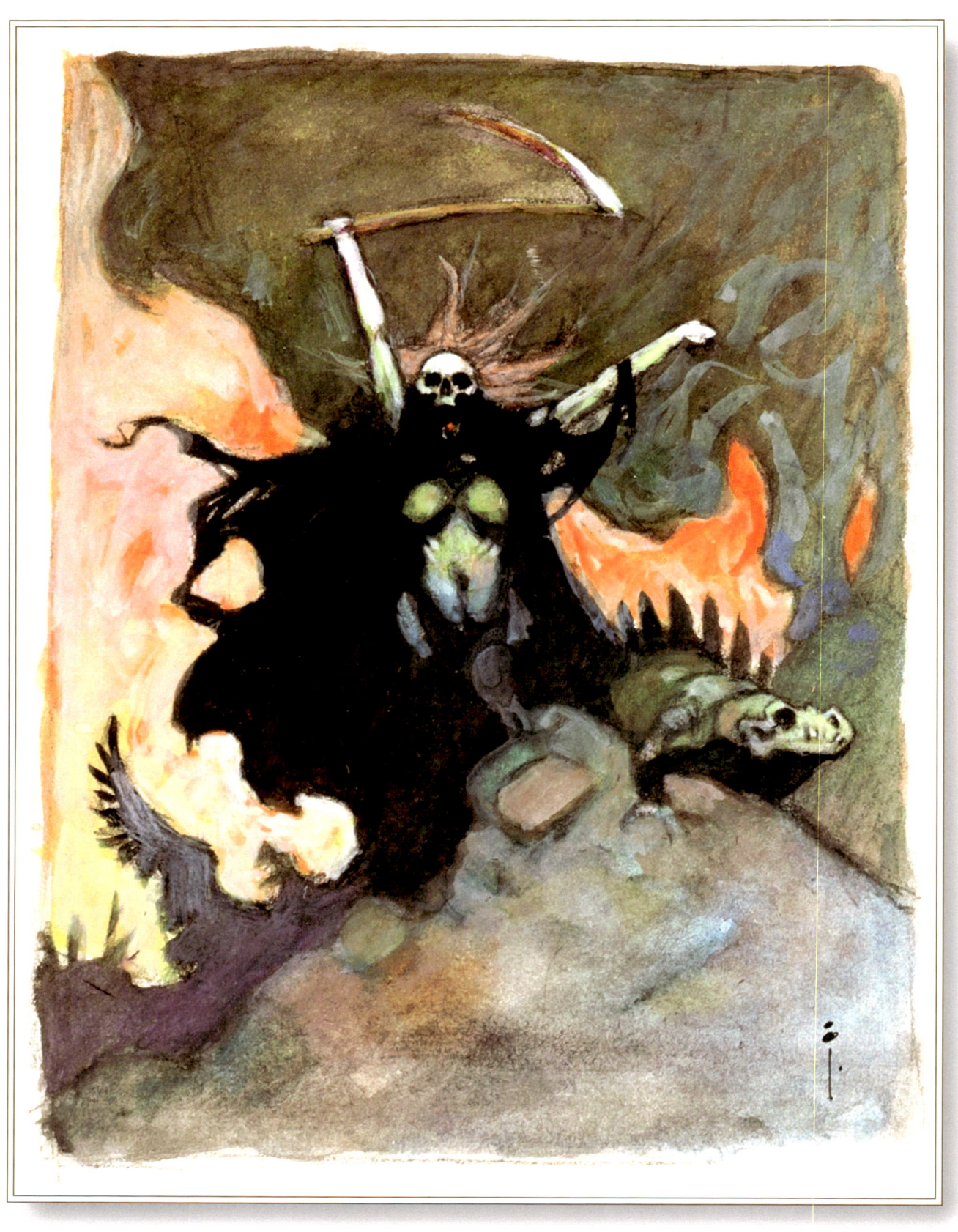

Original 4" x 5" watercolor preliminary,

WOMAN WITH A SCYTHE
Oil on masonite, 1969
First printed as the cover to
Vampirella #11 (Warren, 1971)

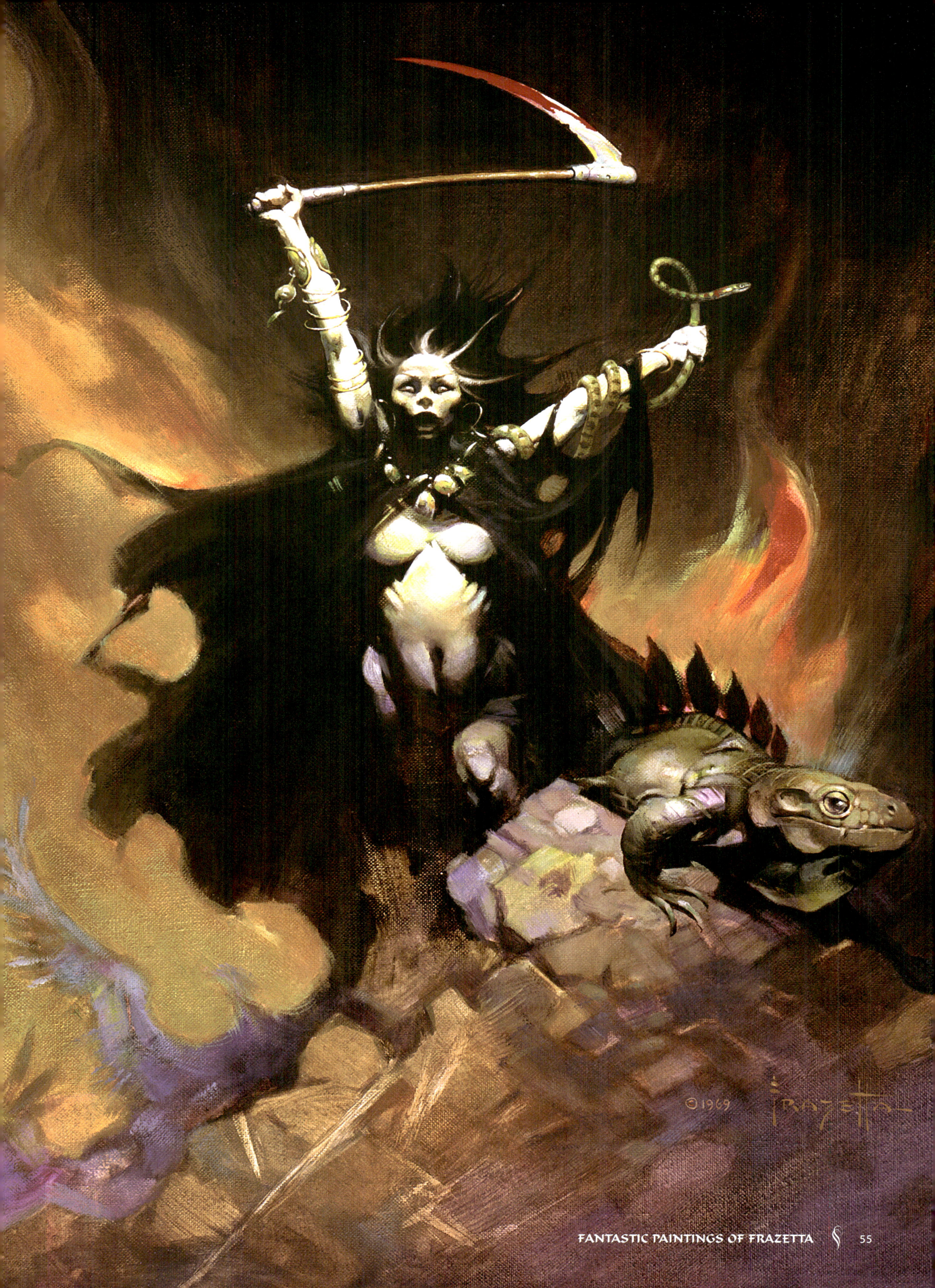

You can easily make jokes about this cover, but you can't really dismiss it, if only for the expression of power in the back and arms of the main character who — contrary to common practice in composition — has his back turned to the viewer. I suppose readers would have known Conan well enough by then that they didn't care that they couldn't see his face.

TERENCE E. HANLEY

Tellers of Weird Tales blogspot

Opposite: **CHAINED**
Oil on academy board, 1967
First printed as the cover to
Conan the Usurper
(Lancer, 1967)

Right: Preliminary sketch 4" x 4.75"

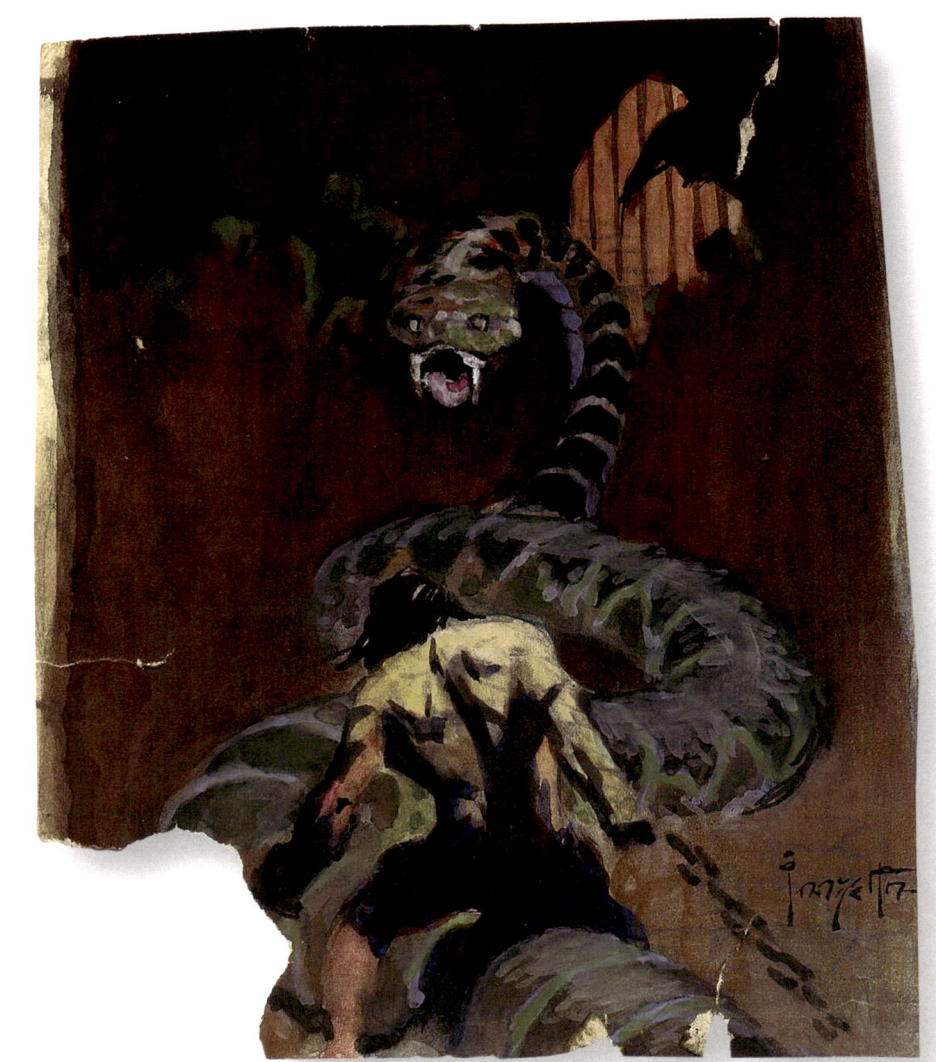

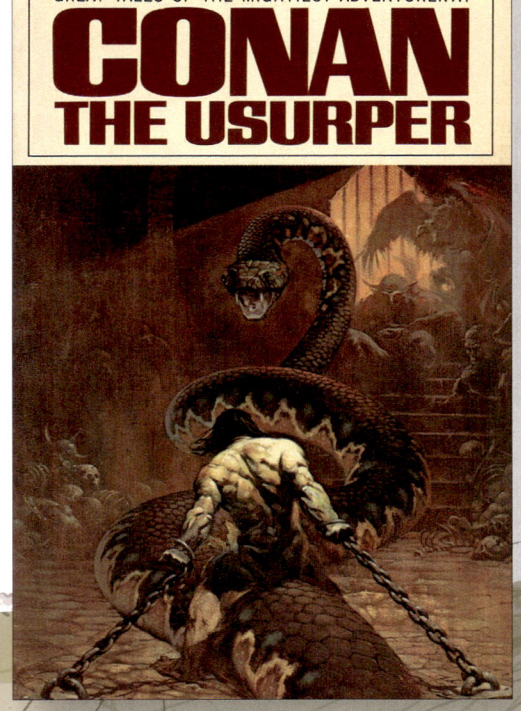

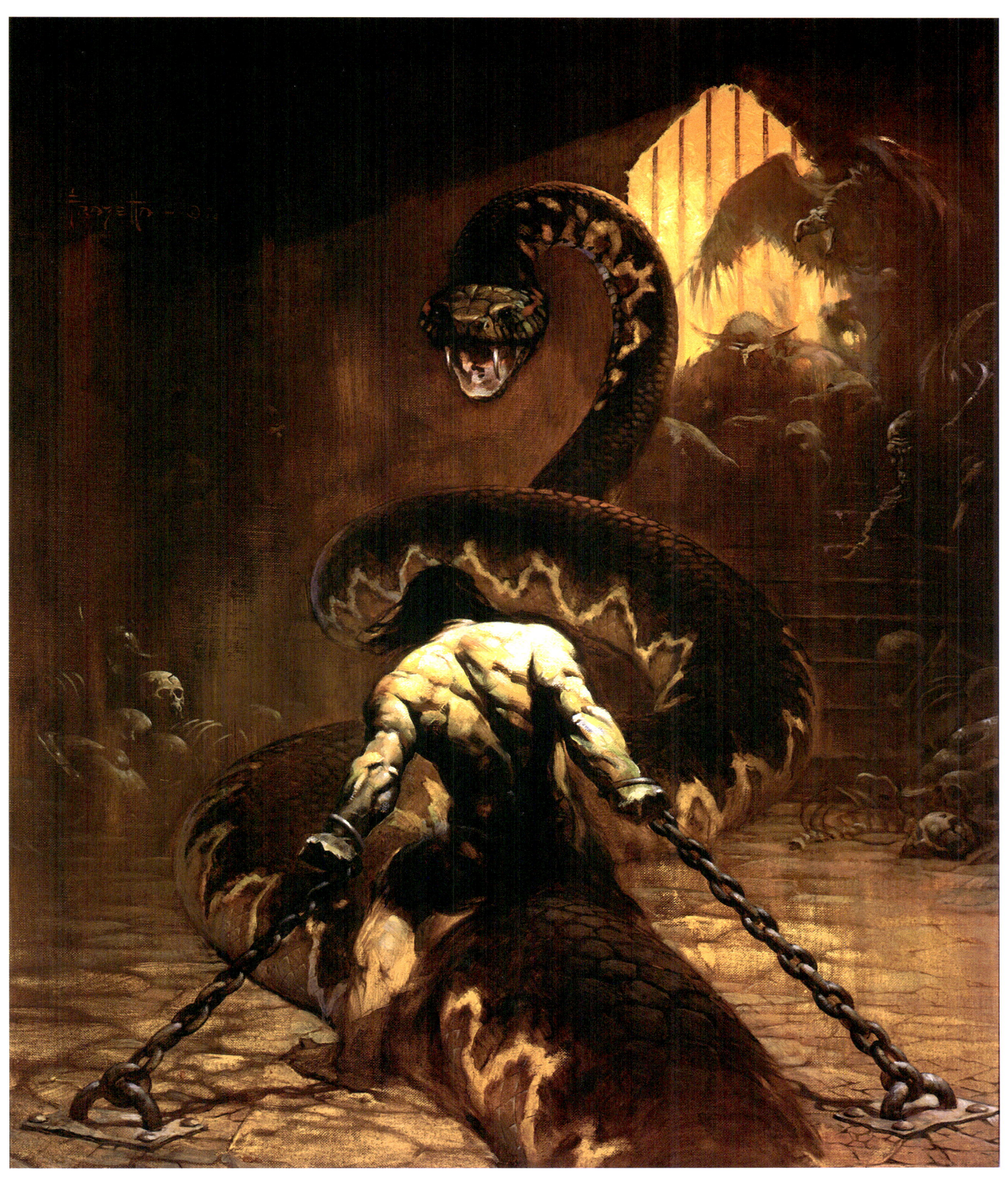

Very few people ever get what is going on with Frazetta's EGYPTIAN QUEEN painting; both in the scene and with Frazetta's post-publication revision to the Queen's face. The original version told the story. That is the job of illustration. The revision is a prettier picture; Frank's idea of Fine Art. The revision is more attractive but, it actually lost the storytelling. The original story/point/intent is HORROR: The deadly man-and-queen-eating wild cat had just broken its chain and the Egyptian Queen was the nearest, most appetizing DINNER! The illustration served its frightful purpose as a horror magazine cover. But upon return of the original to the artist, Frank's interest now became, to have the most beautiful image possible to adorn a wall — eventually a museum wall.

Original painting for Eerie #23 *(Warren, 1969)*

Original preliminary

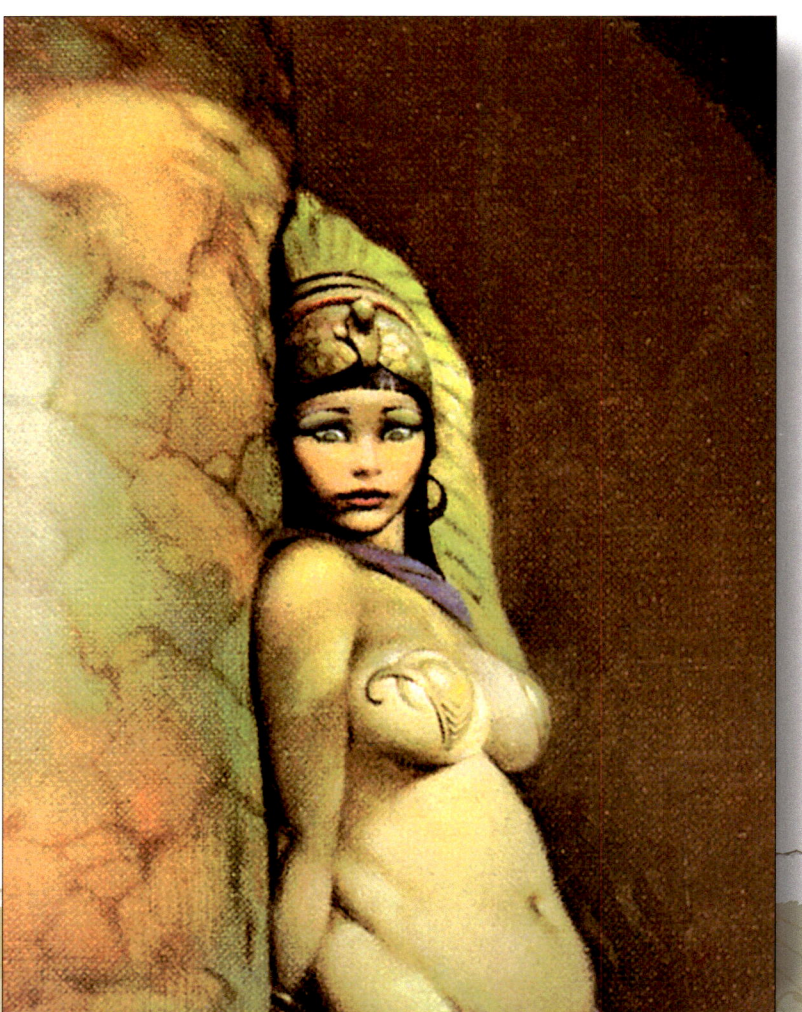

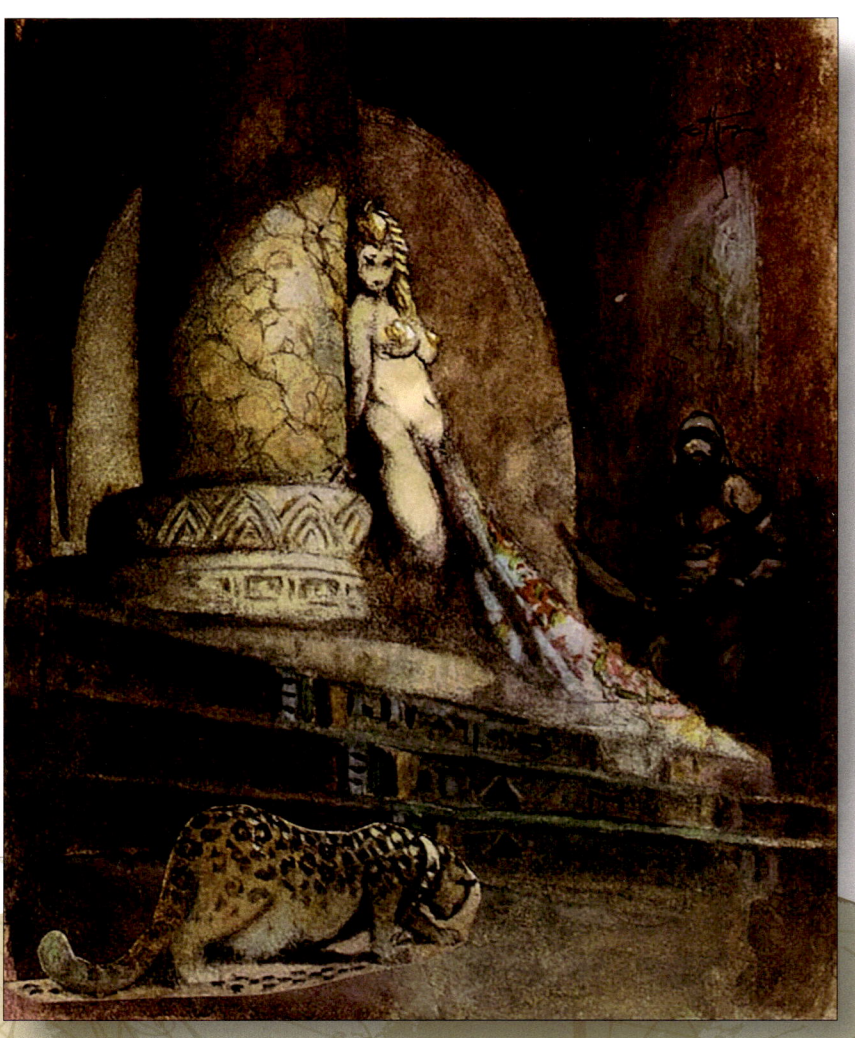

EGYPTIAN QUEEN
Slightly revised oil on canvas, 1968
Imaged by Heritage Auctions (HA.com)

I'll never forget the Egyptian Queen. I got that whole painting done in about a day and a half. Then I looked at her face and I didn't like it. So I started to repaint the face, and I painted the face, and I painted it again, and I painted it again. Well, I was like three days trying to get the right face. I suddenly got sort of blinded to it. I couldn't see any more. I just looked at it and didn't know where I was any more. So I finally just settled for any face, and brought it in, and they printed it that way, and then I forgot about it. So, a couple of months later I get it back; now it was fresh again. And I just looked at it and 'Pow!' I whacked-in the face you see in all the prints. When I got it back, looked at it fresh, her face was painted in five minutes.

FRANK FRAZETTA
Comics Journal *Interview, 1994*

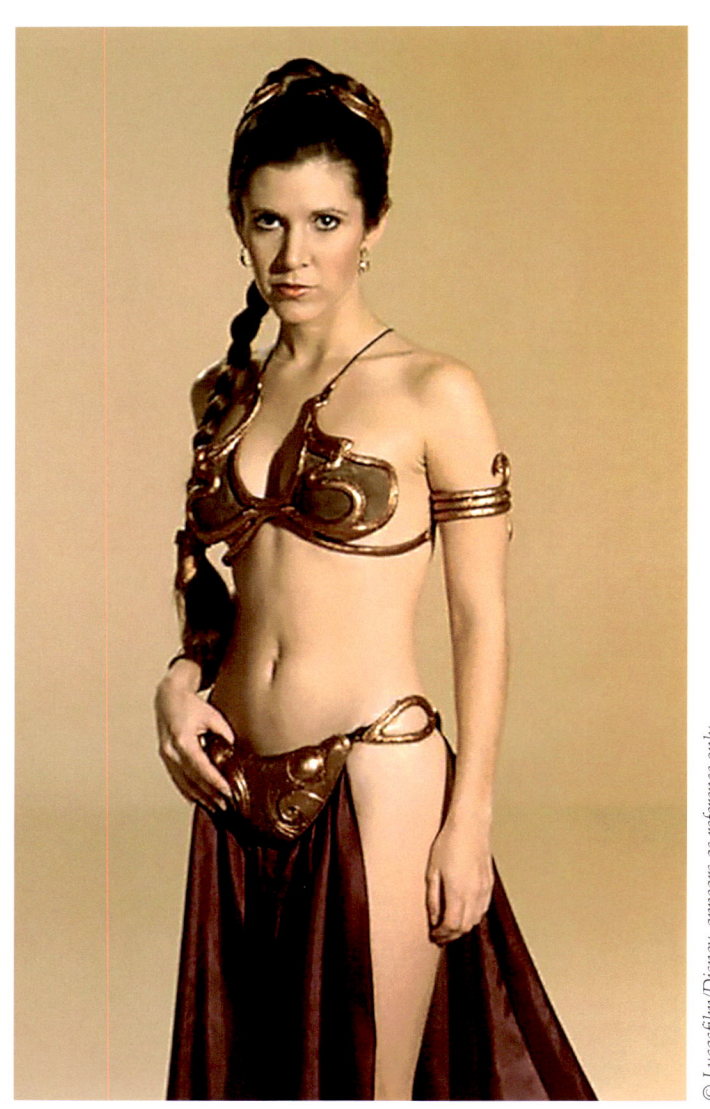

The Princess Leia bikini was inspired in part by the work of Frank Frazetta.
Frazetta's framing of the female form was done out of a love and respect for it.
If you look at his works, you can see a distinct attention to detail when drawing
all human bodies, especially when it came to naked or exposed muscles.
His science fiction and fantasy artwork, along with his use of metal clothing,
also has some clear inspirations on the costume.

AGGIE GUERARD RODGERS

Star Wars Jedi costume designer with Nilo Rodis-Jamero and George Lucas

Detail, **EGYPTIAN QUEEN** *(revised)*
Sold for a world record $5.4 Million at auction in May 2019

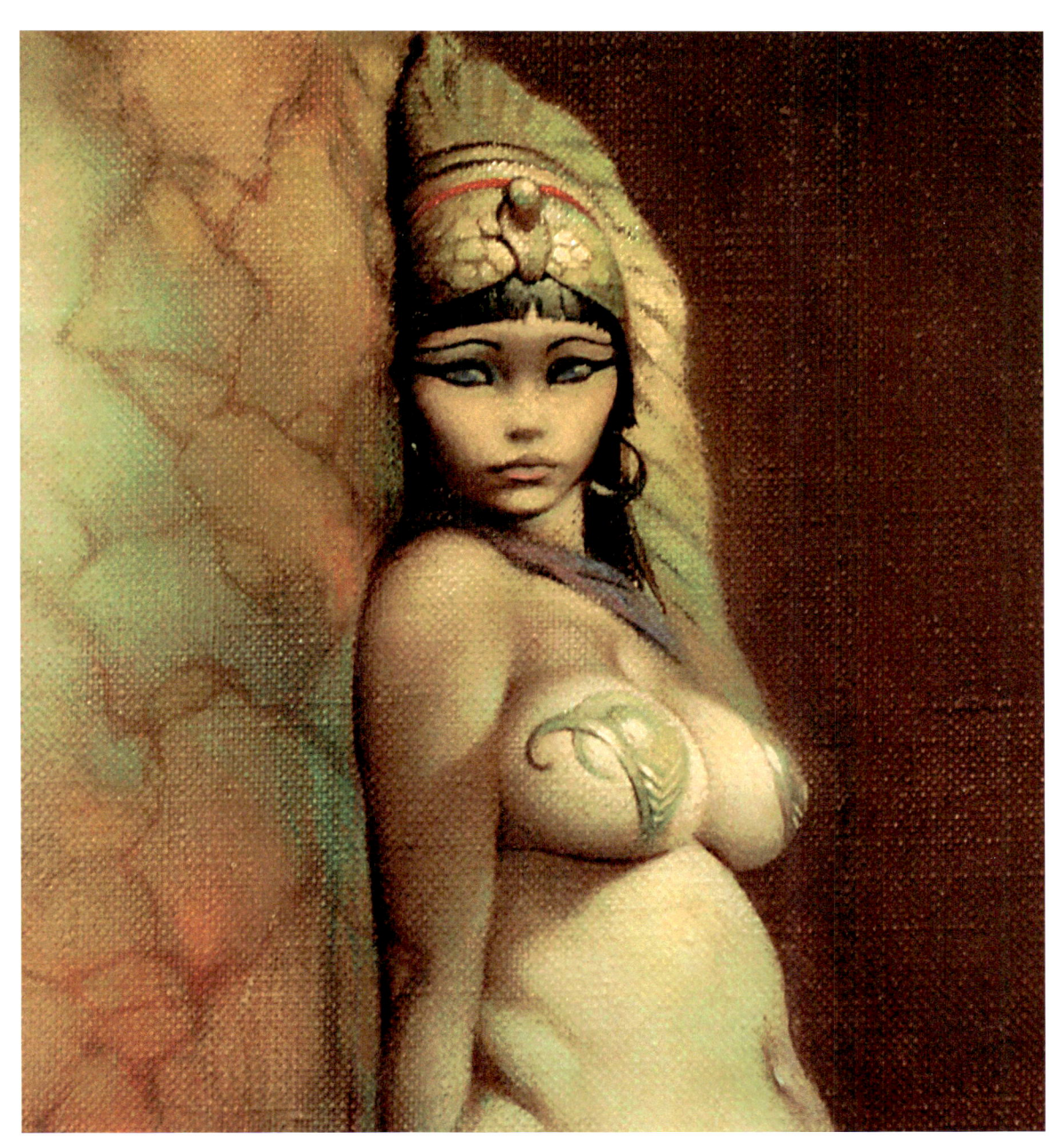

QUEEN KONG: Originally
produced in the early 1970s
for, and based on a concept by
Frazetta's friend, Wally Wood,
as a proposed mature comics
magazine cover — sometimes
referred to as POW — to be
released by Warren Publishing.
Wood dropped the project
when the first paycheck failed
to arrive. The piece ultimately
saw print as the cover to Eerie
#81, released toward the end
of 1976 with a cover date of
February 1977. When Warren
failed to return the original art
to Frazetta, it marked the end of
the artist's relationship
with the publisher.

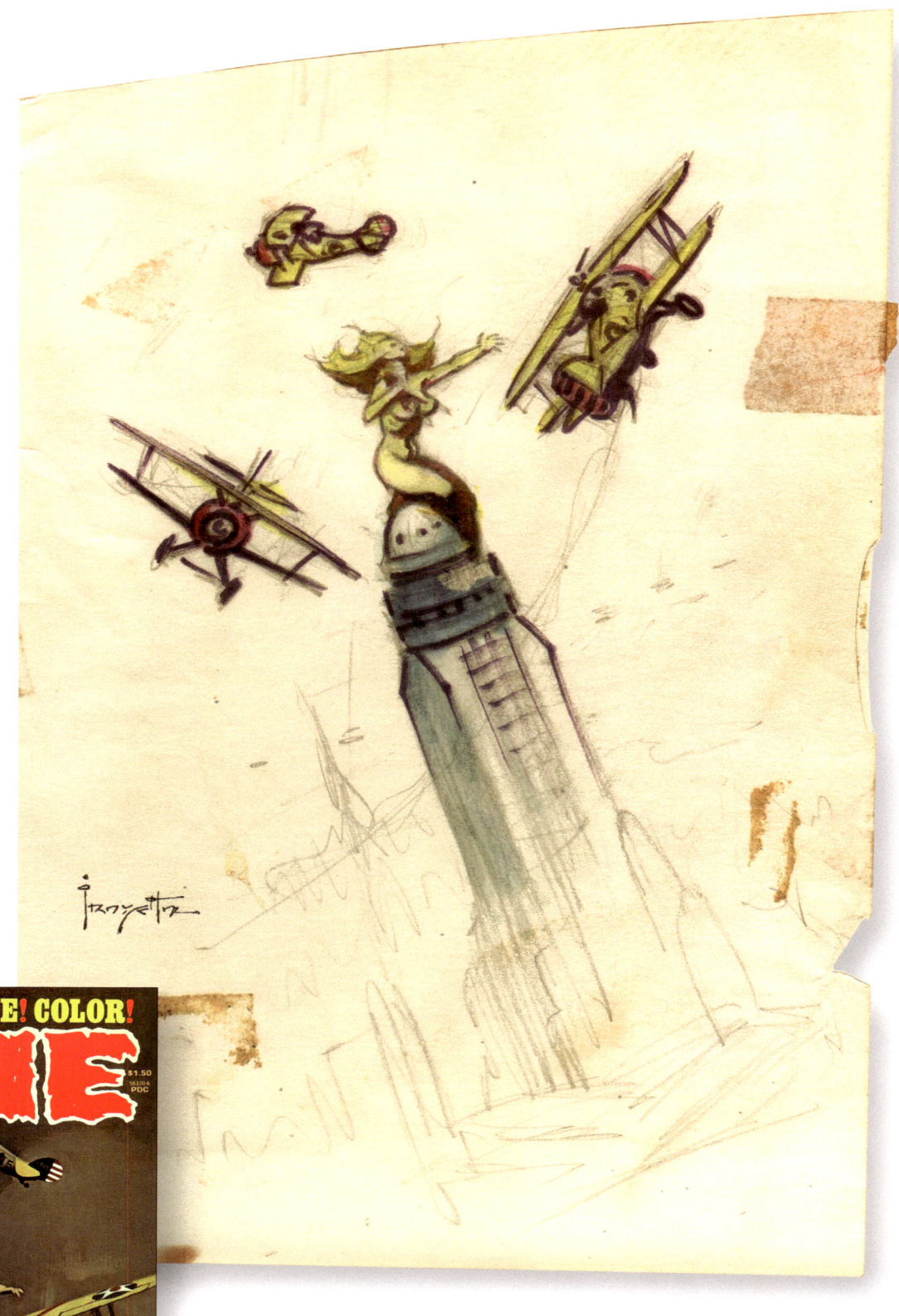

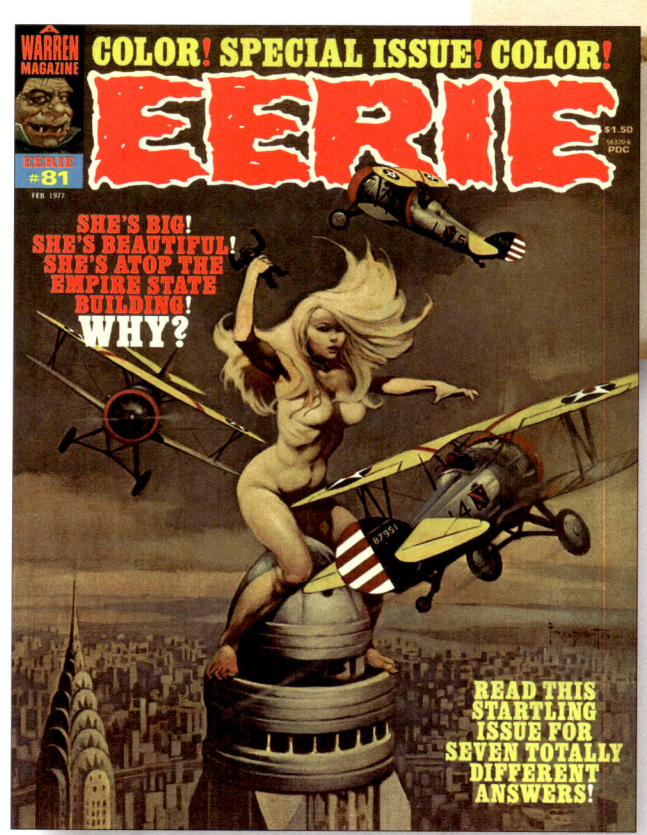

QUEEN KONG

Oil on masonite, 1976
First printed as the cover to Eerie #81
(Warren, 1977)

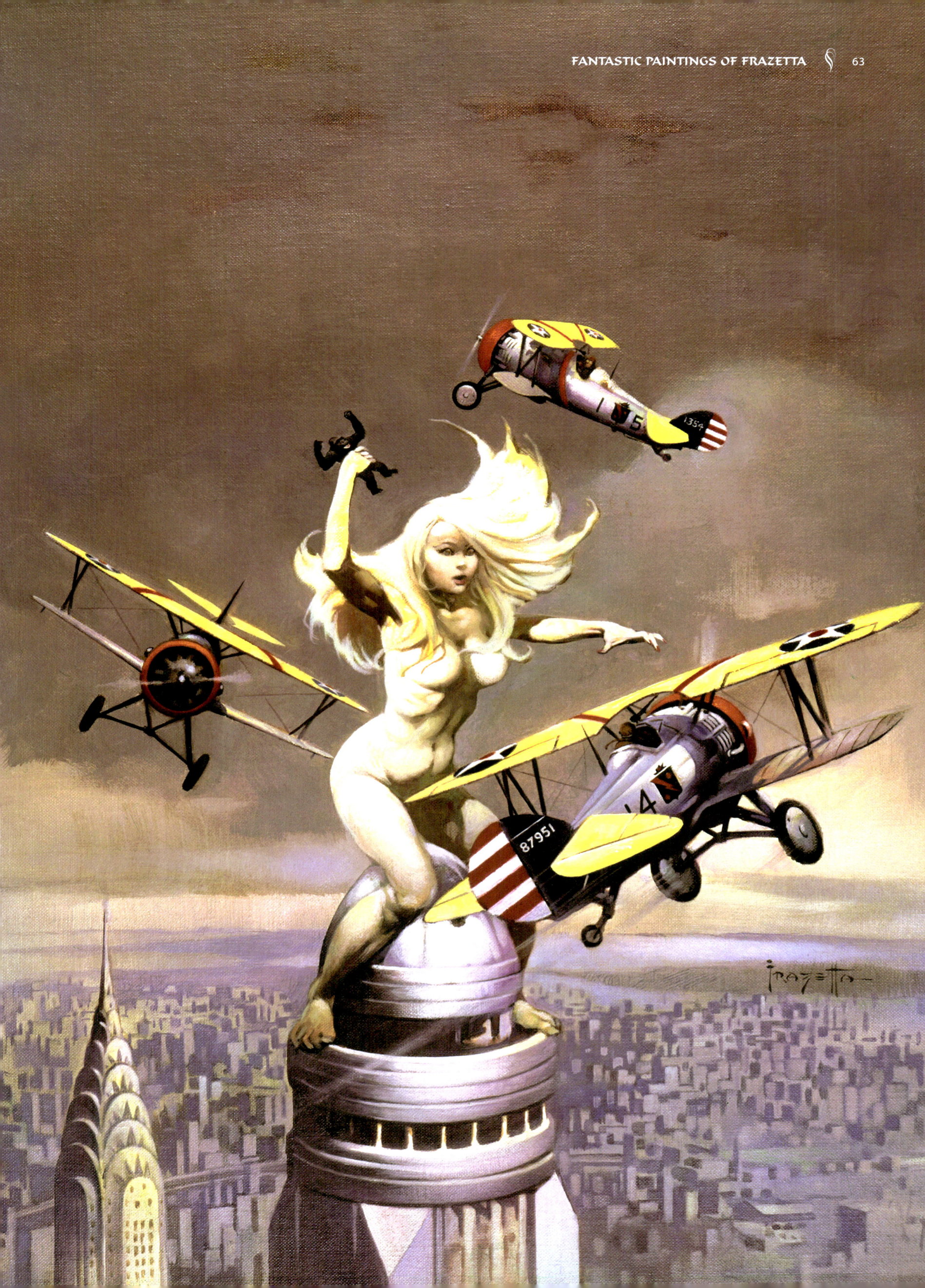

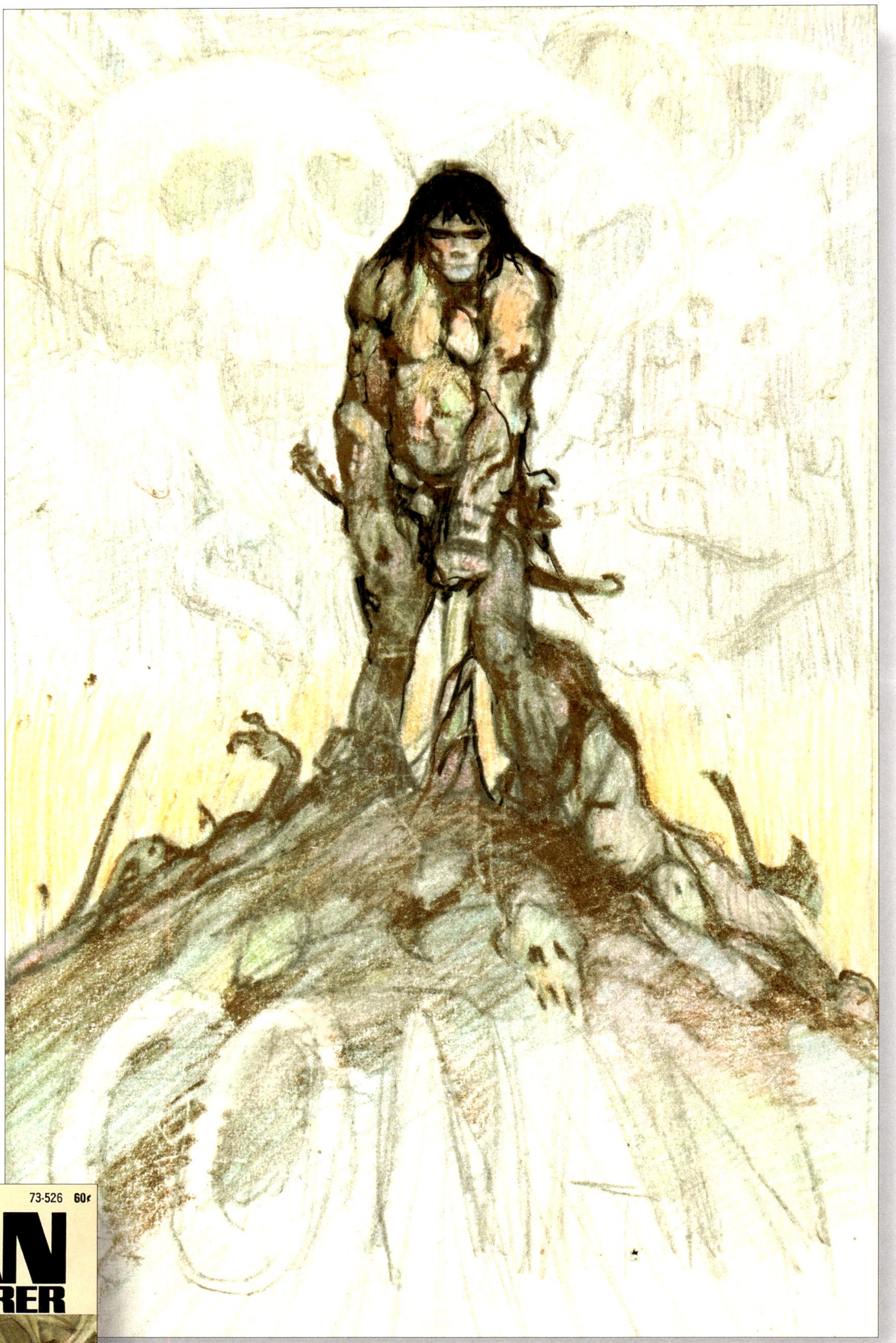

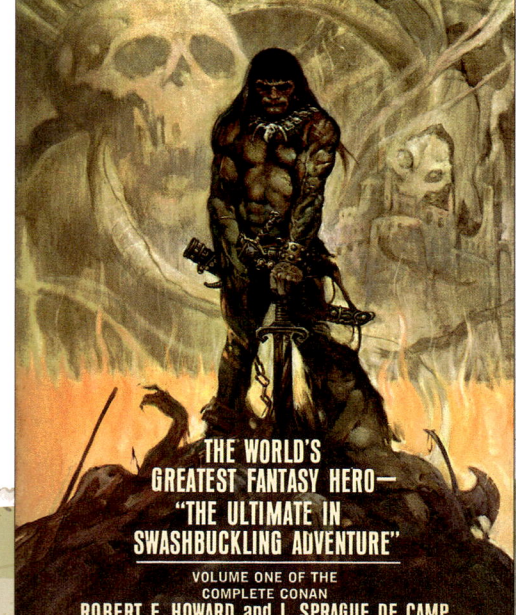

THE BARBARIAN *(revised)*
Oil on canvas, late 1965/early 1966
First printed as the cover to Conan the Adventurer *(Lancer, 1966)*
This revised version first appeared in
The Fantastic Art of Frank Frazetta *(1975)*

Above: Preliminary sketch 4.25" x 7"
Graphite and colored pencils. Previously unpublished

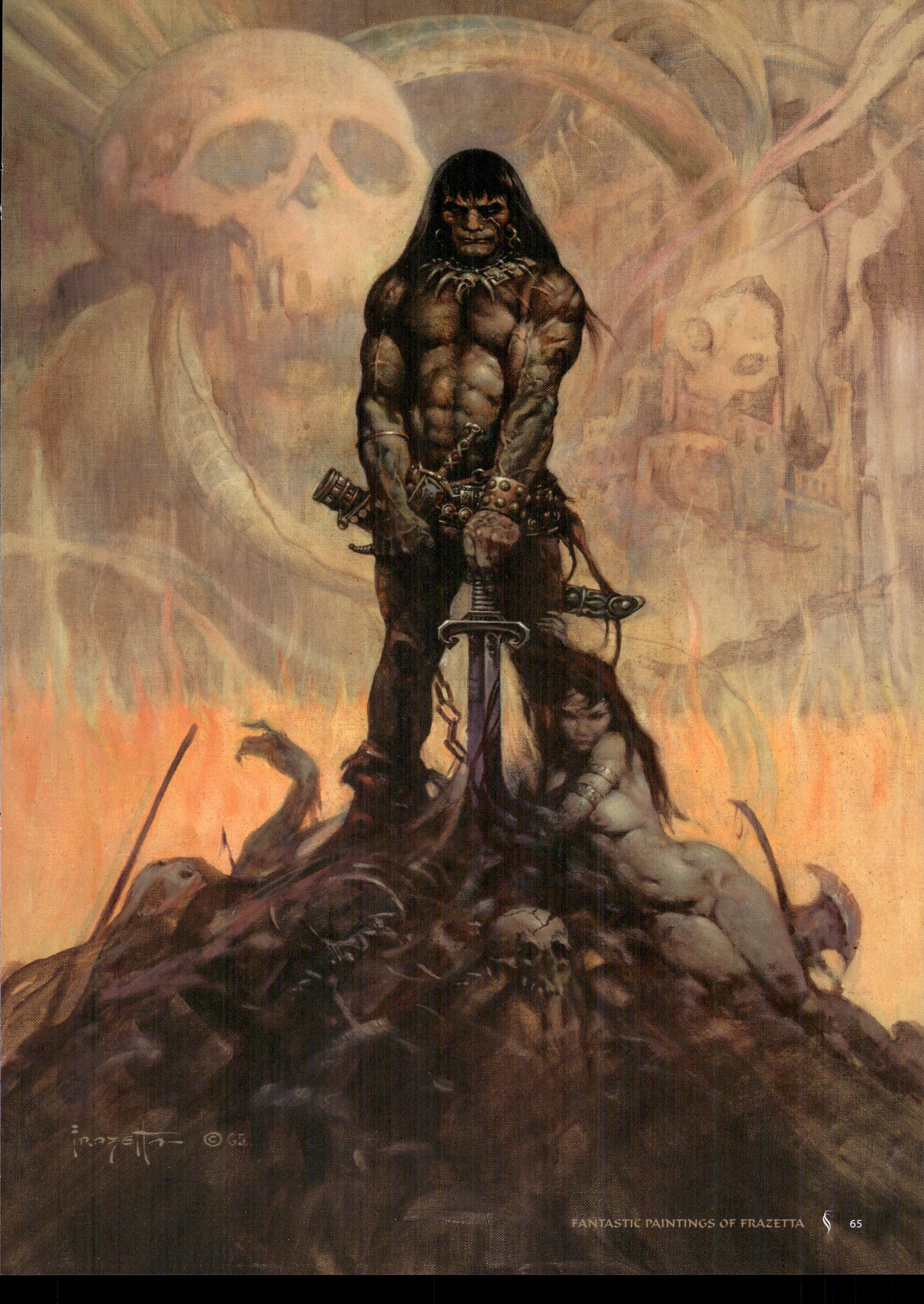

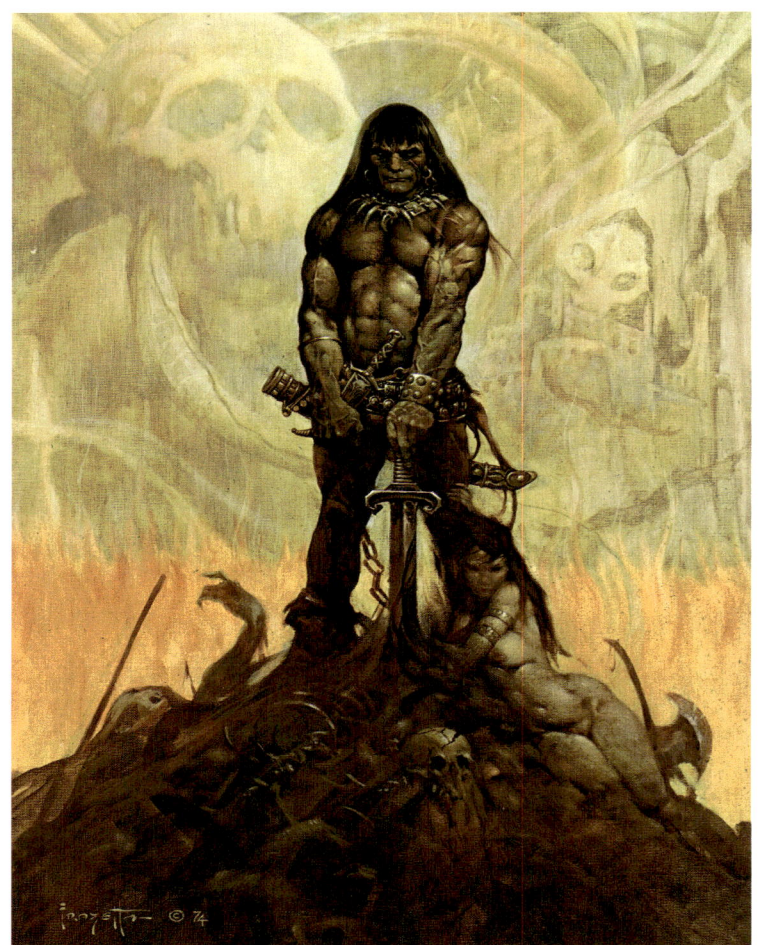

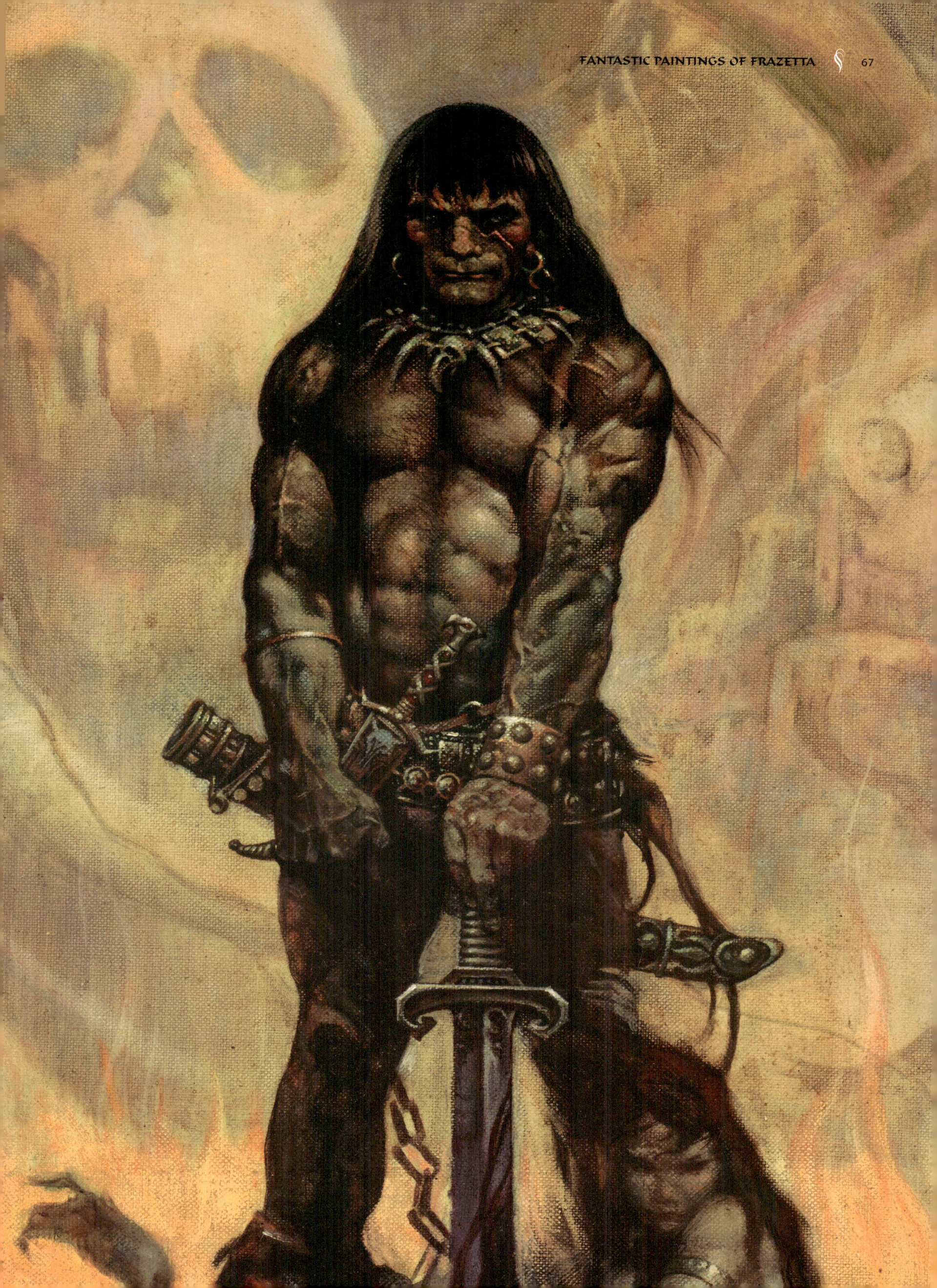

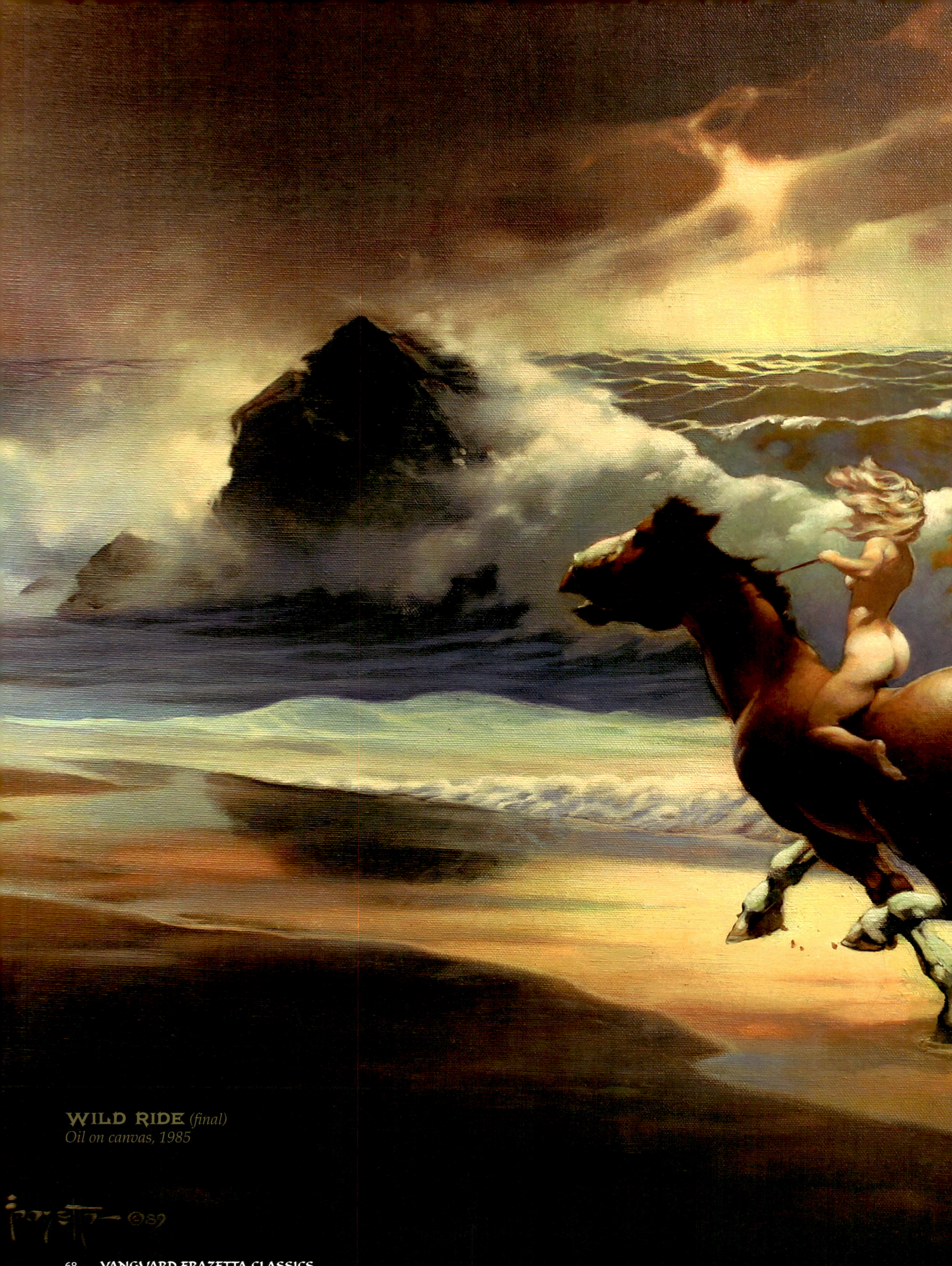

WILD RIDE *(final)*
Oil on canvas, 1985

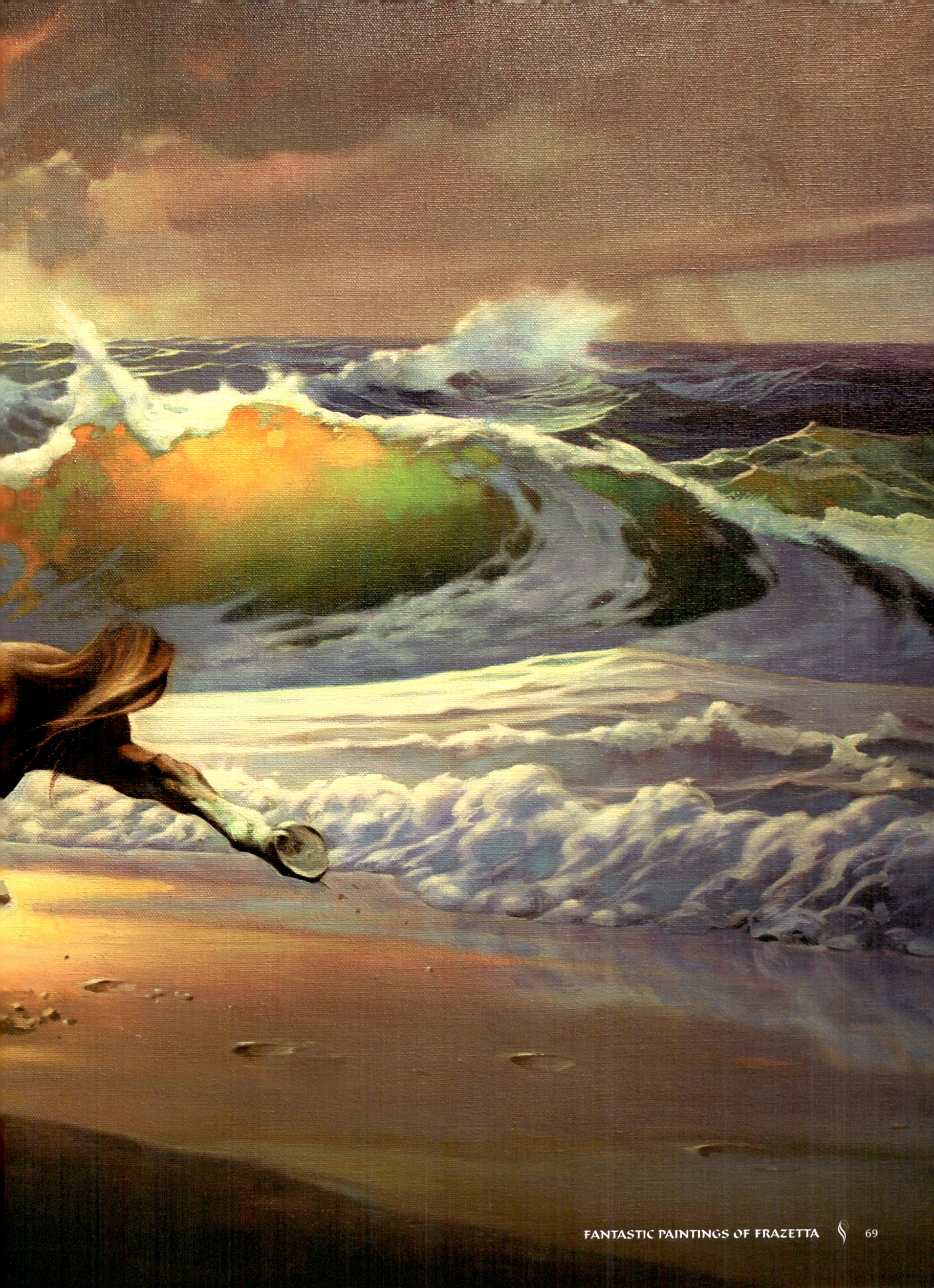

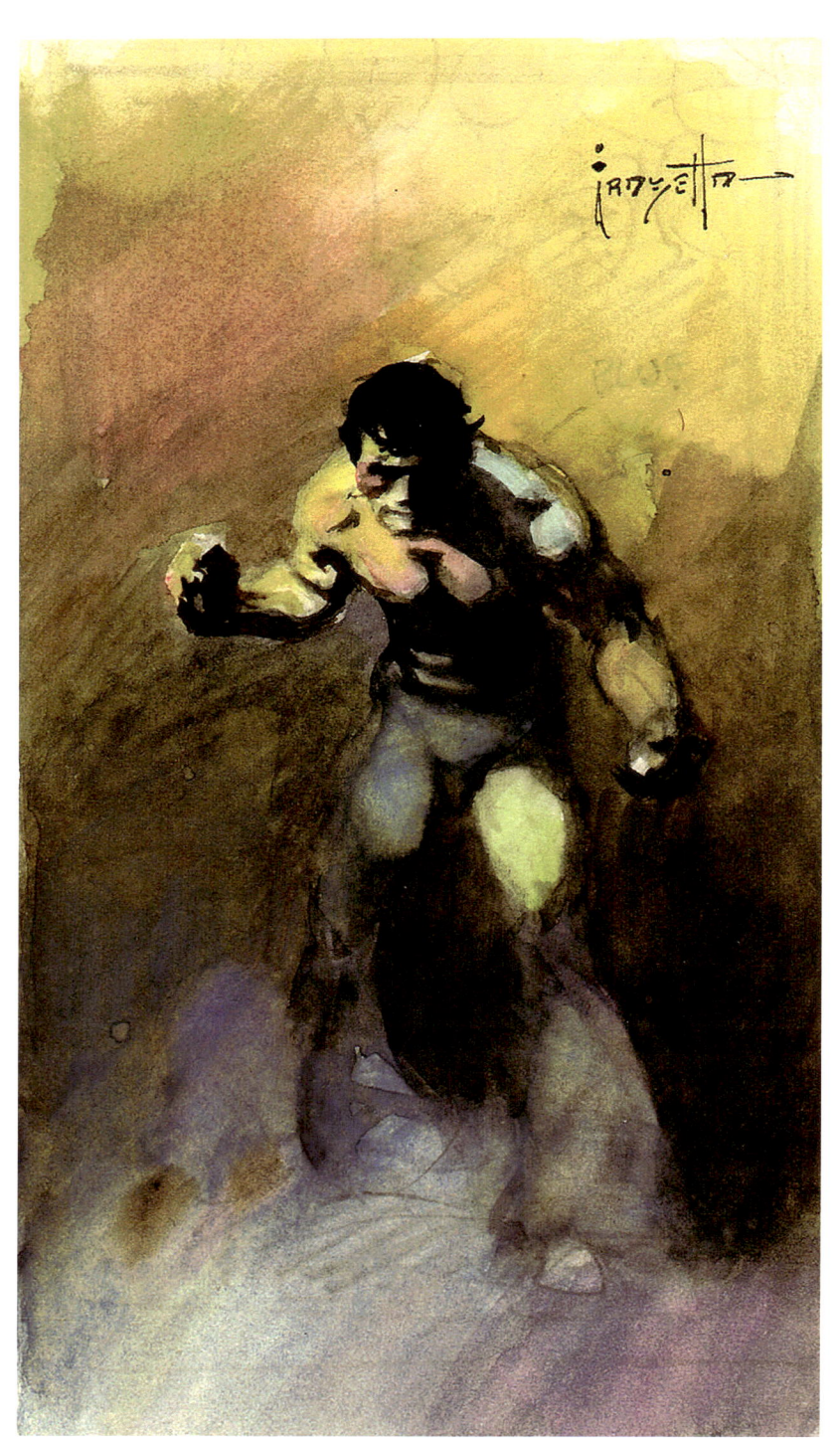

THE MUCKER
Oil on academy board, 1975
First printed as the cover to The Mucker
(Ace, 1974)

THE MUCKER is a rare image that was in none of the 1970s Frazetta art books and never released as a poster. It has been in a private collection all these years.

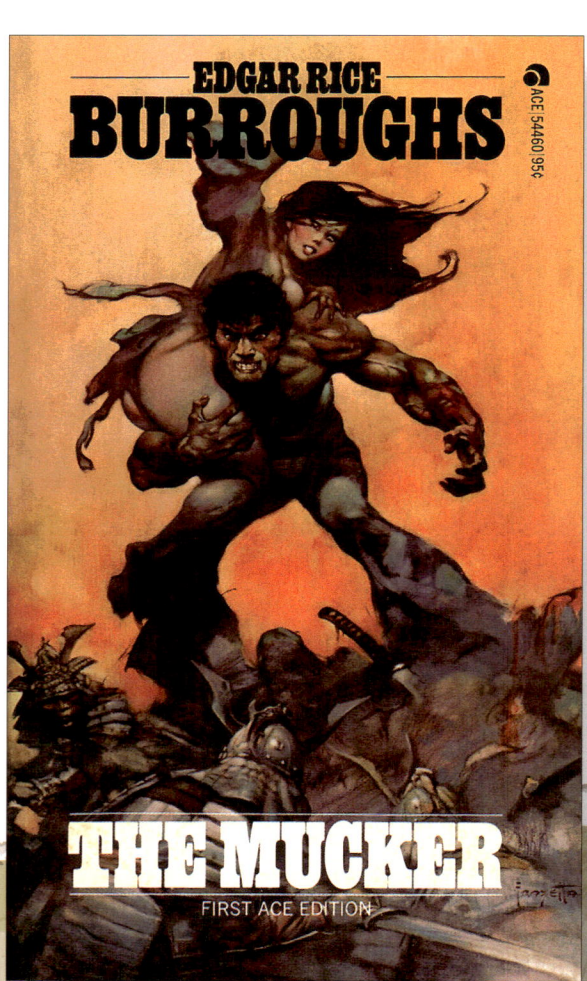

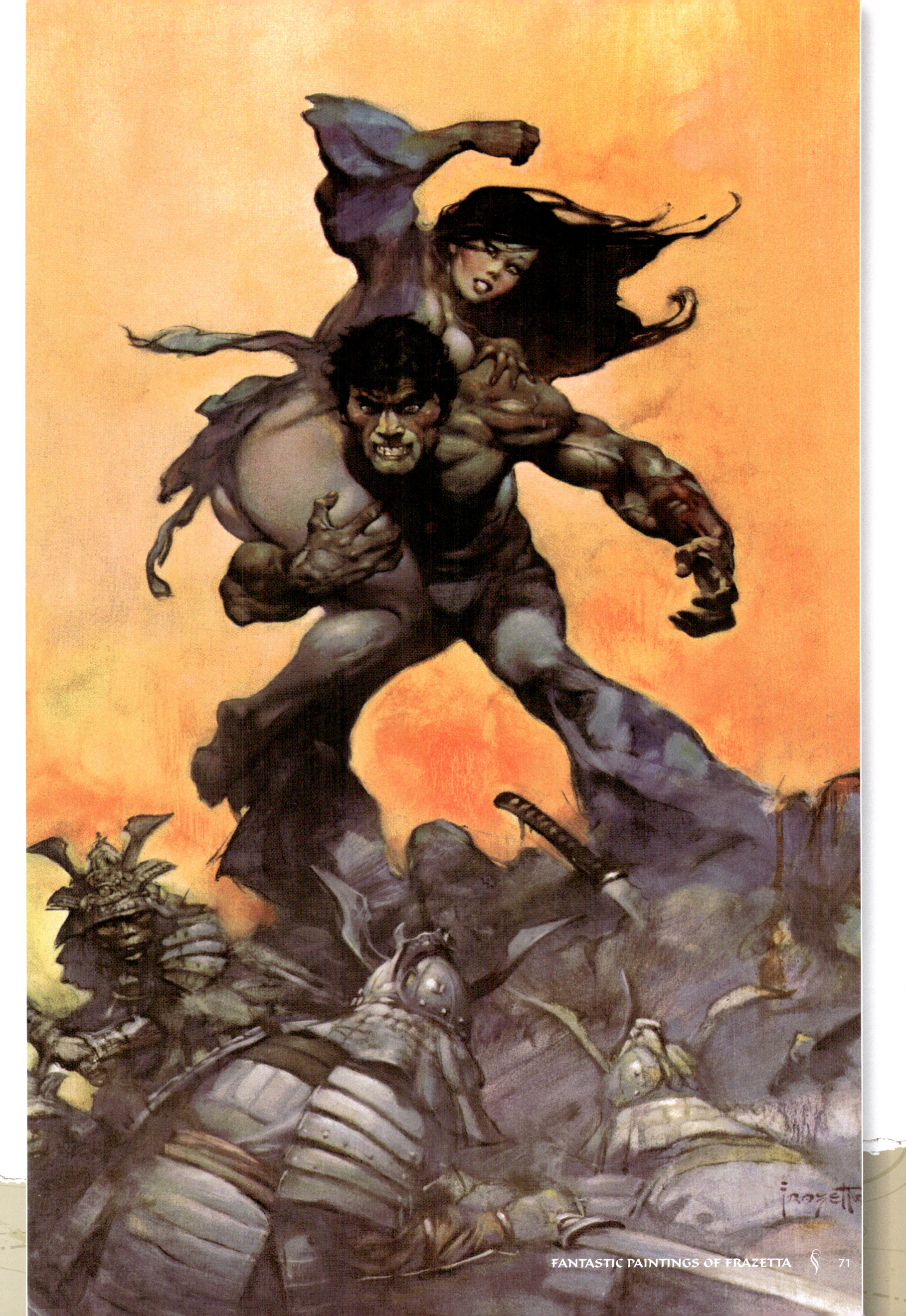

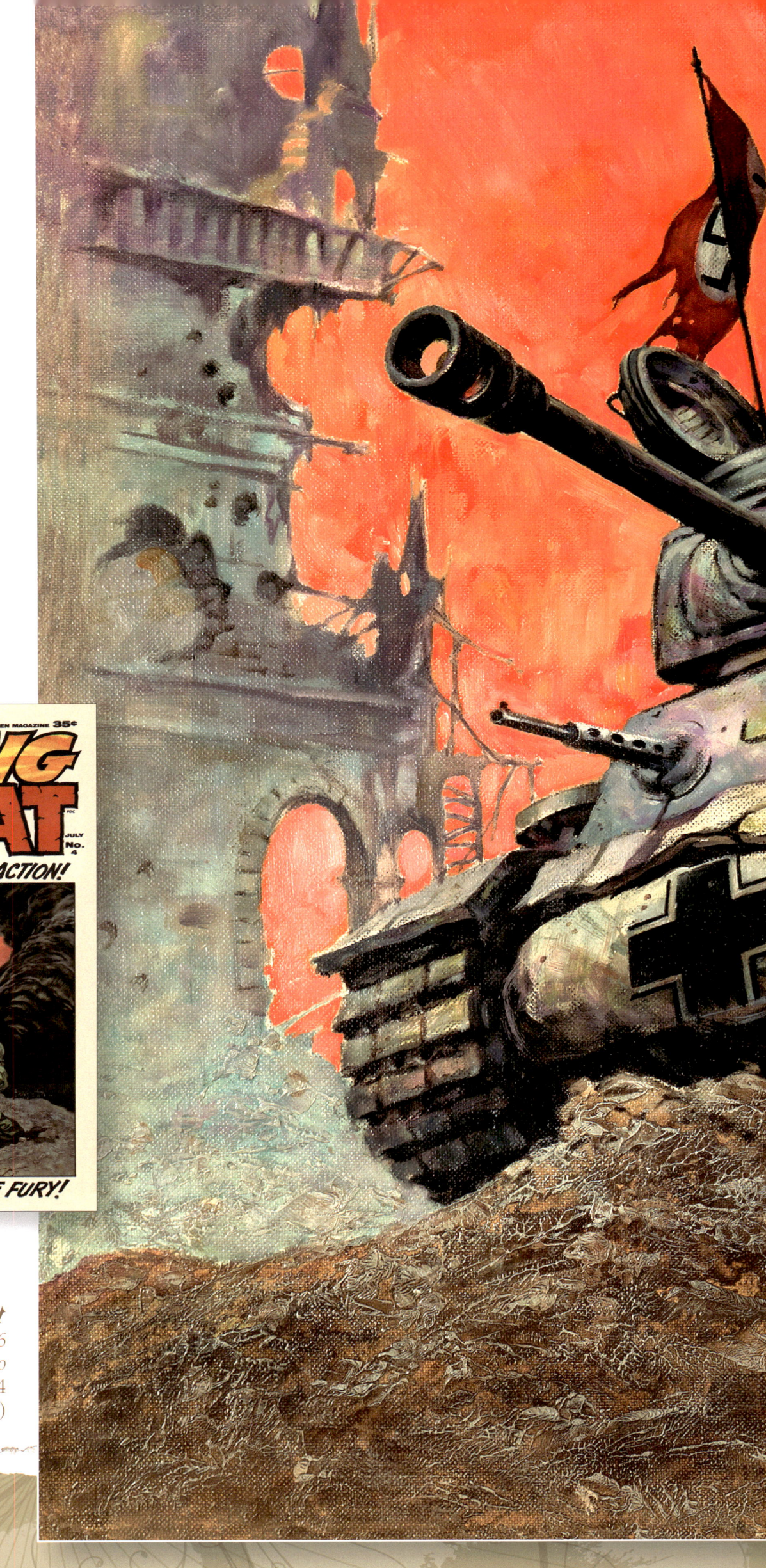

BLAZING COMBAT IV

*Oil on academy board, 1966
First printed as the cover to*
Blazing Combat #4
(Warren, 1966)

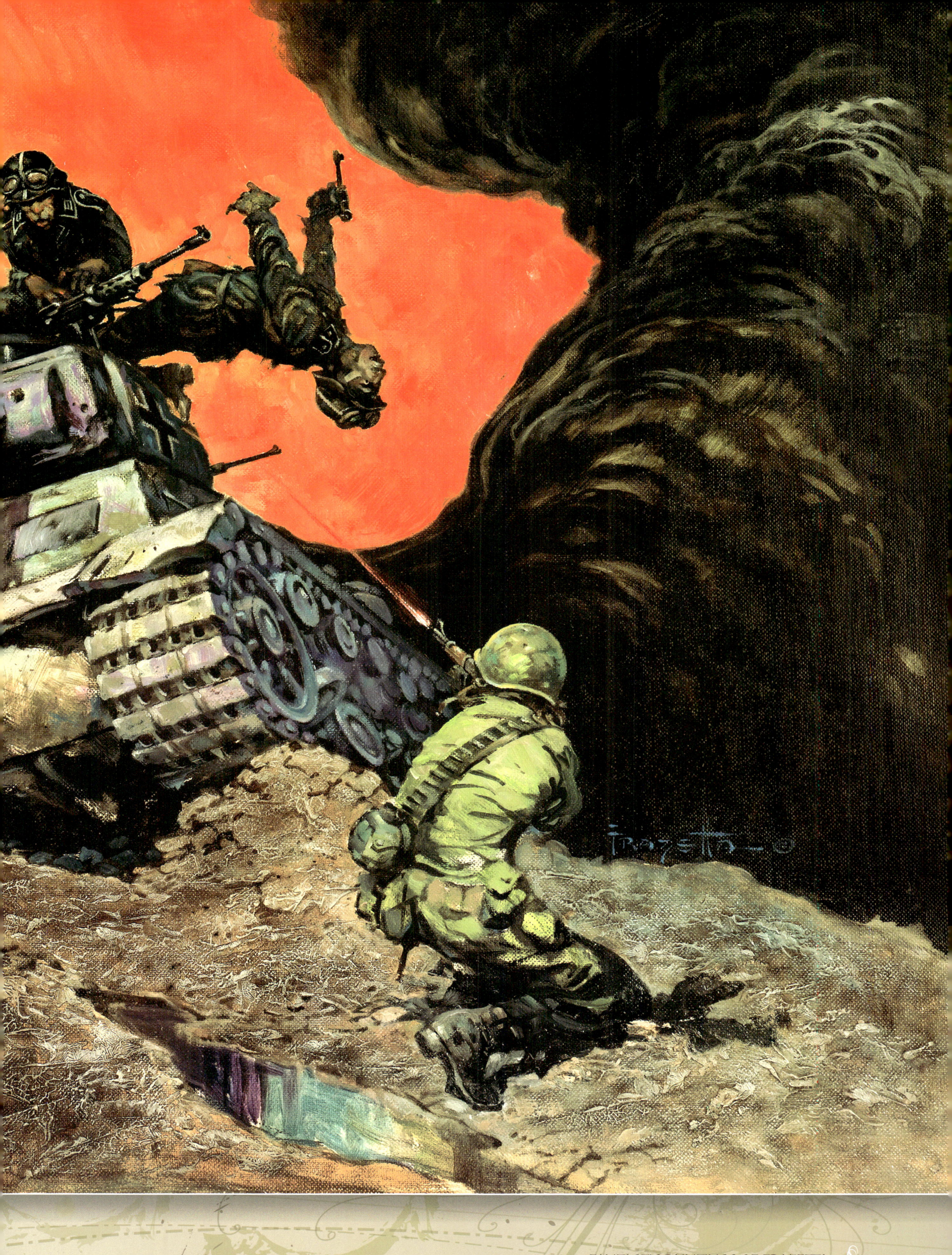

I painted DEATH DEALER and SILVER WARRIOR back to back. I had been sitting on my laurels, just going through the motions. Then, there was a rumor that disturbed me, that I was washed up, that I hadn't done anything [major] in years. They chopped me up for dinner! That's loyalty for you. It made me decide to show them the old spirit. I sat down, DEATH DEALER was born, then SILVER WARRIOR, [in some ways] better than anything I'd ever done.

FRANK FRAZETTA

Preview #54, January 1984

THE SILVER WARRIOR

Oil on masonite, 1972
First printed as the cover to
The Silver Warriors
(Dell, 1973)

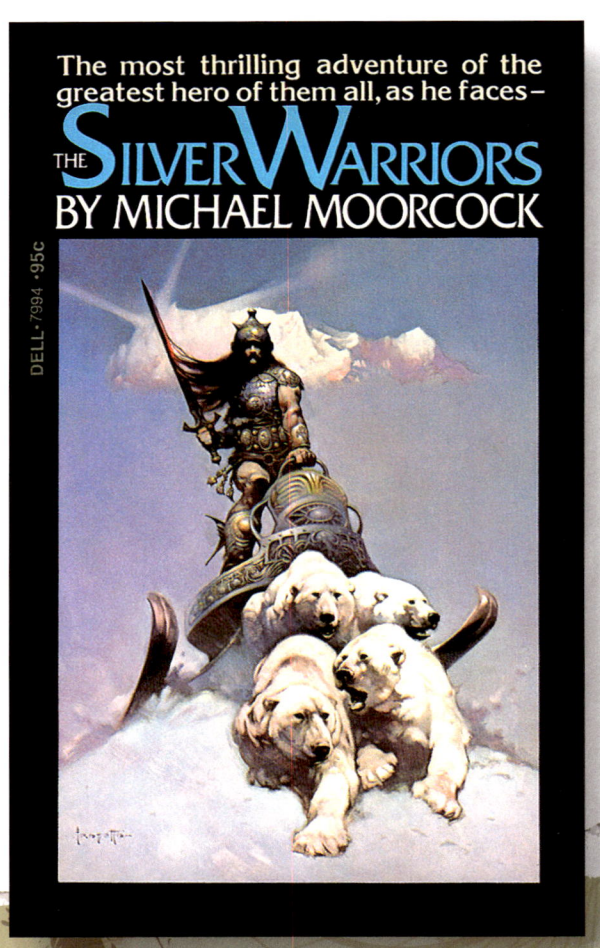

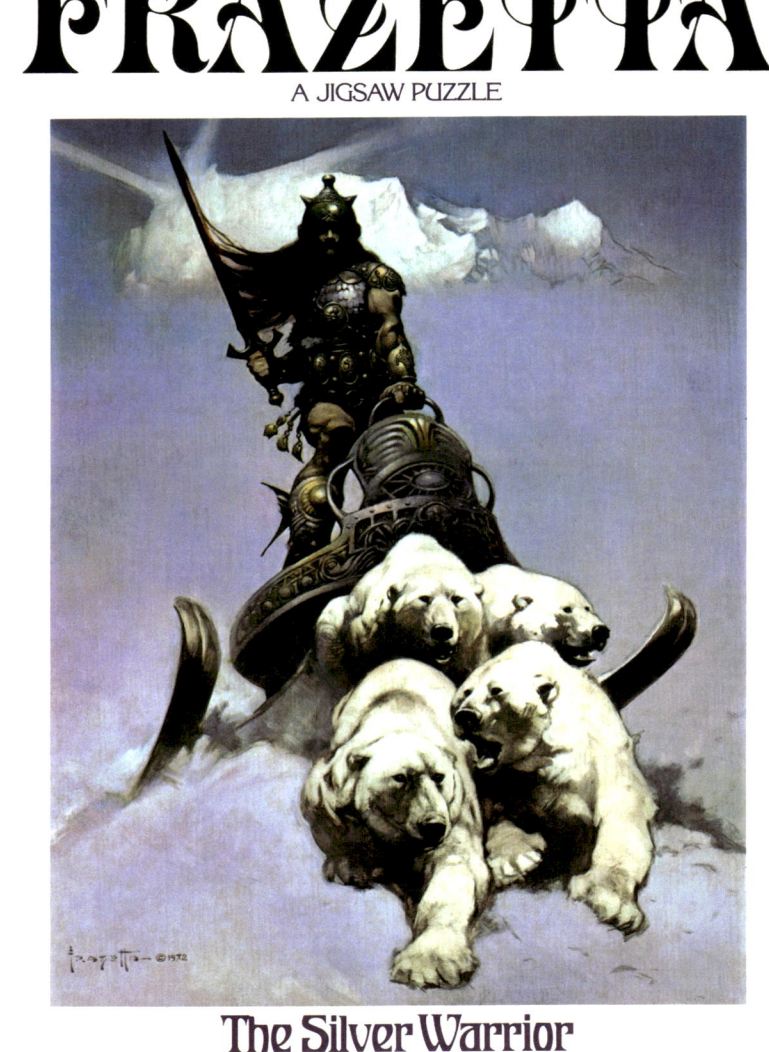

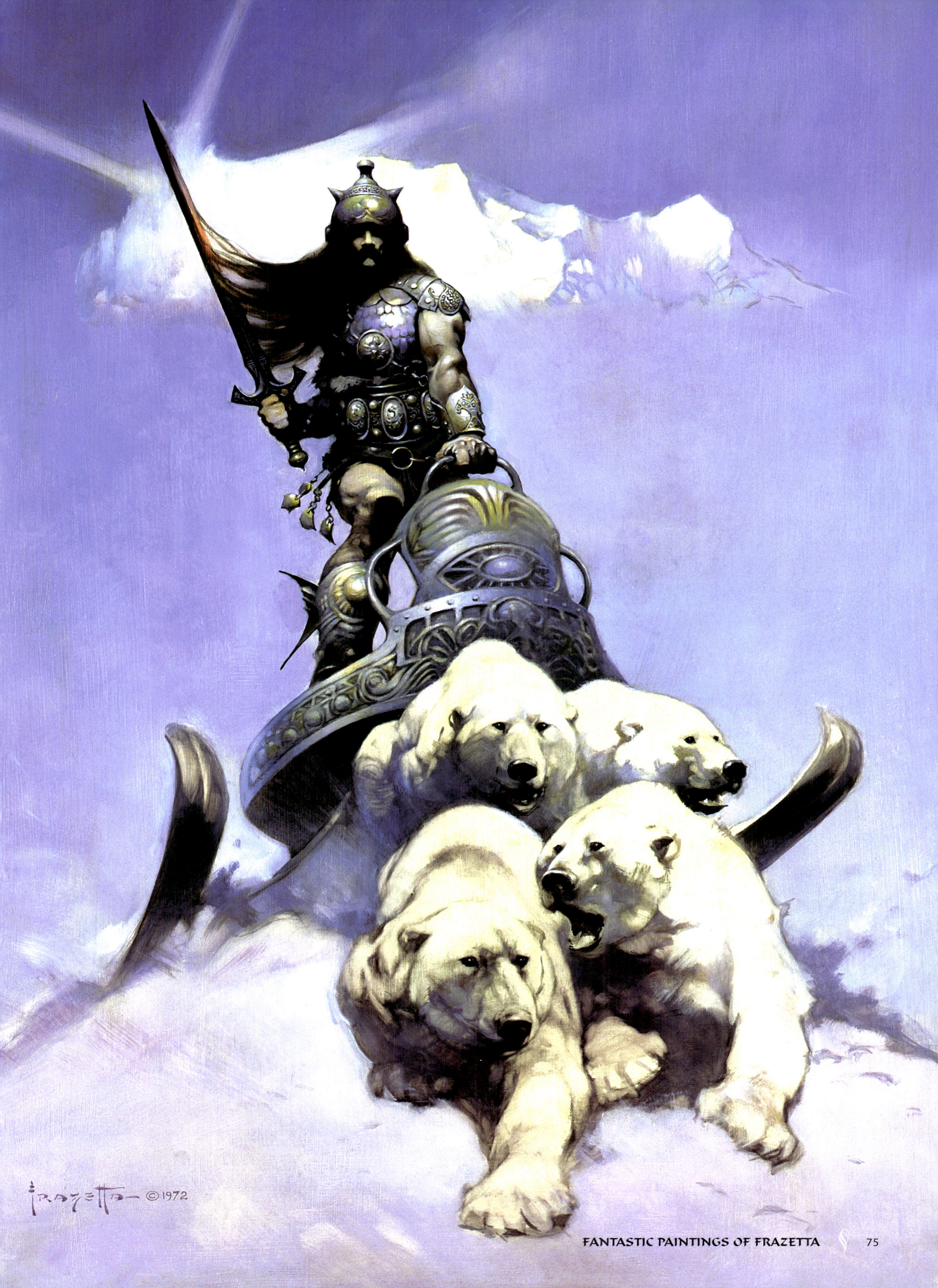

> *I loved the original versions of* Conan The Buccaneer *and I was very distressed when Frank changed the basic concept. I have grown to really like the current version and I realize why Frank wanted the changes. Frank said that he wanted to give Conan a fighting chance in battle. An axe is more firepower than bare hands, especially when all the other warriors are heavily armed.*

DOC DAVE WINIEWICZ

Frazetta Blogspot

THE DESTROYER *(Final version)*
Oil on academy board, 1971
First printed as the cover to
Conan the Buccaneer *(Lancer, 1971)*

This revised version first appeared in
The Fantastic Art of Frank Frazetta *(Ballantine, 1975)*

In 2010, THE DESTROYER sold for $1.5 Million

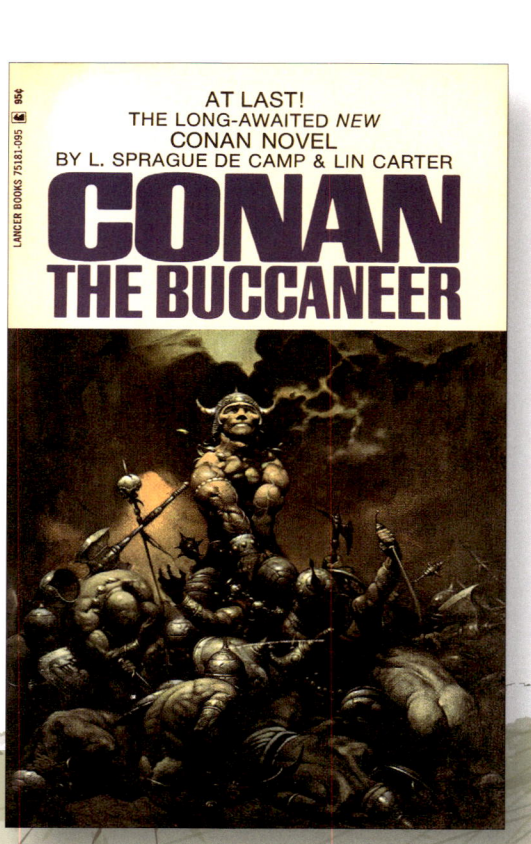

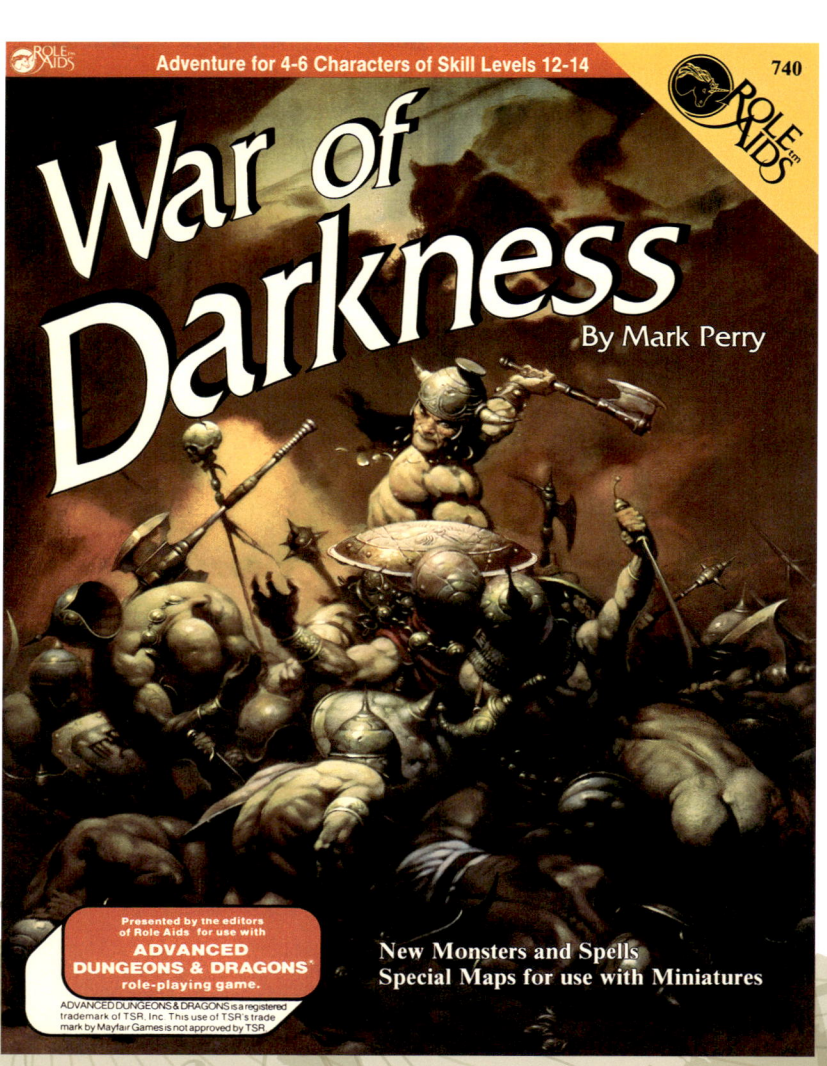

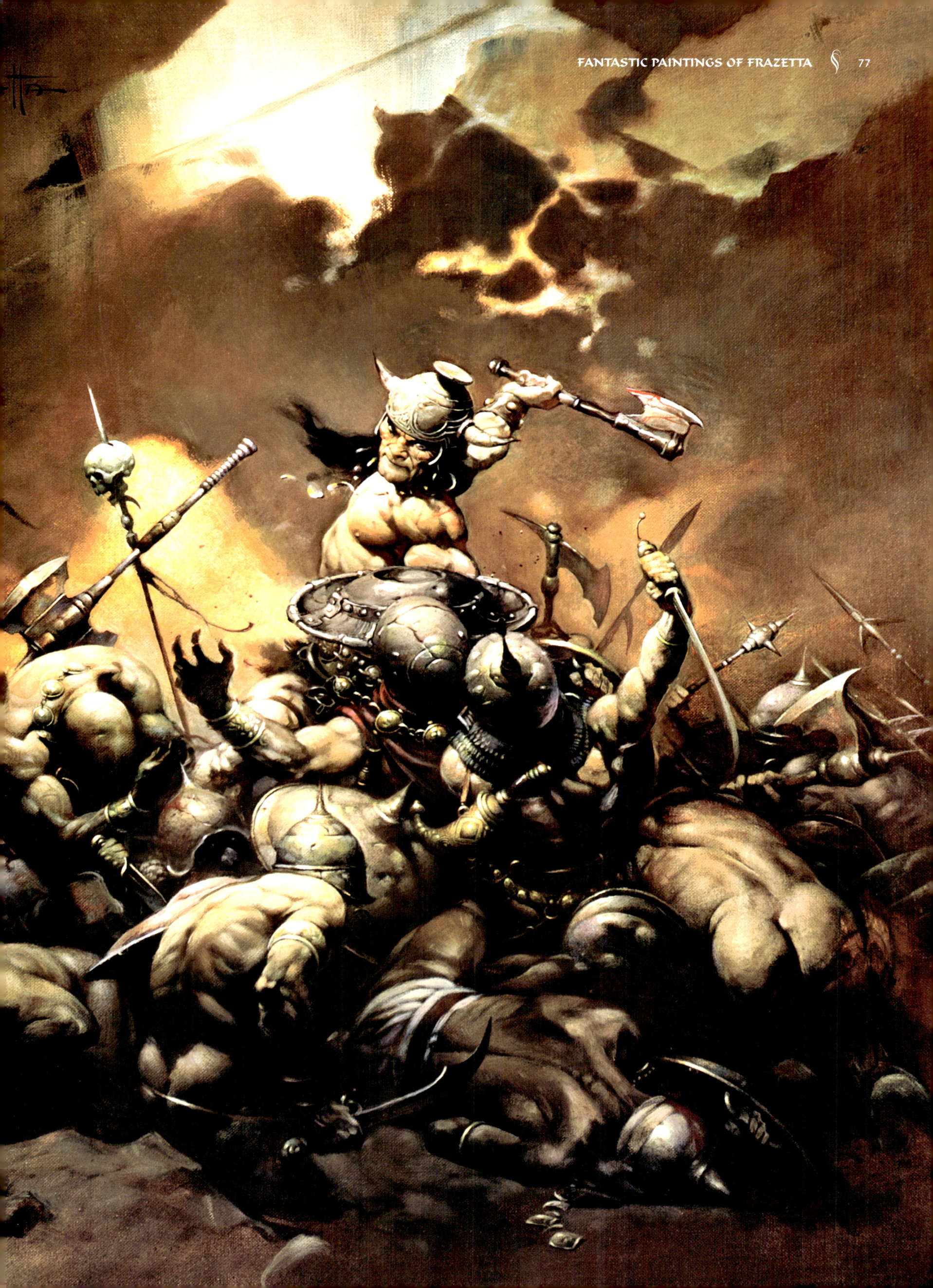

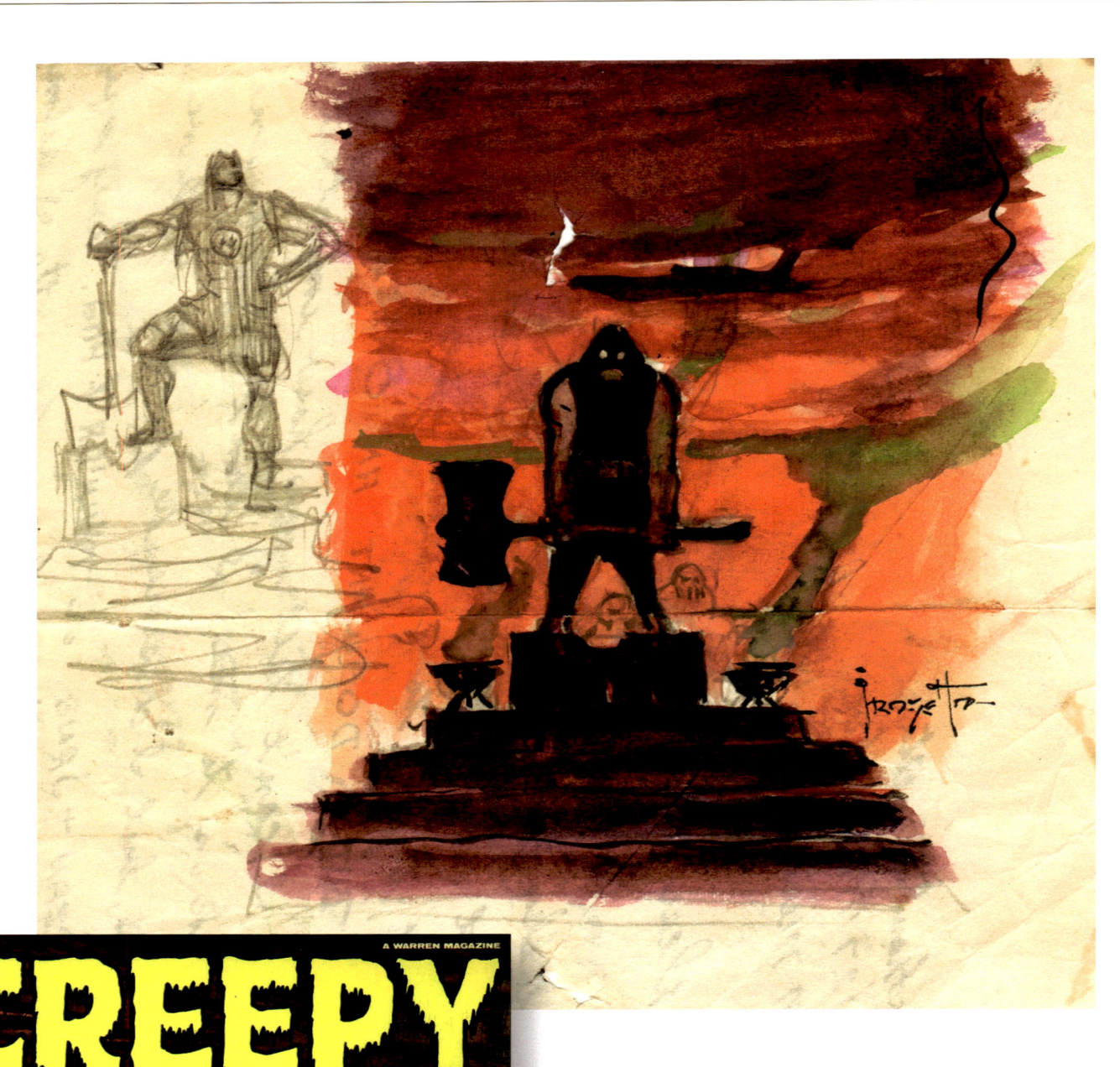

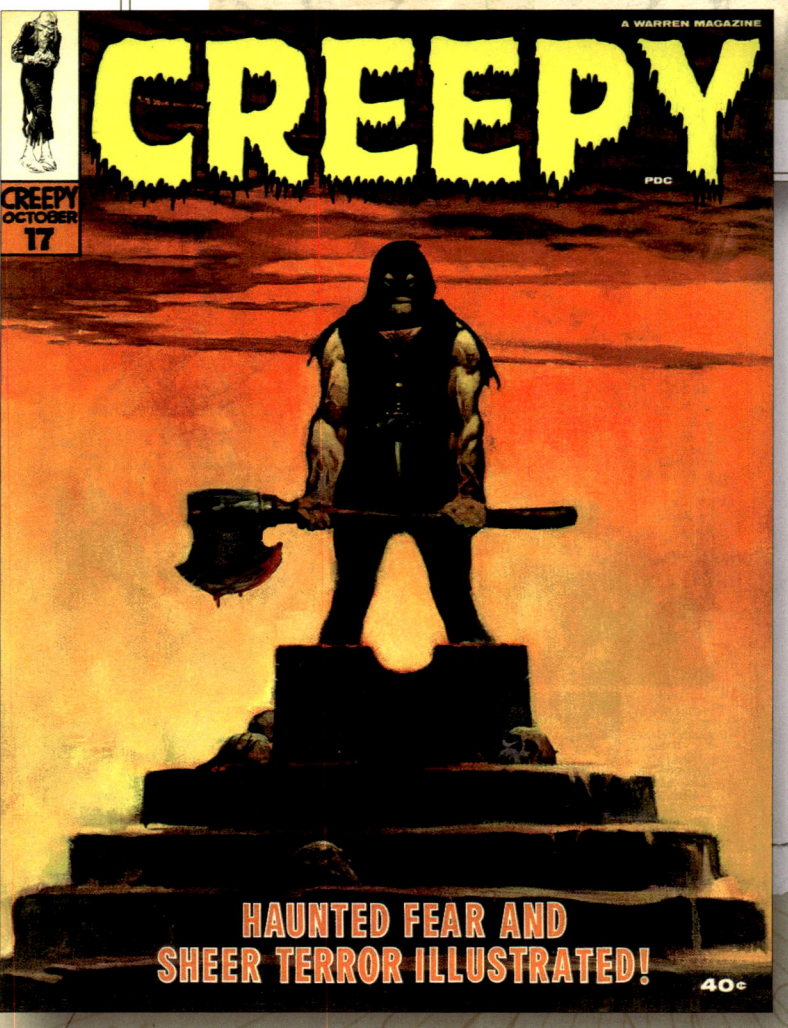

EXECUTIONER *(Slightly modified)*
Oil on masonite, 1967
First printed as the cover to Creepy #17
(Warren, 1967)
Unlike most of Frazetta's paintings, this image was never issued by the artist as a poster in the 1970s or '80s.

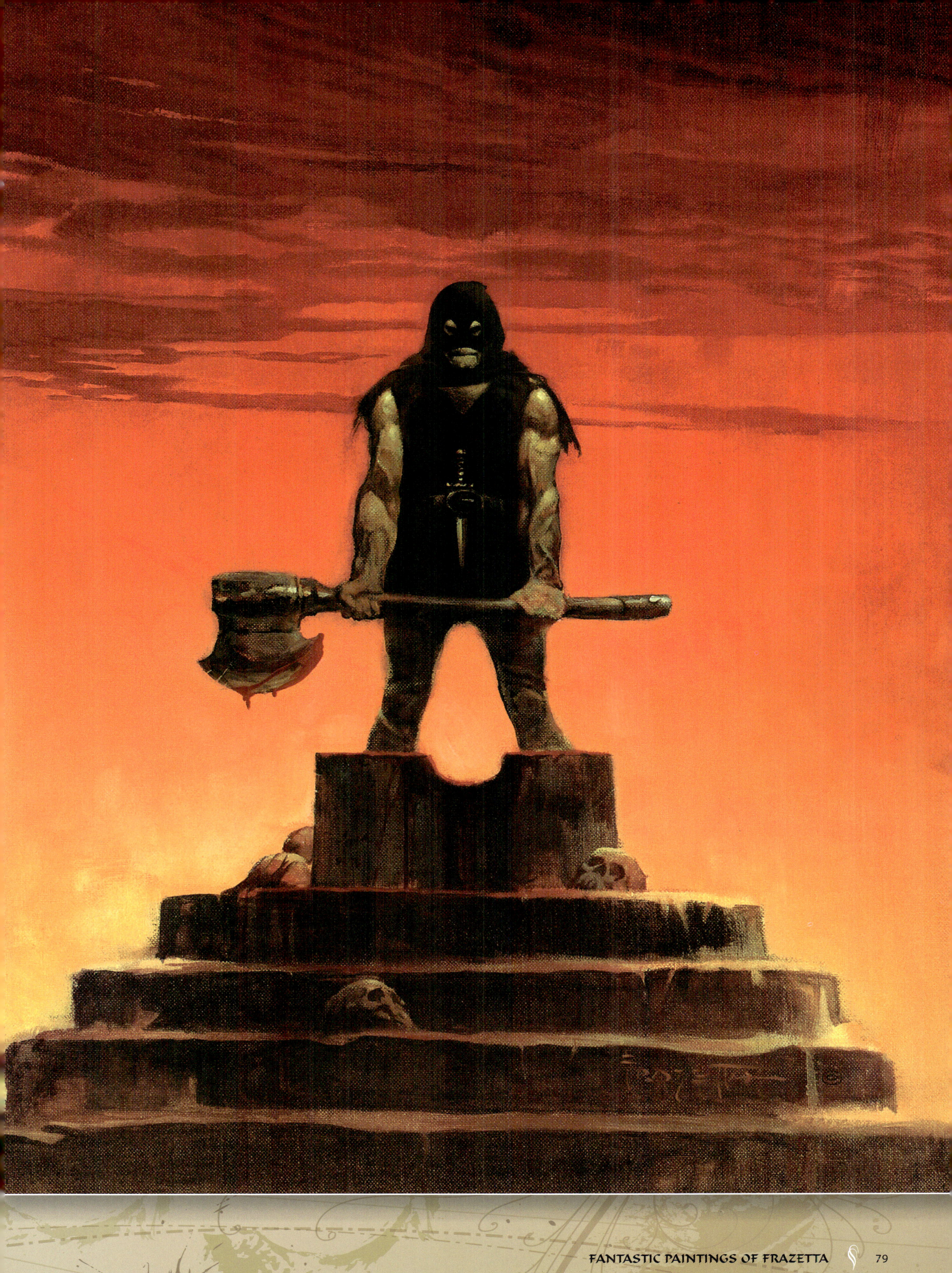

*I was attracted to Fantasy originally
because it wasn't a defined genre. Like rock
and roll, you could make something of
your own out of it.*

MICHAEL MOORCOCK

Mythmakers & Lawbreakers: Anarchist Writers on Fiction

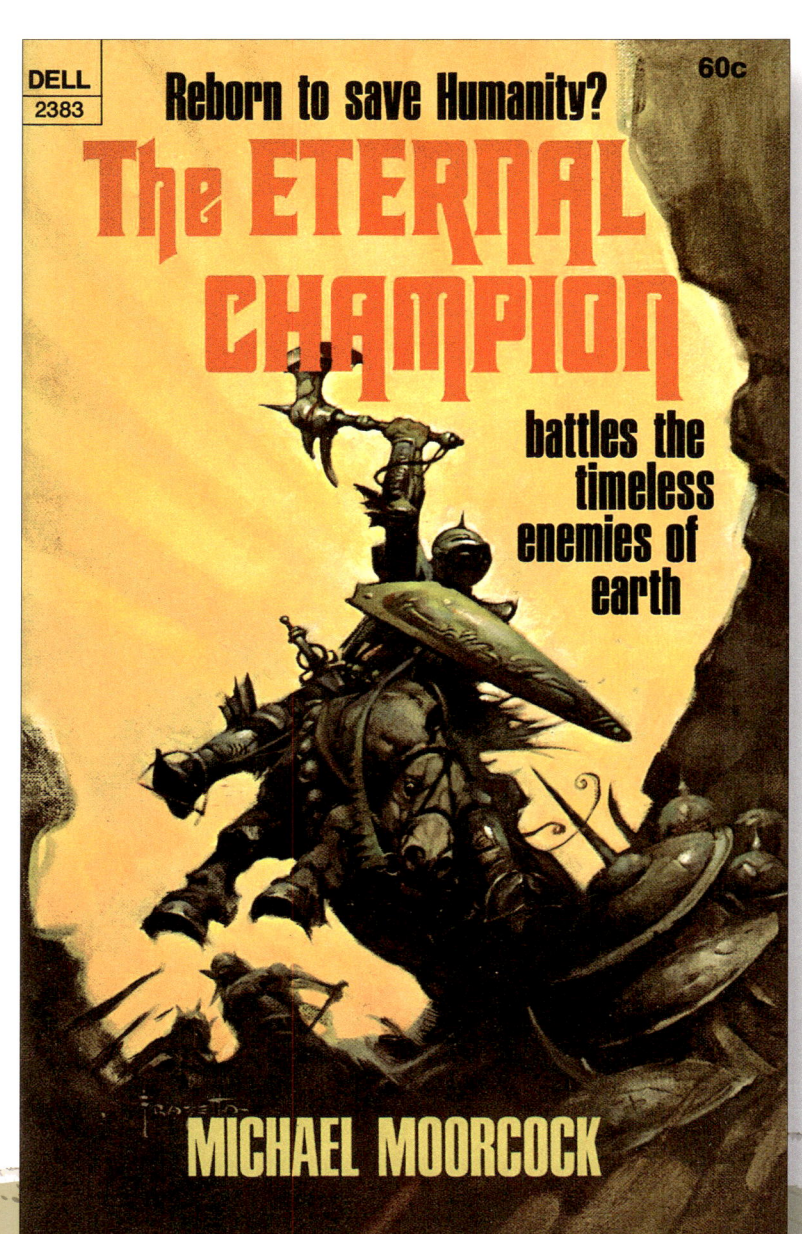

DELL
2383

Reborn to save Humanity?

The ETERNAL CHAMPION

60c

**battles the
timeless
enemies of
earth**

MICHAEL MOORCOCK

ETERNAL CHAMPION *(Original version)
Oil on masonite, 1970
First printed as the cover to*
The Eternal Champion
(Dell, 1970)

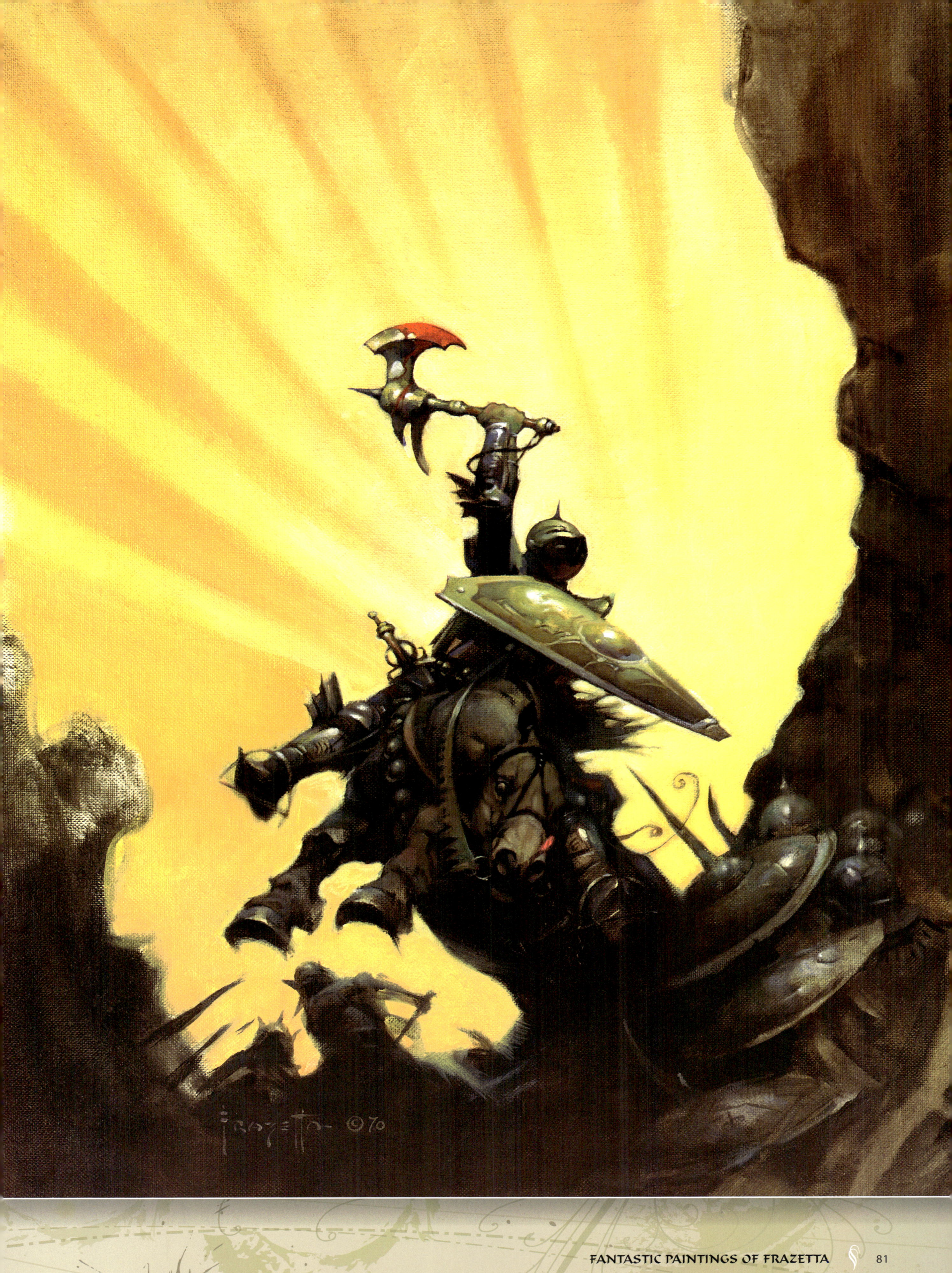

I use the ideas of Law and Chaos precisely because I am suspicious of simplistic notions of good and evil. In my multiverse, Law and Chaos are both legitimate ways of interpreting and defining experience. Ideally, the Cosmic Balance keeps both sides in equilibrium. By playing "the Game of Time"… the various participants maintain that equilibrium. When the scales tip too far toward Law we move toward rigid orthodoxy and social sterility, a form of decadence. When Chaos is uppermost we move too far towards undisciplined and destructive creativity.

MICHAEL MOORCOCK

1994, re: his multiverse Eternal Champion who is endlessly reincarnated

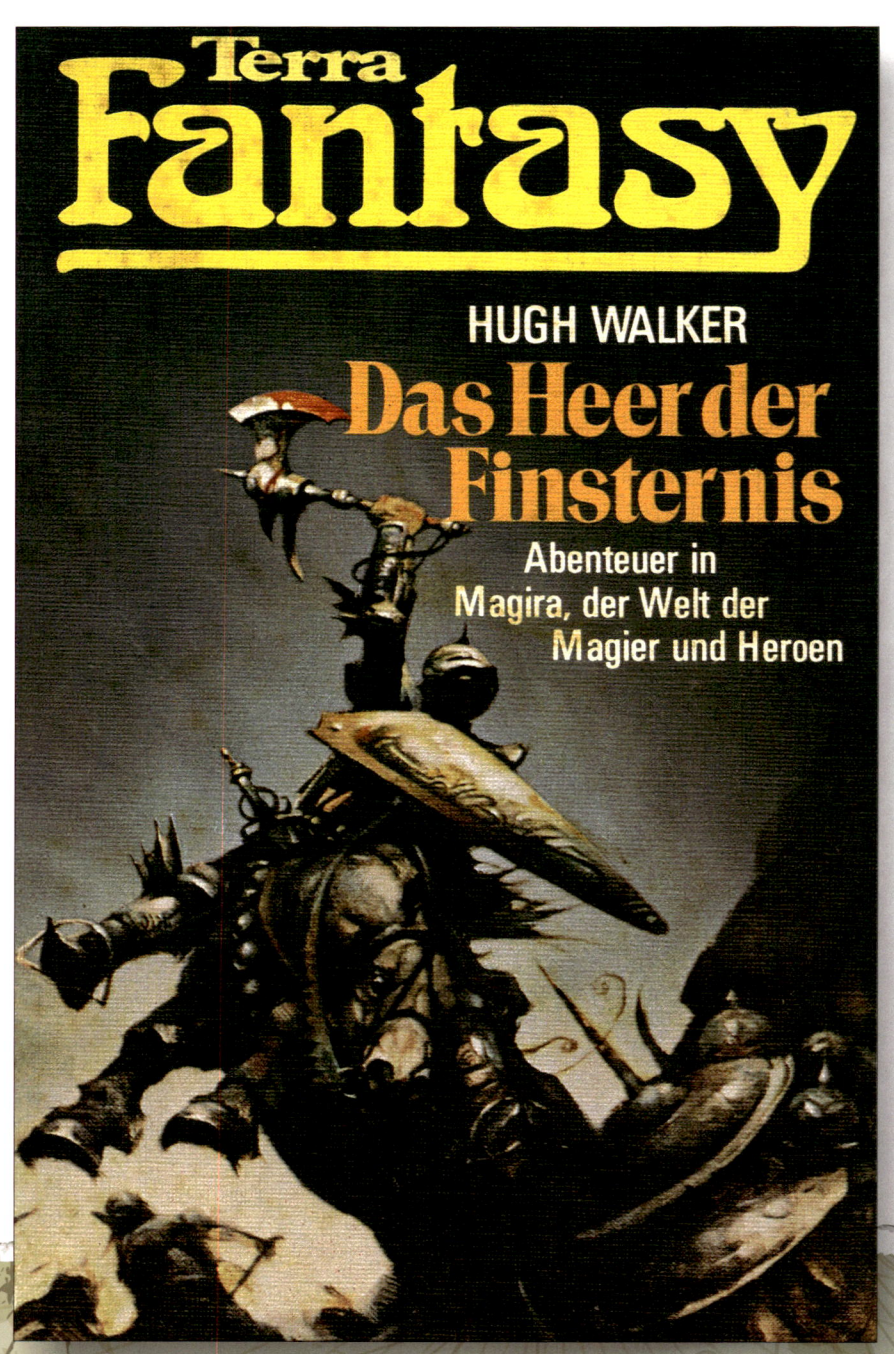

ETERNAL CHAMPION *(revised)*
Oil on masonite, 1994
First printed in Legacy
(Underwood, 1999)

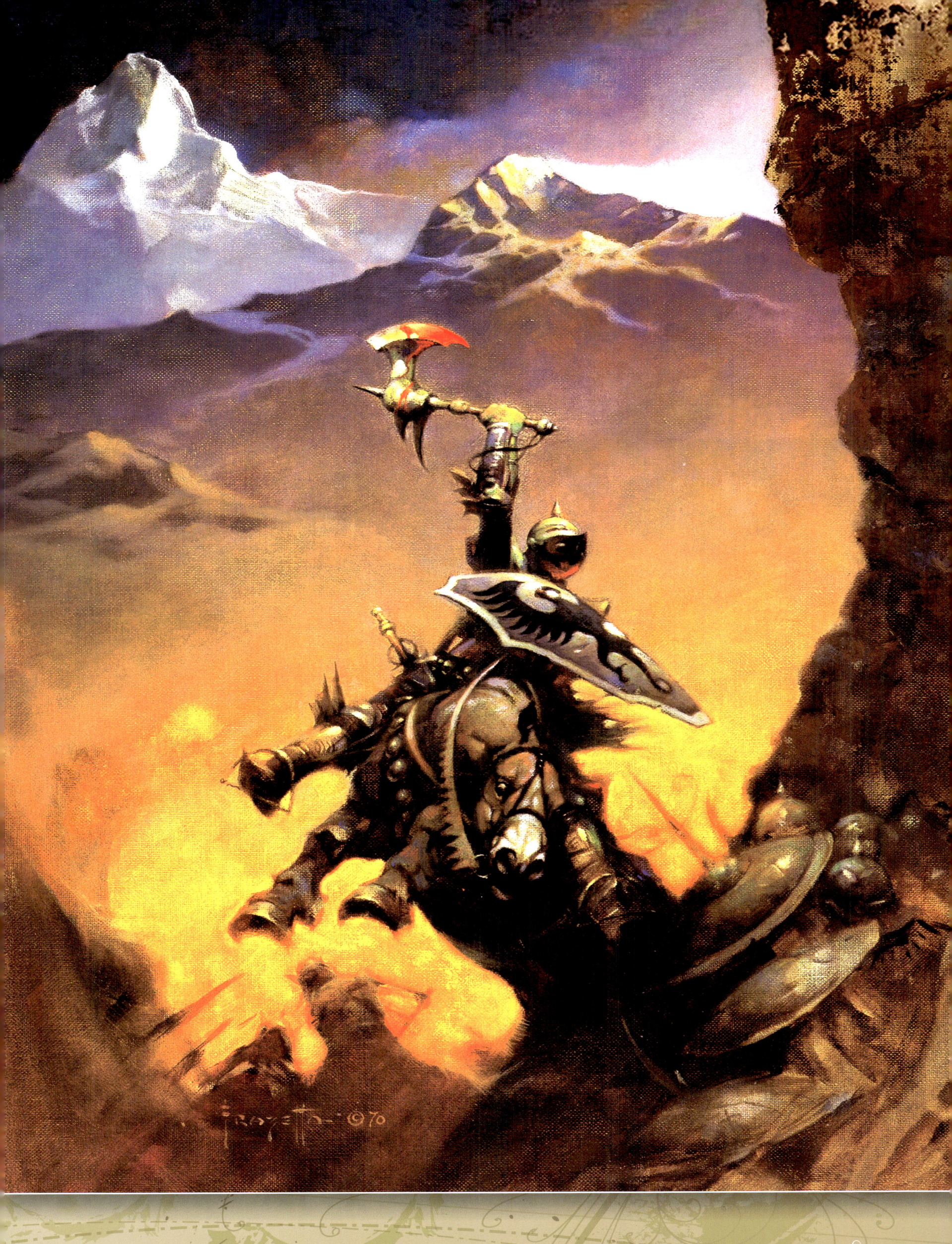

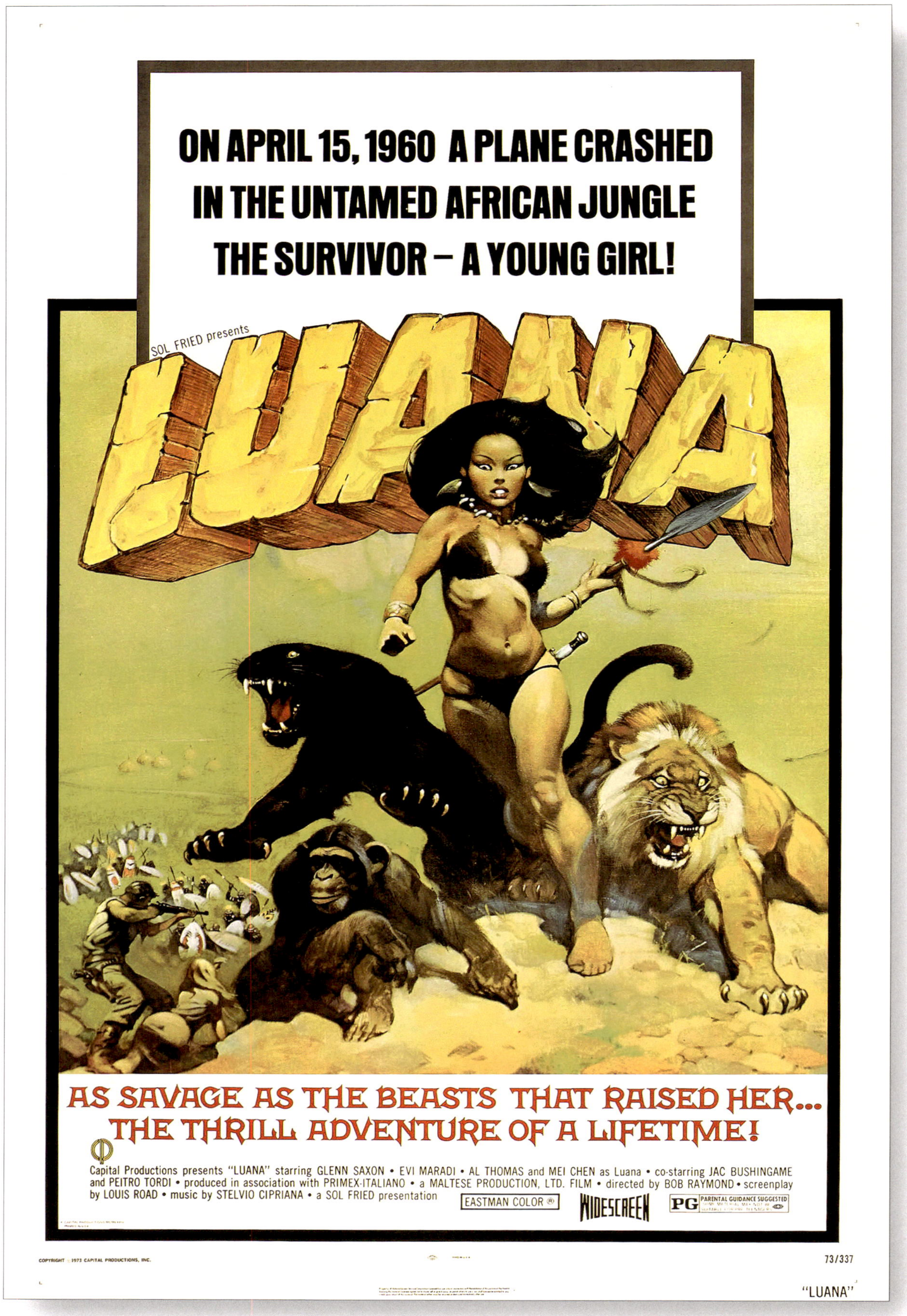

ON APRIL 15, 1960 A PLANE CRASHED
IN THE UNTAMED AFRICAN JUNGLE
THE SURVIVOR – A YOUNG GIRL!

SOL FRIED presents

LUANA

AS SAVAGE AS THE BEASTS THAT RAISED HER...
THE THRILL ADVENTURE OF A LIFETIME!

Capital Productions presents "LUANA" starring GLENN SAXON • EVI MARADI • AL THOMAS and MEI CHEN as Luana • co-starring JAC BUSHINGAME and PEITRO TORDI • produced in association with PRIMEX-ITALIANO • a MALTESE PRODUCTION, LTD. FILM • directed by BOB RAYMOND • screenplay by LOUIS ROAD • music by STELVIO CIPRIANA • a SOL FRIED presentation

EASTMAN COLOR ® | WIDESCREEN | PG PARENTAL GUIDANCE SUGGESTED

COPYRIGHT © 1973 CAPITAL PRODUCTIONS, INC.

73/337

"LUANA"

LUANA
First printed as a One-sheet A movie poster
(Capital Productions, 1973)

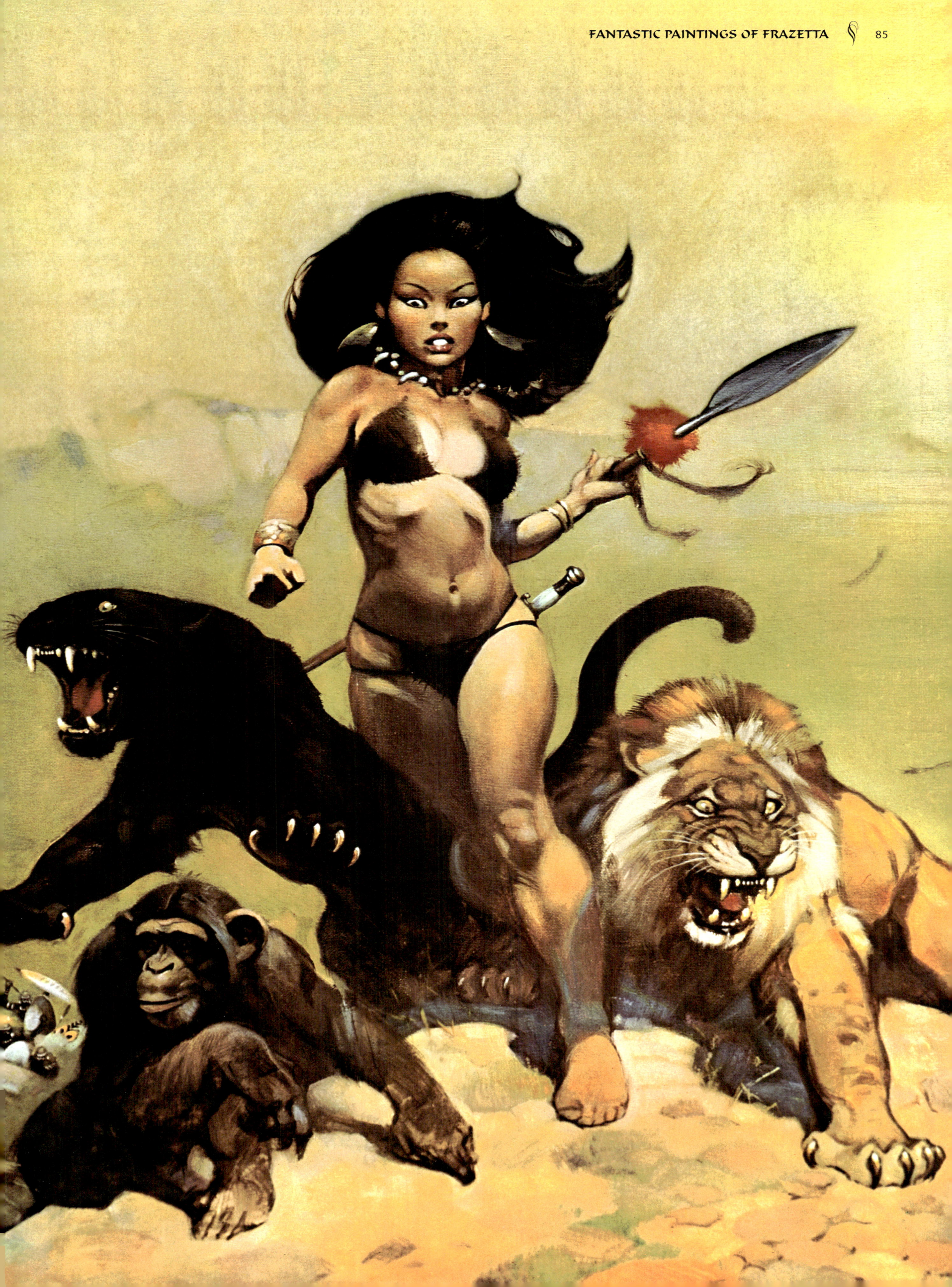

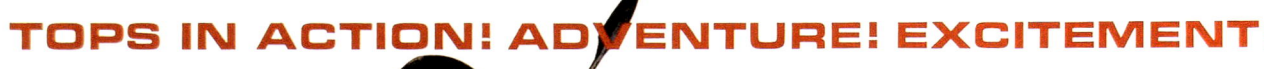

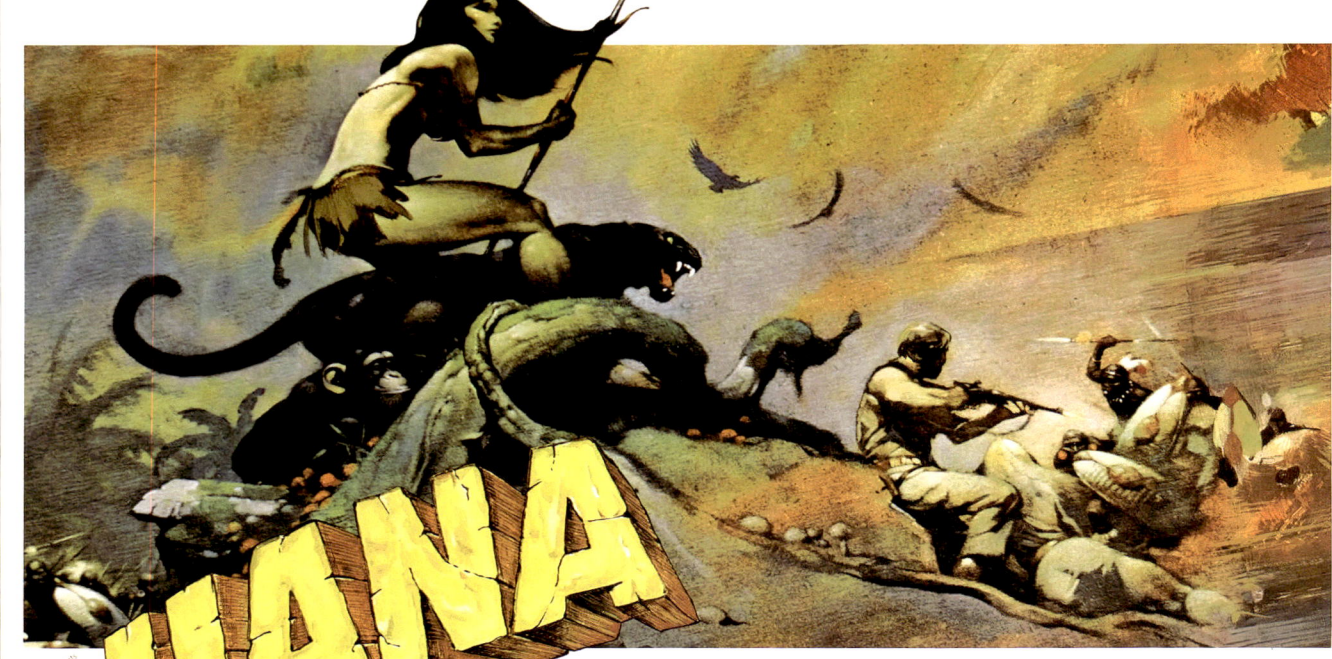

TOPS IN ACTION! ADVENTURE! EXCITEMENT!

...GE AS THE BEASTS THAT RAISED HER...

UNDERWATER ADVENTURE! · MAN-EATING PLANTS!
· FORBIDDEN JUNGLE TREACHERY! · ATTACK OF THE POISON DARTS!
...ST DEADLY SCORPIONS! · RIVER OF MADDENED CROCODILE HORDES!

...ring GLENN SAXON · EVI MARADI · AL THOMAS and MEI CHEN as Luana · co-starring JAC BUSHINGAME
...with PRIMEX-ITALIANO · a MALTESE PRODUCTION, LTD. FILM · directed by BOB RAYMOND · screenplay
...NA · a SOL FRIED presentation

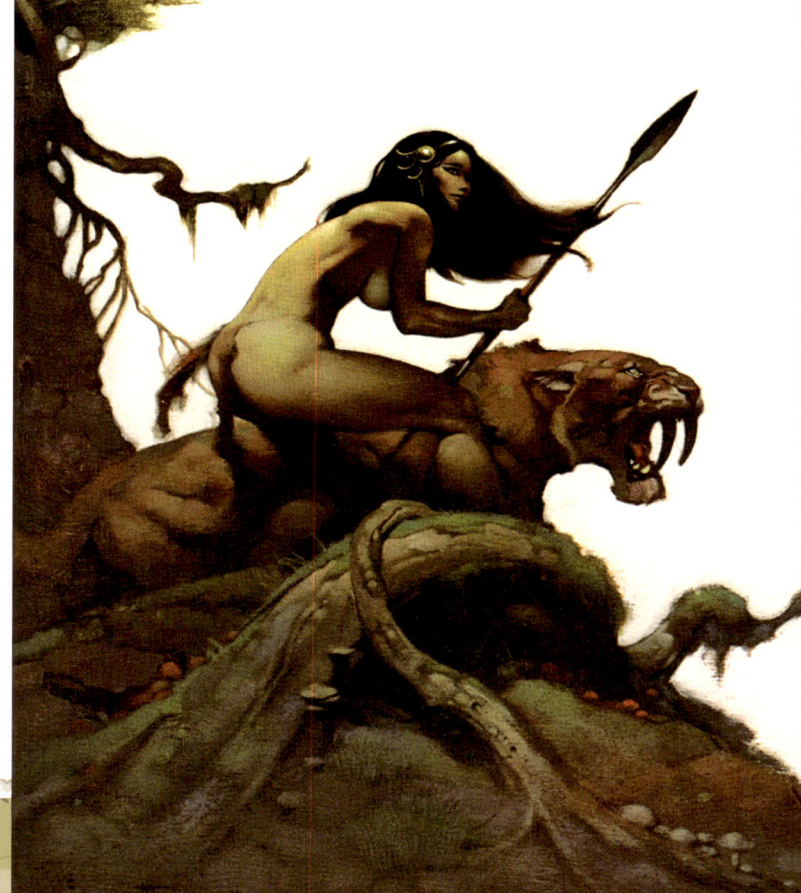

AN ACE BOOK | 75132 | 75¢

EDGAR RICE BURROUGHS
SAVAGE PELLUCIDAR

SAVAGE PELLUCIDAR
Oil on academy board, 1973
First printed as Luana B-sheet movie poster
and was cut down and revised to become
Savage Pellucidar *(Ace, 1973)*

NOTE: Frazetta had nothing to do
with the censoring of the poster.
(Capital Productions, 1973)

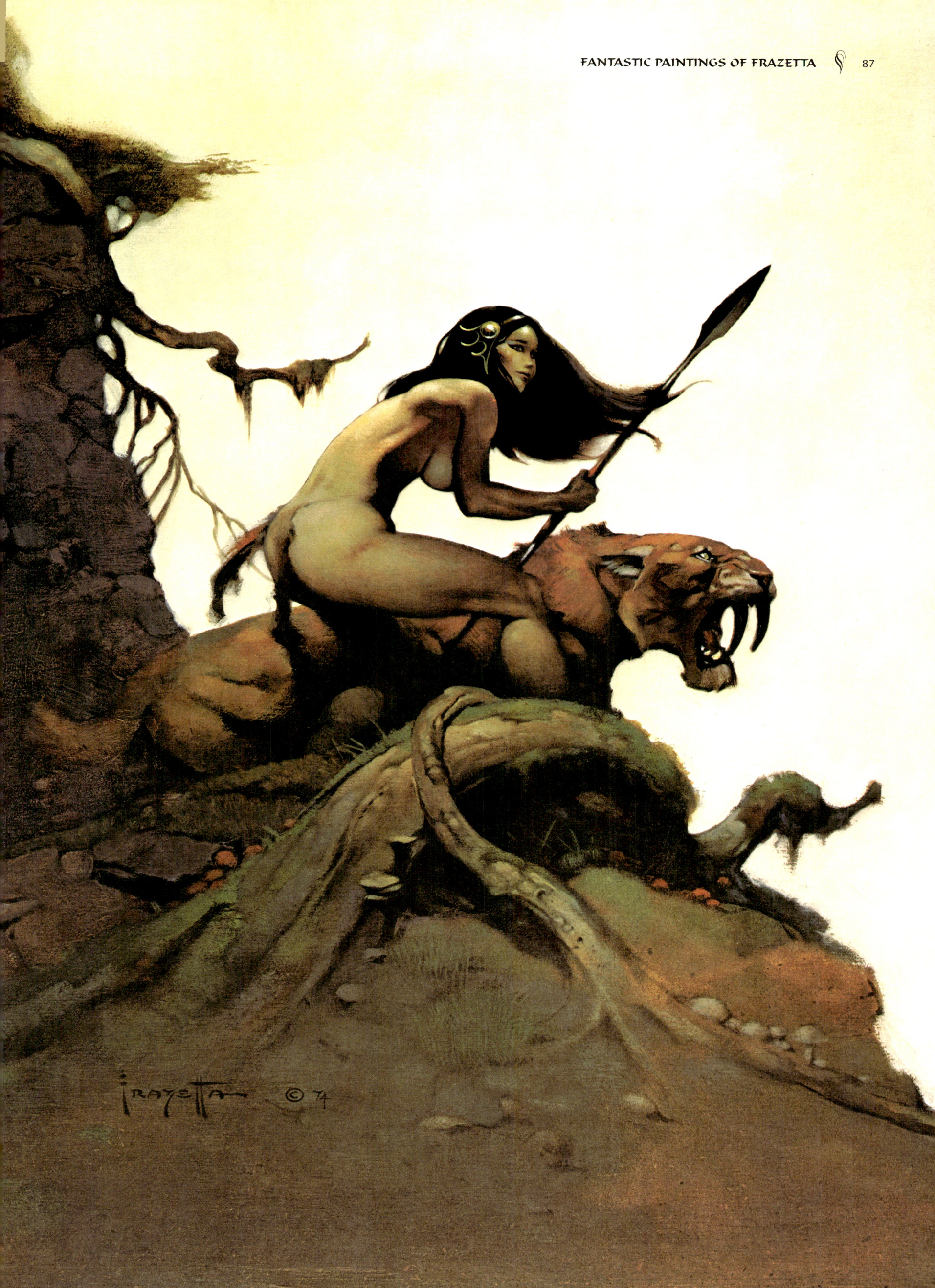

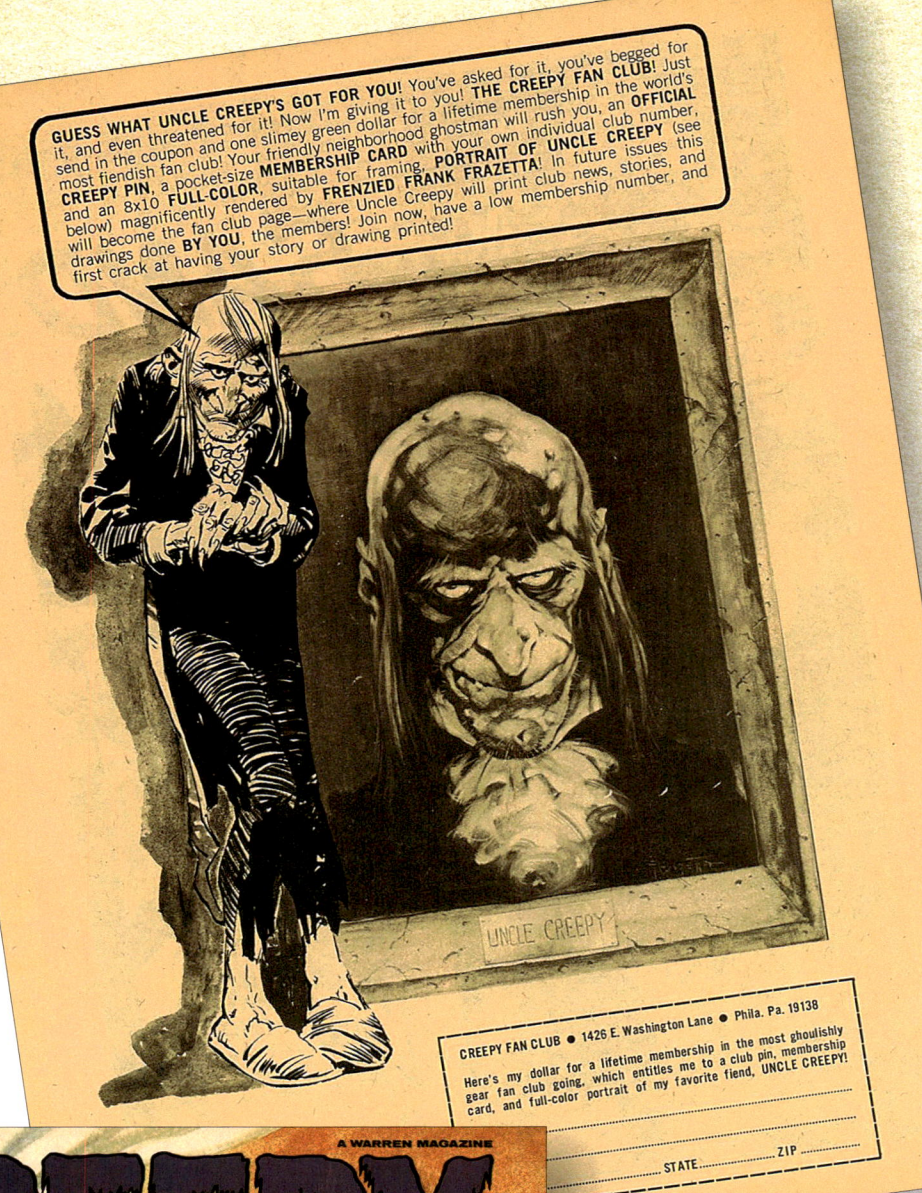

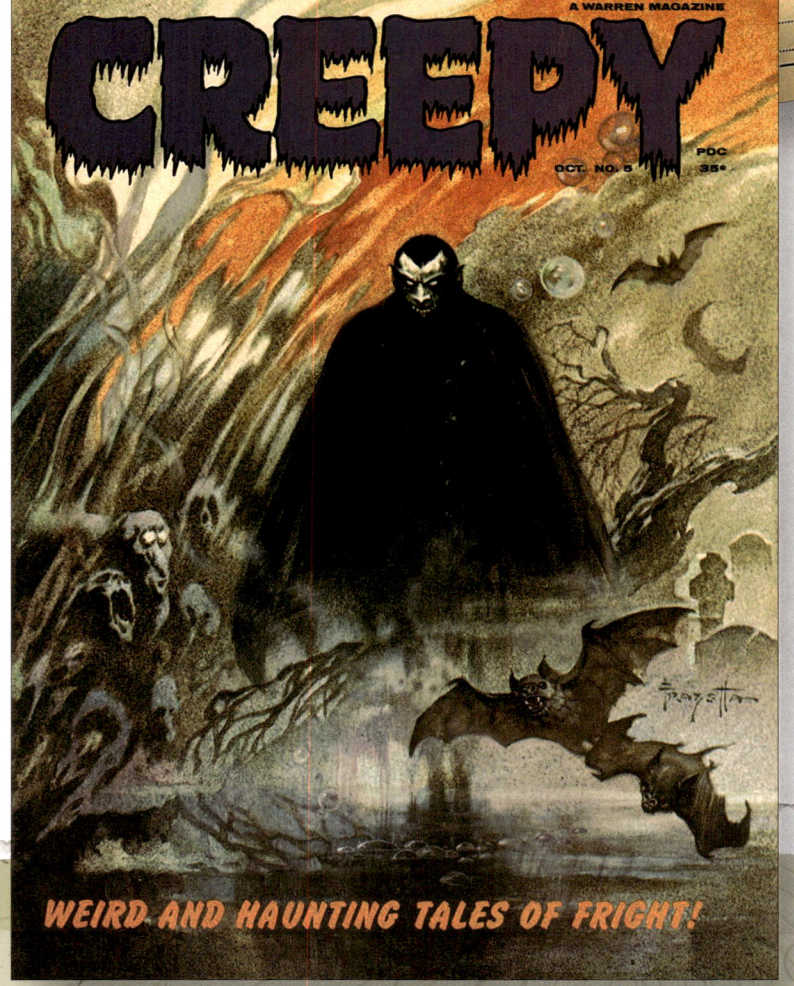

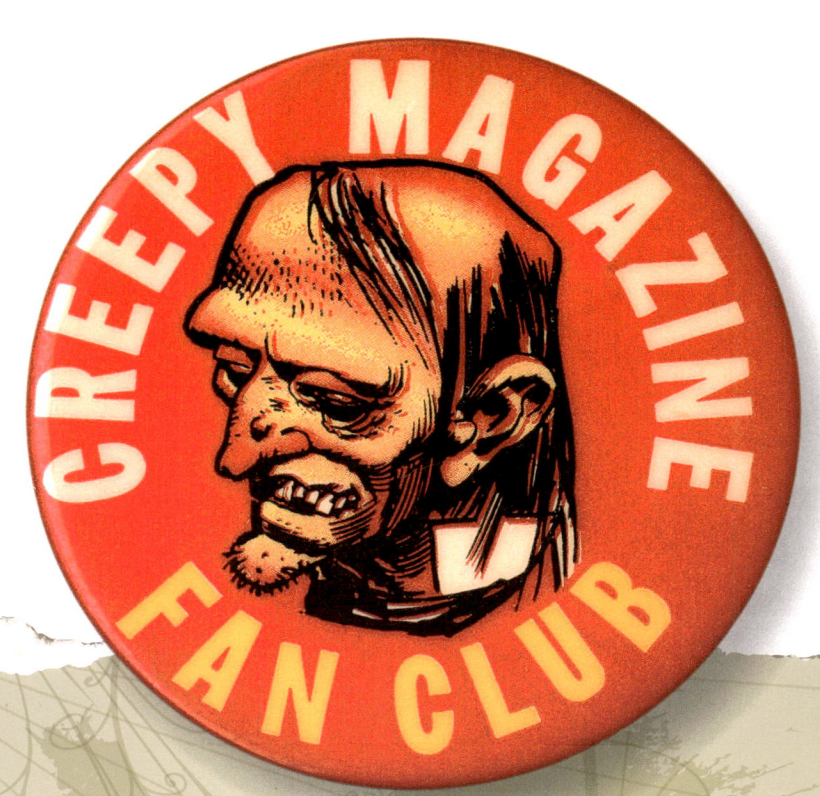

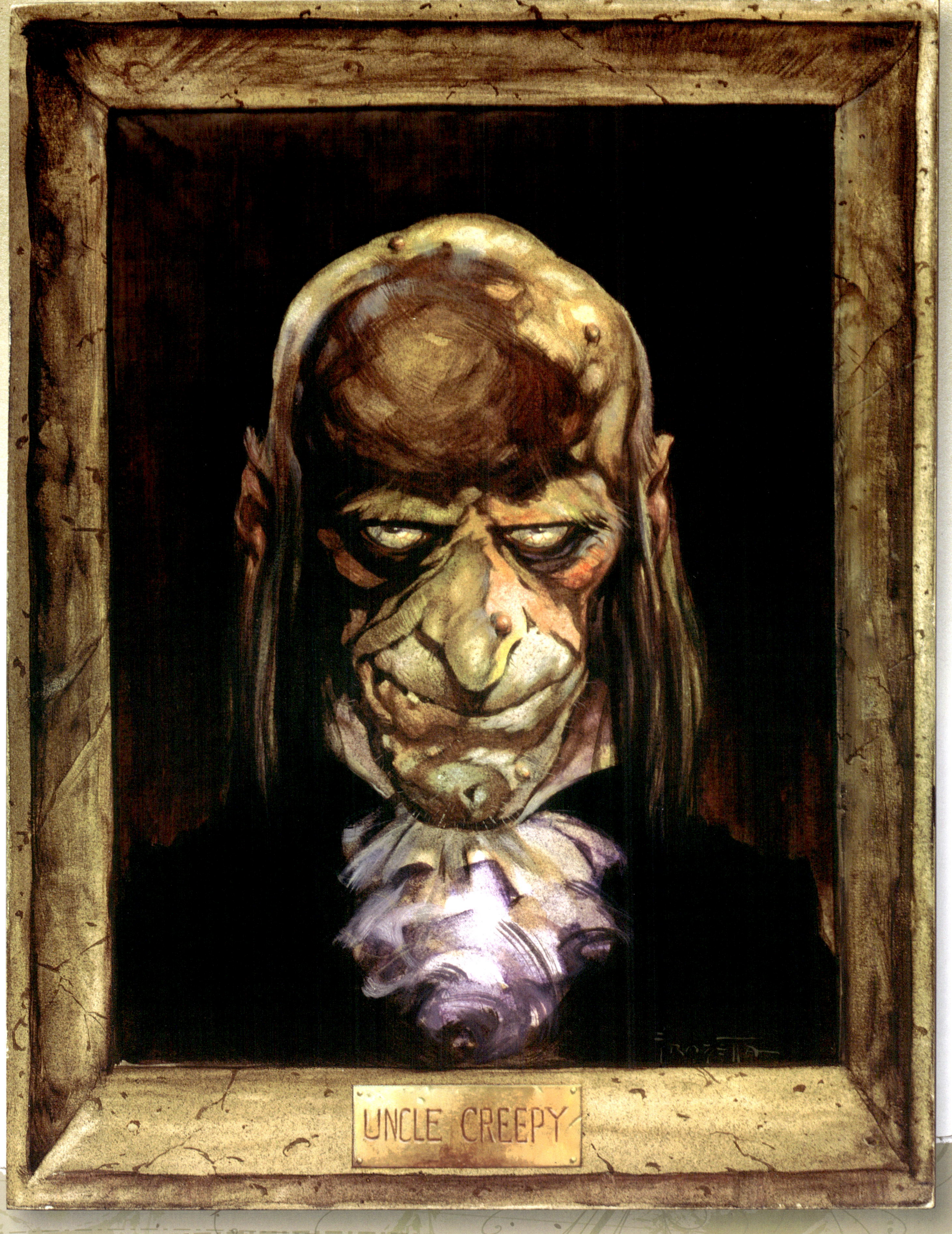

UNCLE CREEPY

Tarzan and the Jewels of Opar was one of Frazetta's personal favorites and exhibits the qualities that would make Frazetta a world famous creative artist: dramatic lighting, furious action and wonderfully subtle color tints. In this oil, Frazetta has taken a standard scene of heroic rescue and re-energized it with his own special magic. This painting also features a rare instance of Frazetta photographing himself as the model for the Tarzan figure.

DOC DAVE WINIEWICZ

November 1995 Christie's East Auction catalog

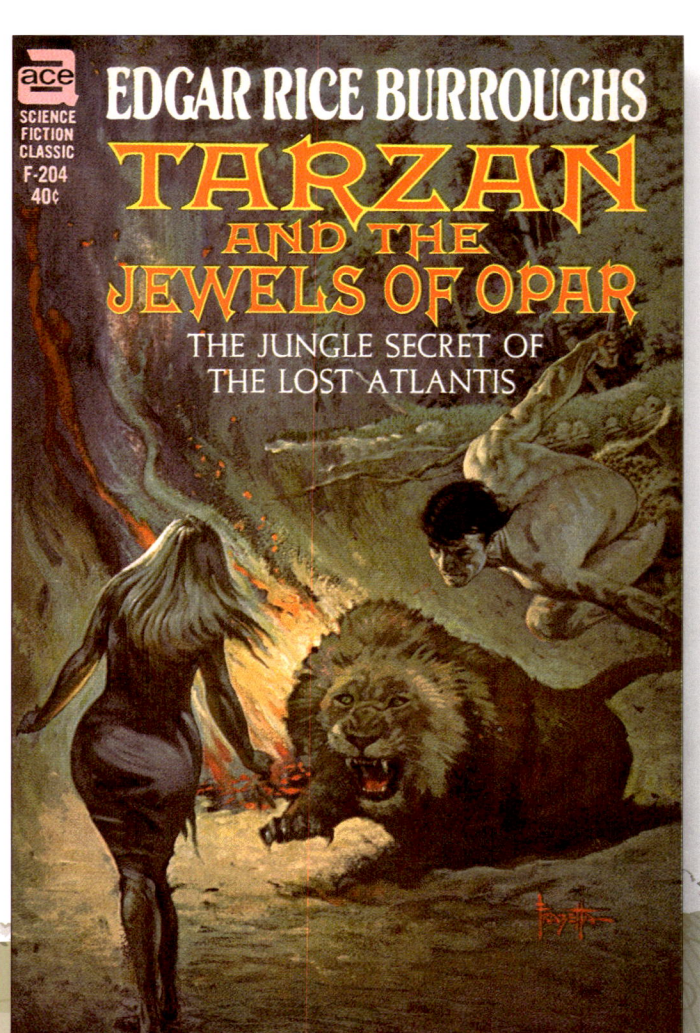

TARZAN AND THE JEWELS OF OPAR

Oil on canvas, 1963
First printed as the cover to
Tarzan and the Jewels of Opar
(Ace, 1963)

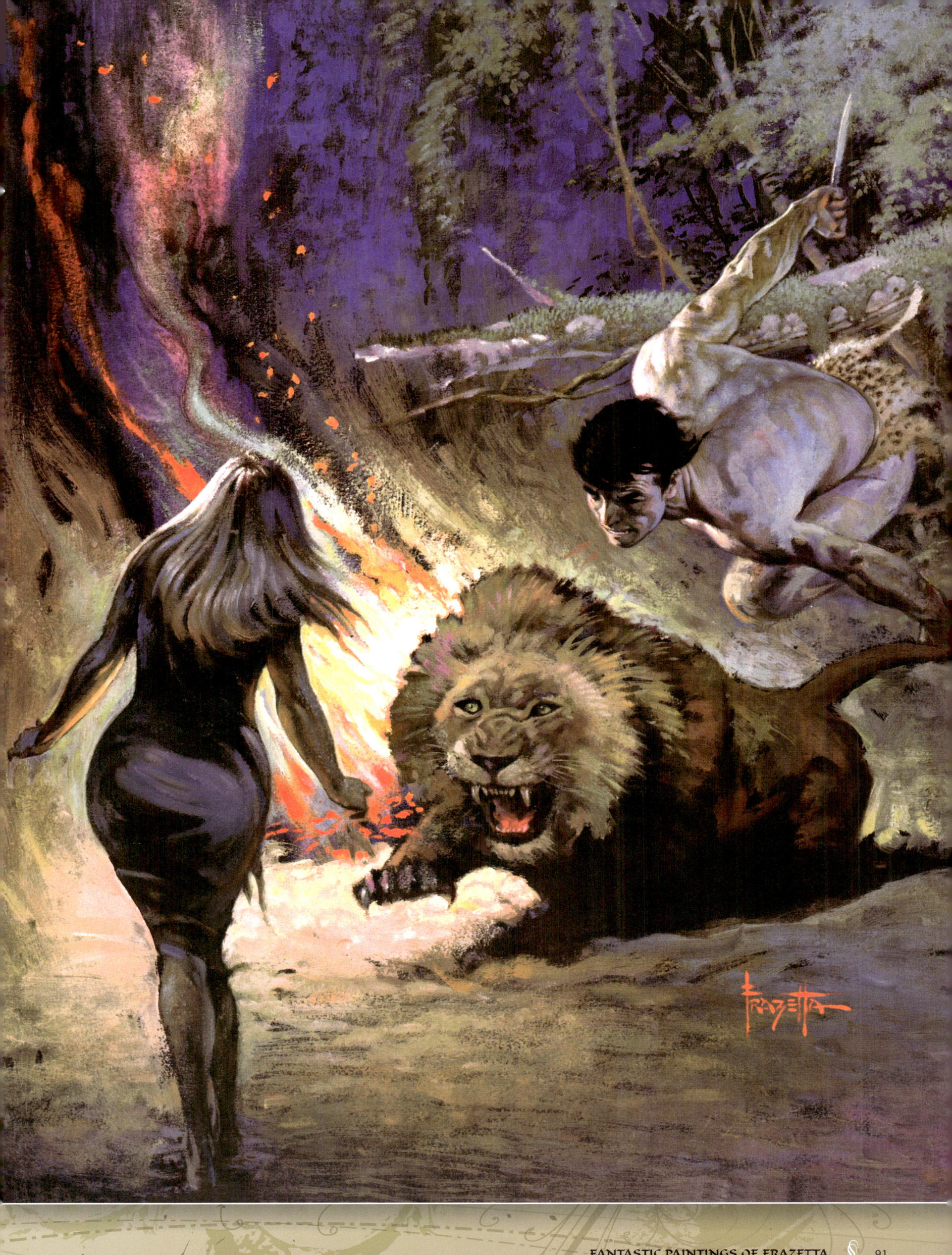

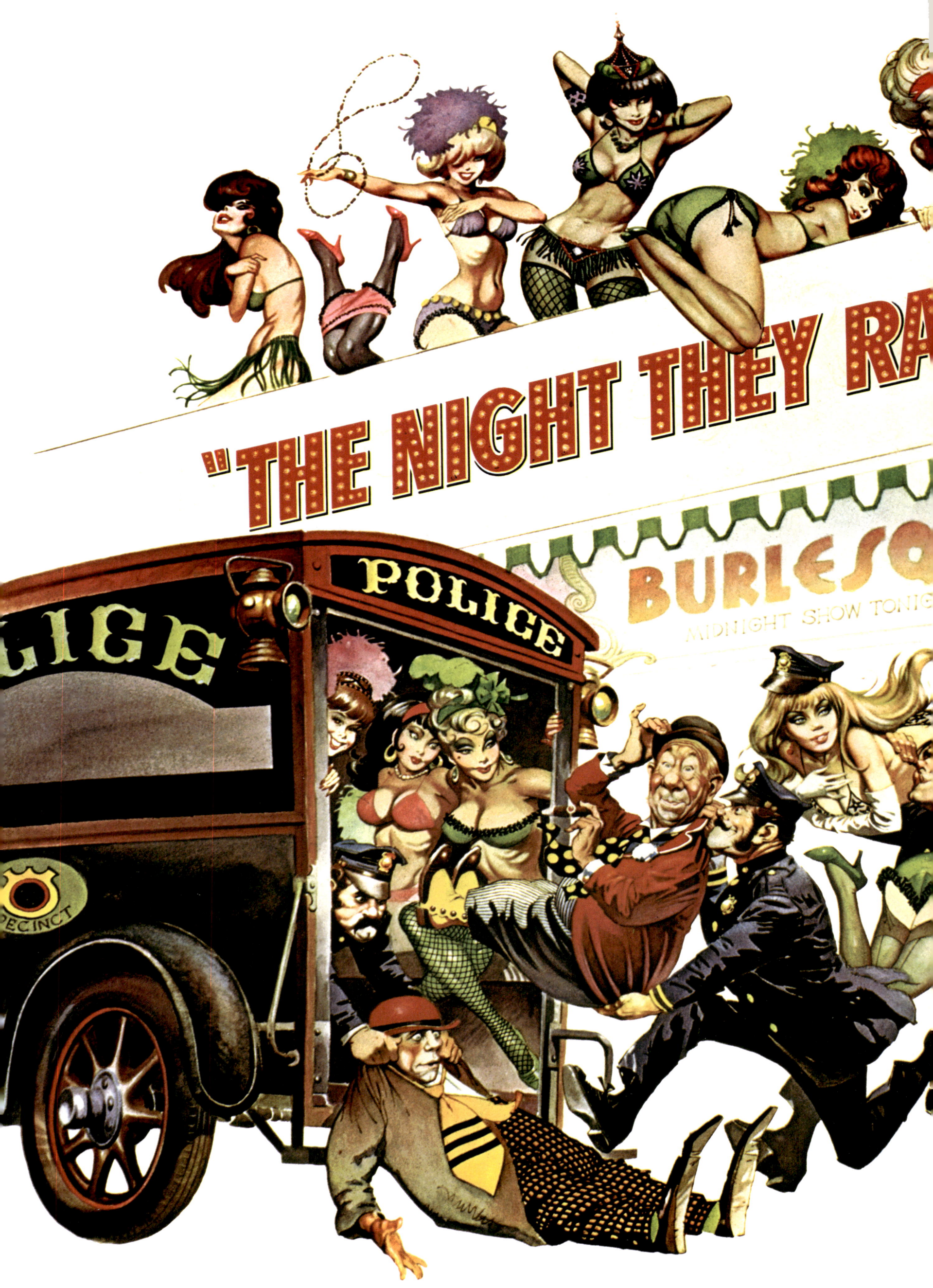

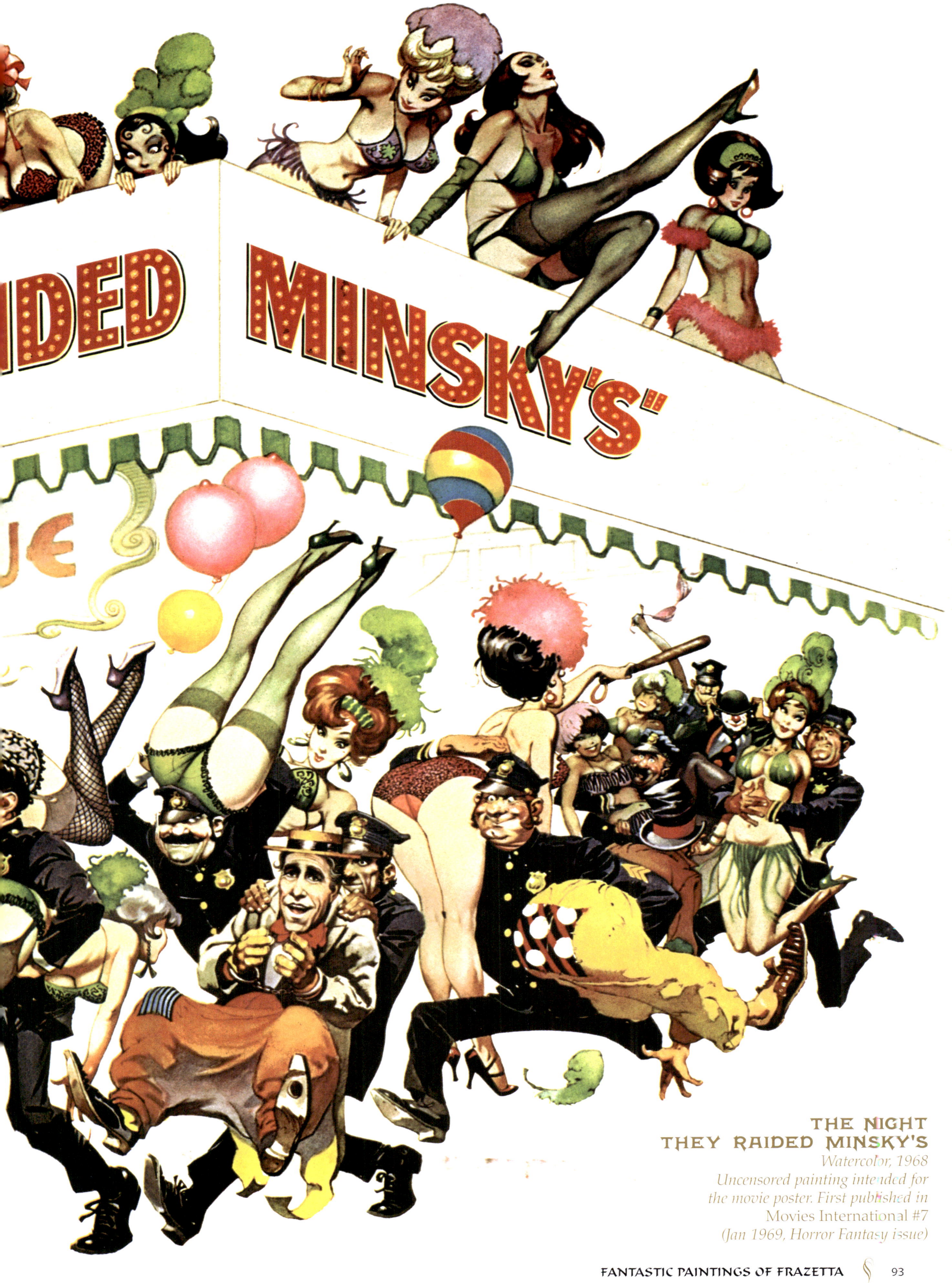

THE NIGHT
THEY RAIDED MINSKY'S
Watercolor, 1968
Uncensored painting intended for
the movie poster. First published in
Movies International #7
(Jan 1969, Horror Fantasy issue)

They told me about [Howard's barbarian] character. I sped through the first few chapters to visualize this character. I didn't seriously read any of it. I went right ahead and developed this character that barely resembled Howard's description. Quite a different guy. It was what I thought a barbarian should look like, the ultimate barbarian. His description was quite different. He was leaner with tousled hair and hawkish features. I instead saw a bruised, battered, scarred, monster of a guy. That's just the way I felt a guy should look like at this point. Once again, it's all personal.

FRANK FRAZETTA

Seconds *interview*

BERSERKER

Oil on academy board, 1967
First printed as the cover to Conan the Conqueror
(Lancer, 1967)

In 2009, this painting sold for $1 Million. The record sell during the artist's life was to Kirk Hammett, lead guitarist for Metallica.

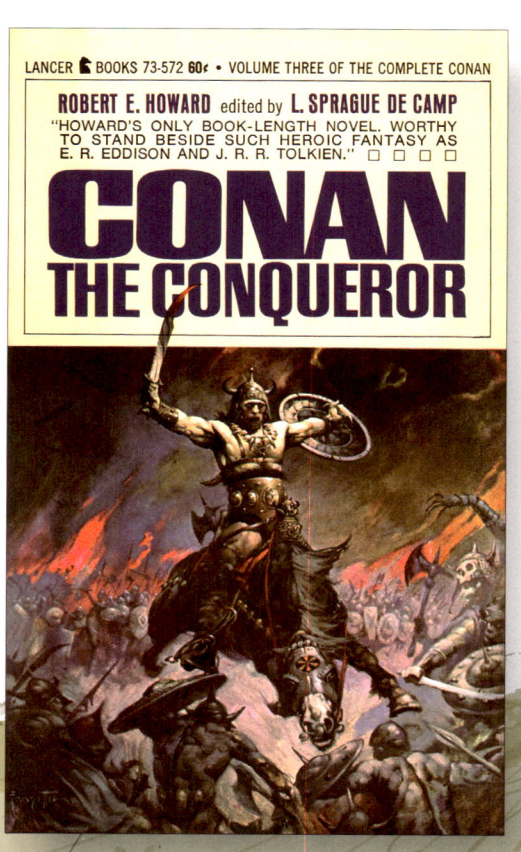

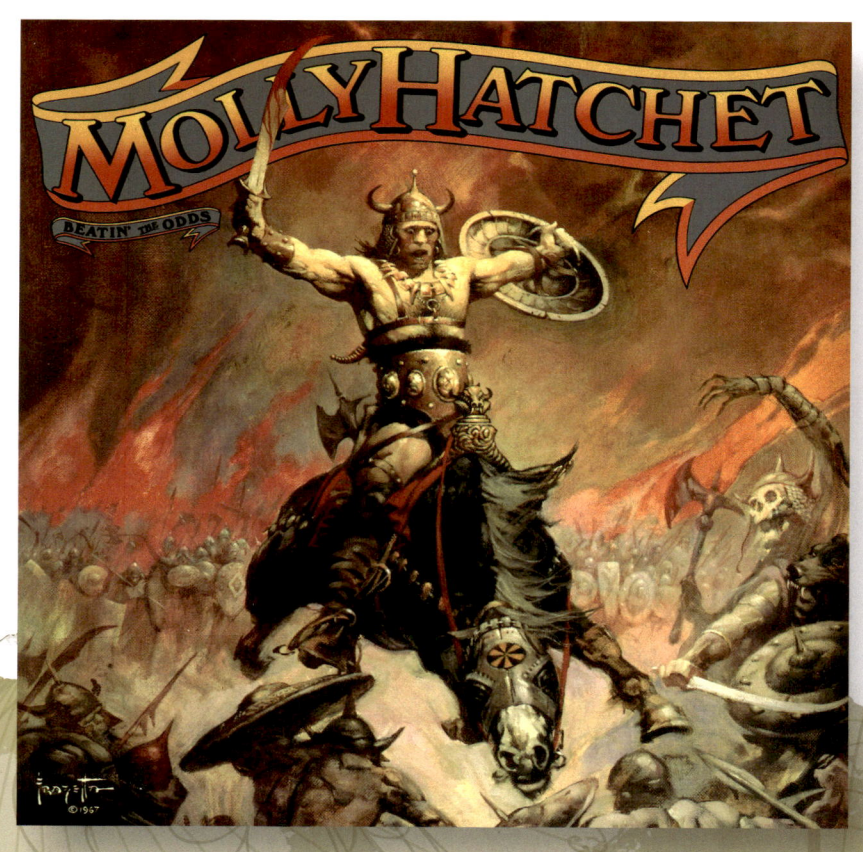

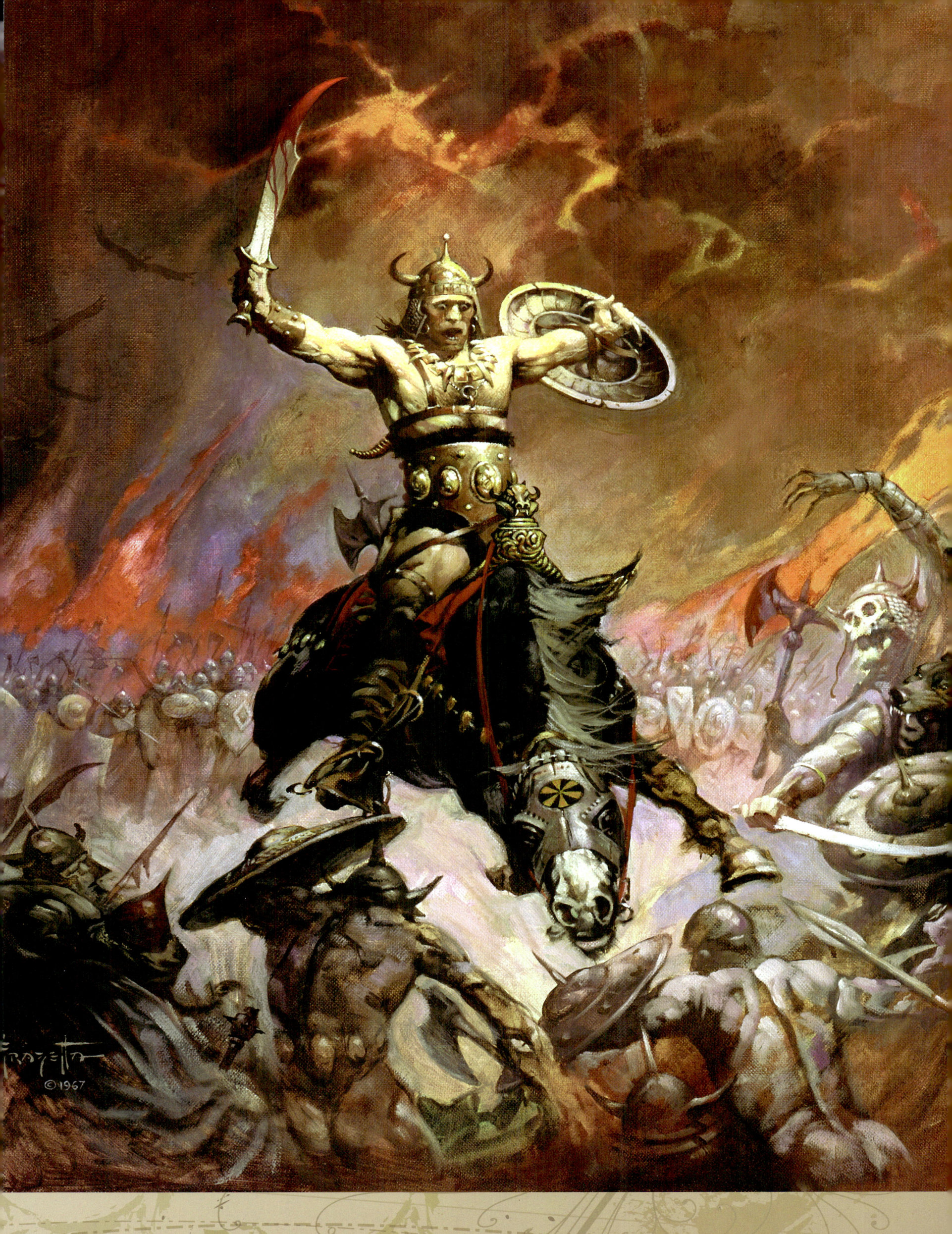

Lord Greystoke — he who had been "Tarzan of the Apes" — sat in silence in the apartments of his friend, Lieutenant Paul d'Arnot, in Paris, gazing meditatively at the toe of his immaculate boot. His mind revolved many memories, recalled by the escape of his arch-enemy from the French military prison to which he had been sentenced for life upon the testimony of the ape-man. He thought of the lengths to which Rokoff had once gone to compass his death, and he realized that what the man had already done would doubtless be as nothing by comparison with what he would wish and plot to do now that he was again free.

EDGAR RICE BURROUGHS

from The Beasts of Tarzan

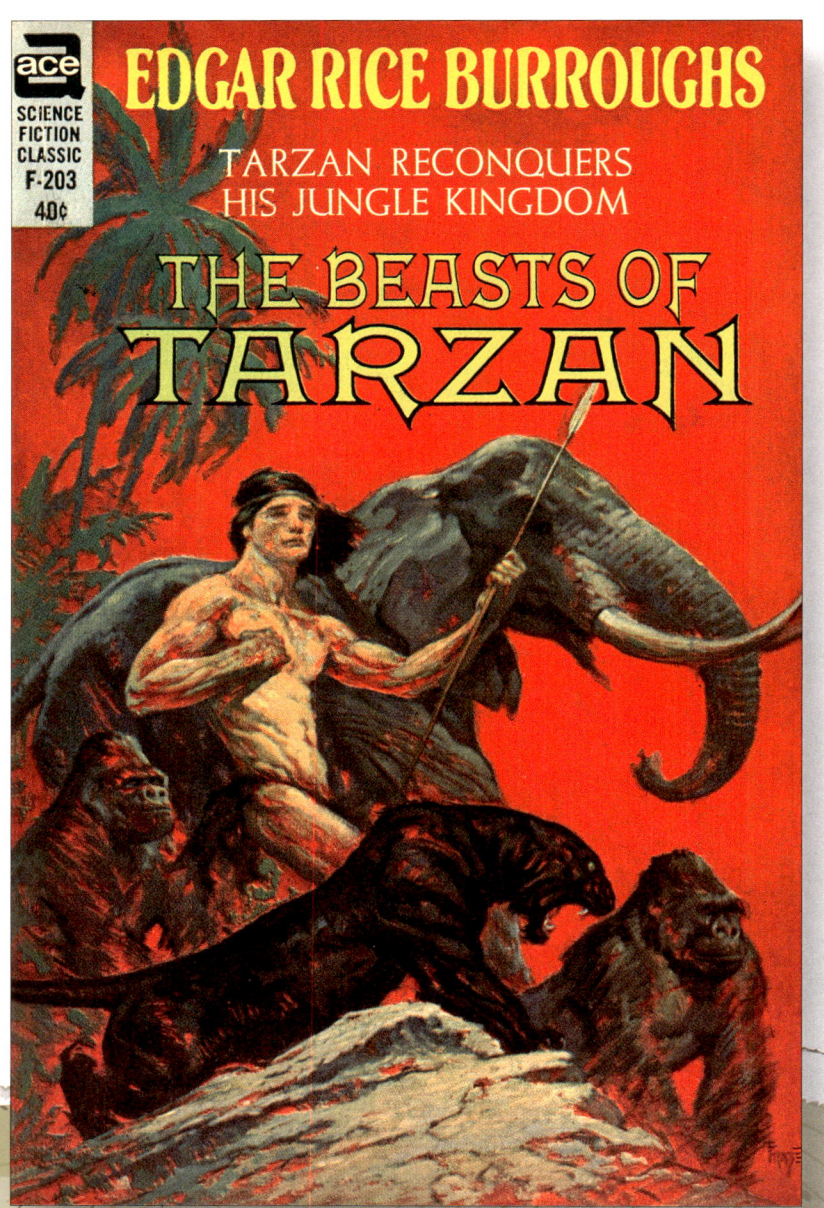

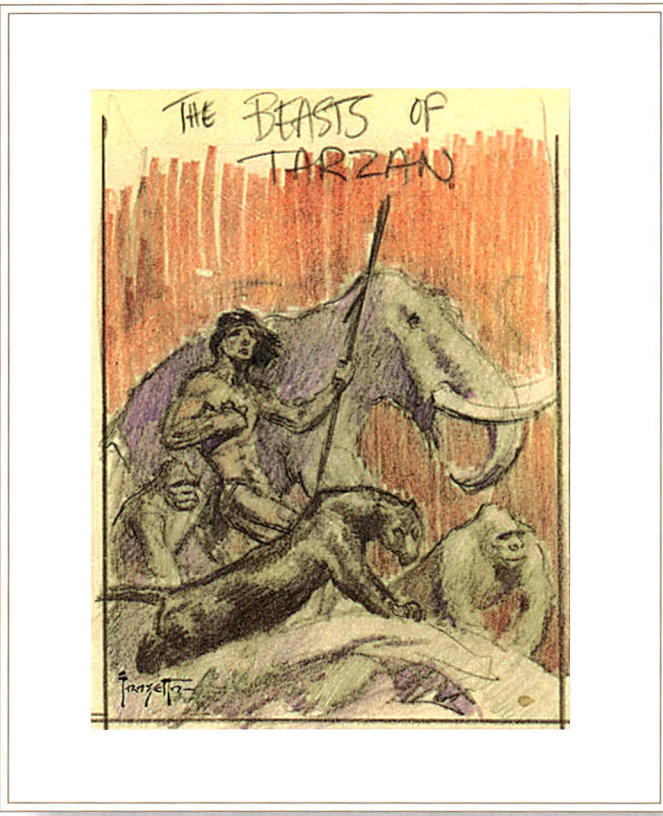

THE BEASTS OF TARZAN

Oil on academy board, 1964
First printed as the cover to
The Beasts of Tarzan *(Ace, 1964)*

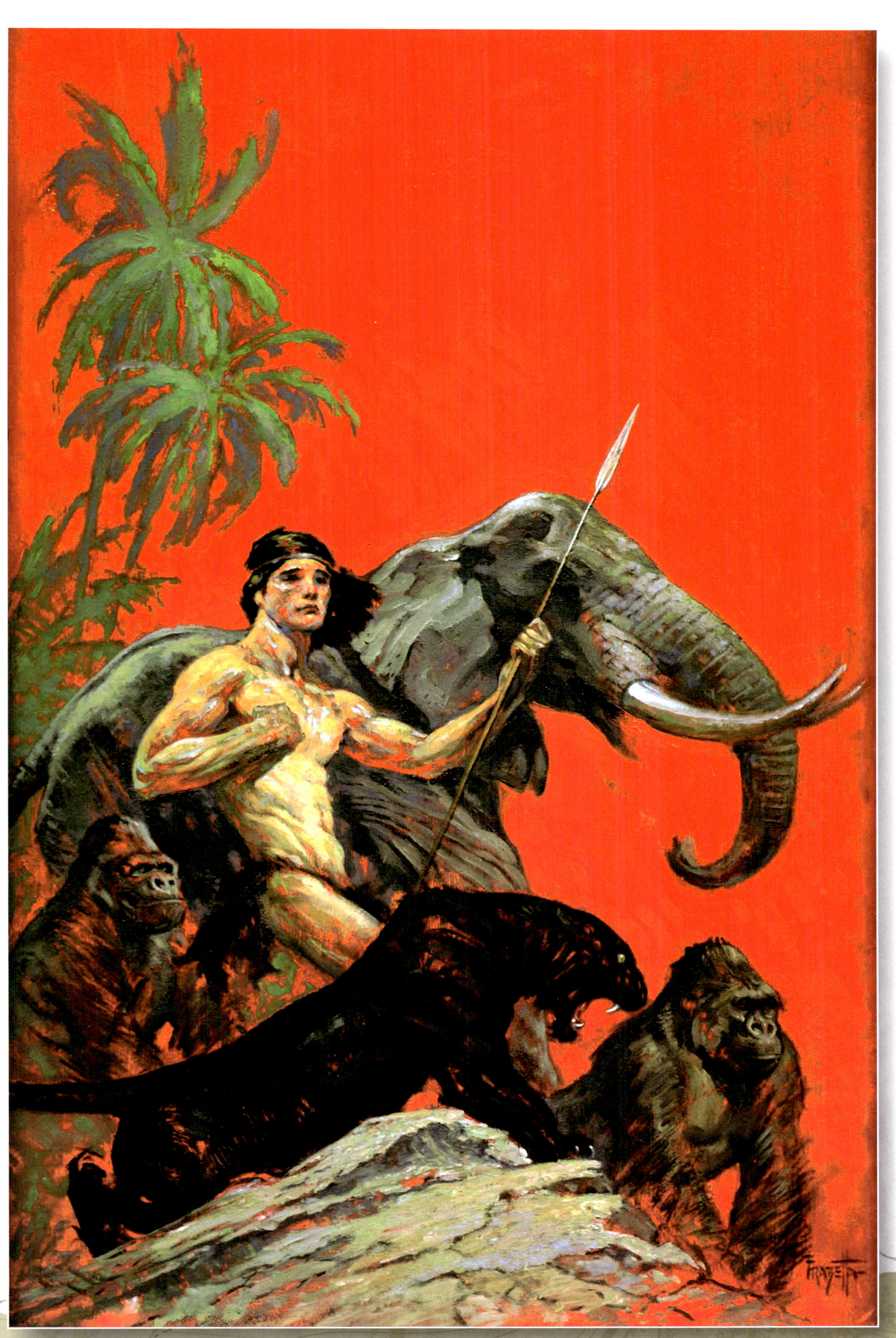

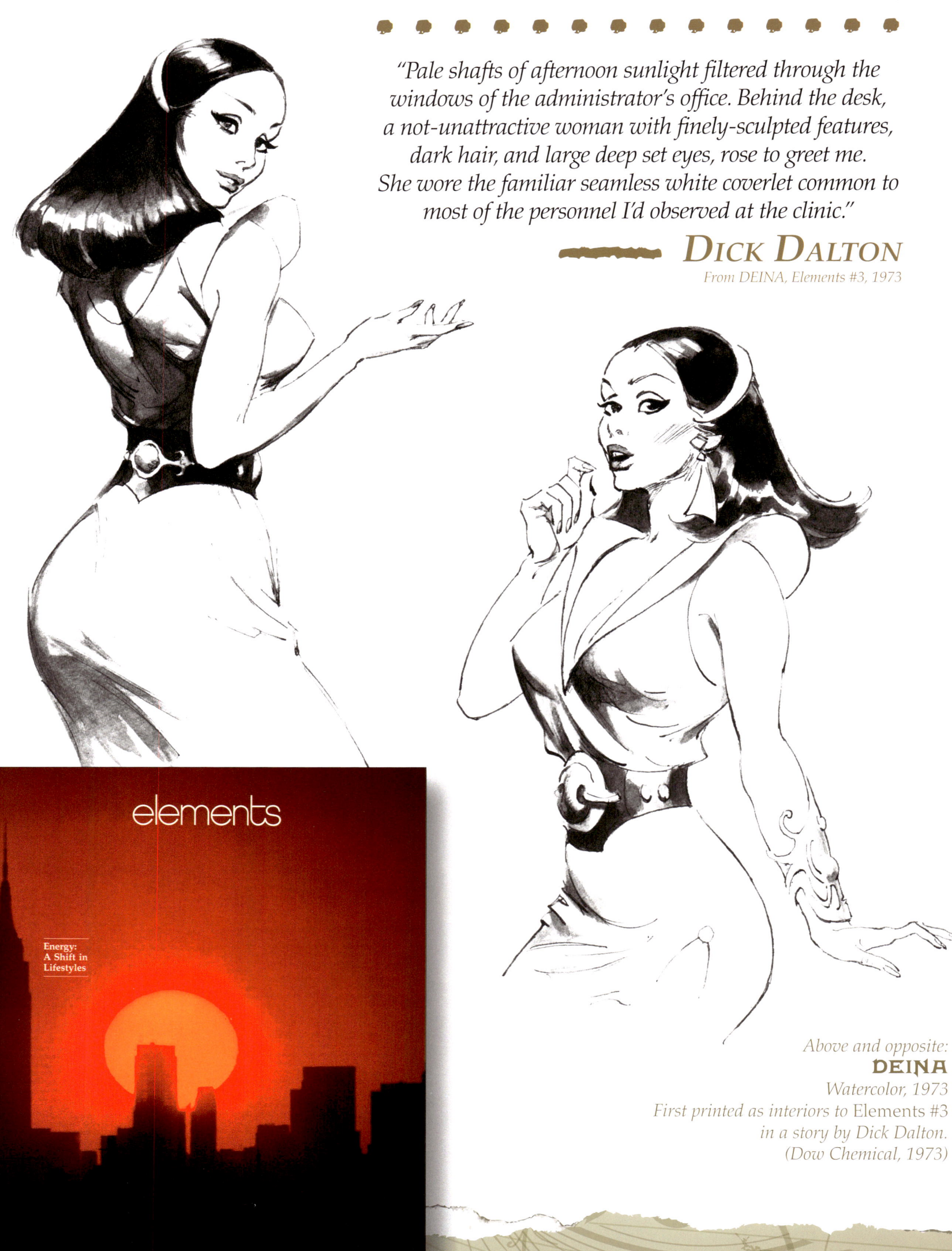

"Pale shafts of afternoon sunlight filtered through the windows of the administrator's office. Behind the desk, a not-unattractive woman with finely-sculpted features, dark hair, and large deep set eyes, rose to greet me. She wore the familiar seamless white coverlet common to most of the personnel I'd observed at the clinic."

DICK DALTON
From DEINA, Elements #3, 1973

elements

Energy:
A Shift in
Lifestyles

Above and opposite:
DEINA
Watercolor, 1973
First printed as interiors to Elements #3
in a story by Dick Dalton.
(Dow Chemical, 1973)

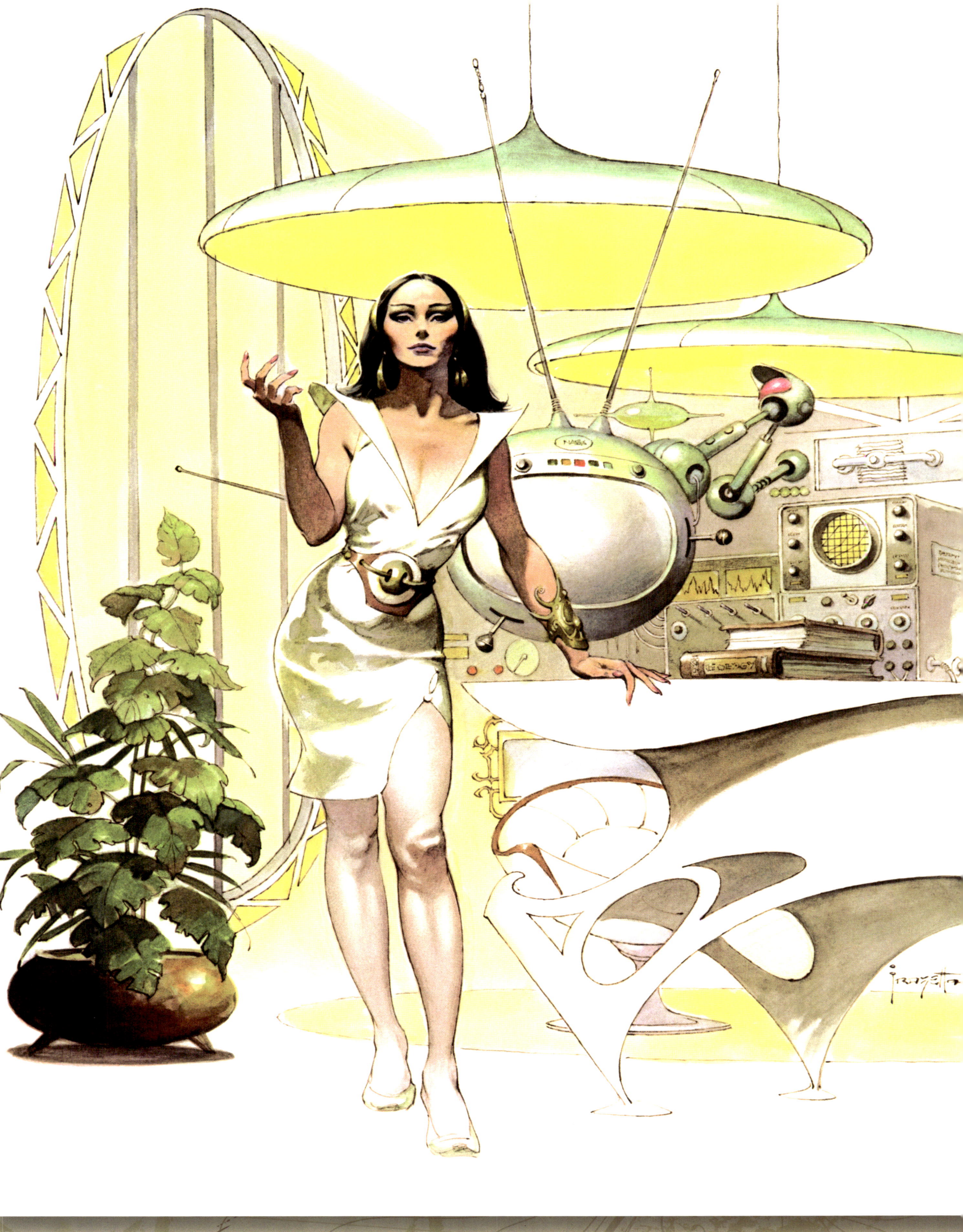

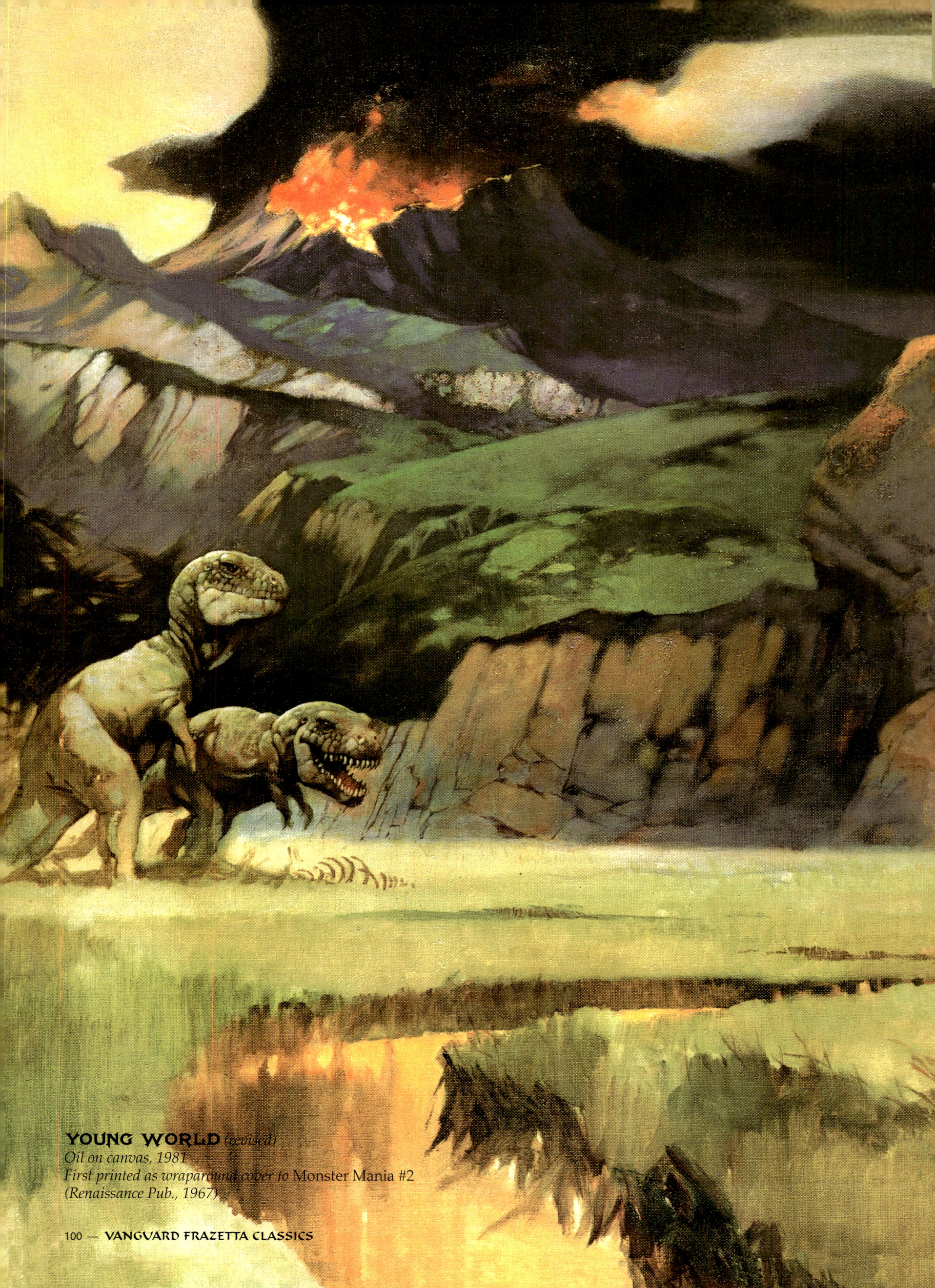

YOUNG WORLD *(revised)*
Oil on canvas, 1981
First printed as wraparound cover to Monster Mania #2
(Renaissance Pub., 1967)

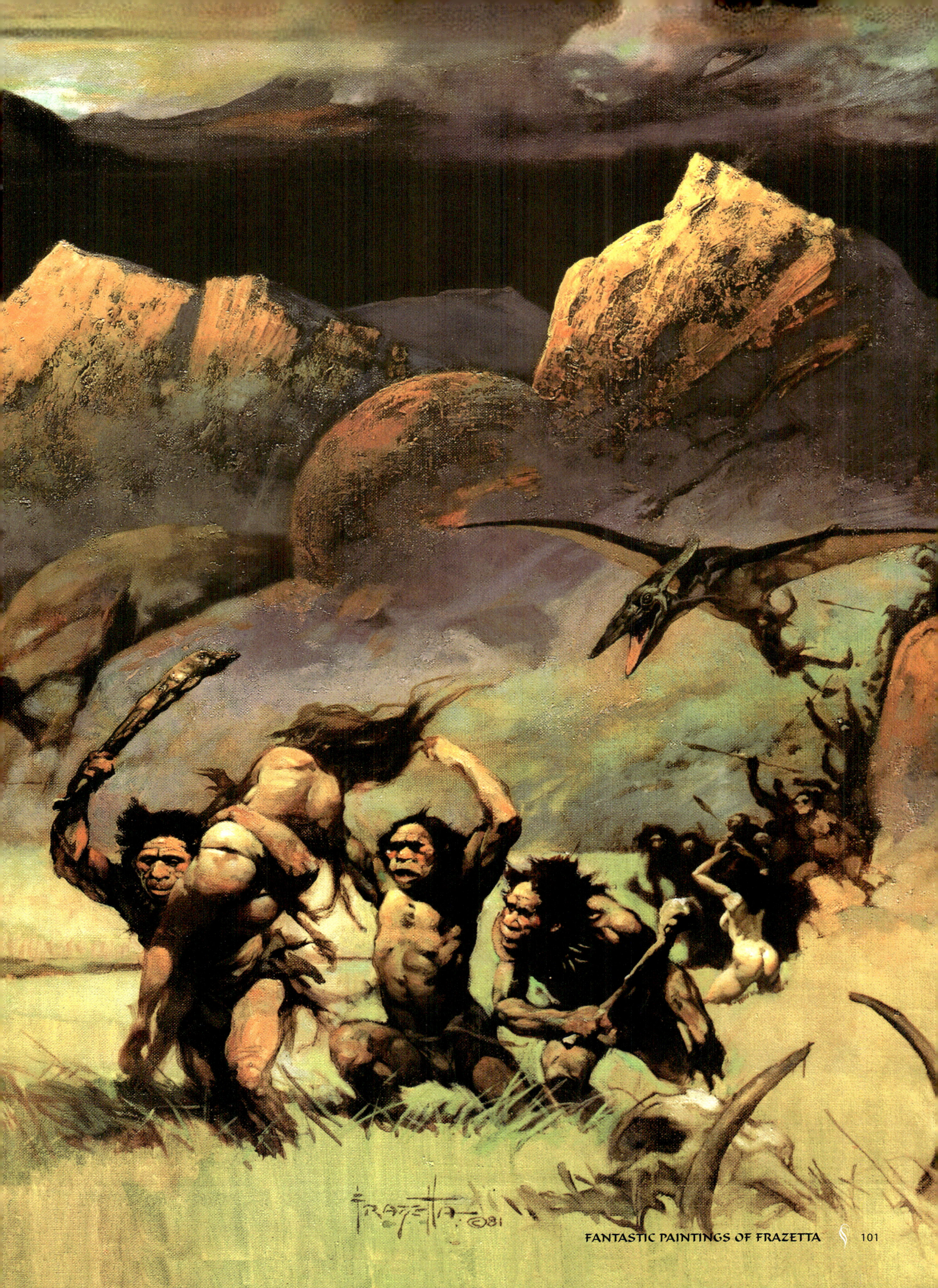

*L. Sprague de Camp was a popular writer of science fiction and fantasy.
He also edited and placed Howard's Conan stories in both the Gnome Press
hardbacks and the Lancer paperback series. De Camp managed Conan for many
years. In de Camp's autobiography* Time and Chance, *he commented on how
different Frazetta's Conan was from Howard's: "Conan the Adventurer, had
a cover by Frank Frazetta, who painted covers for most of the Lancer Conans.
Frazetta's work was superior to that of most illustrators, but he gave Conan
something I have objected to ever since. Robert Howard described Conan's hair as a
'square cut black mane,' implying a Prince Valiant bob. [But] Frazetta gave Conan
hair down to his solar plexus, and long-haired Conan has been ever since."
While de Camp may have objected to Frazetta rendering his own barbarian instead
of Howard's, the audience loved it and as de Camp said, "long-haired
Conan has been ever since."*

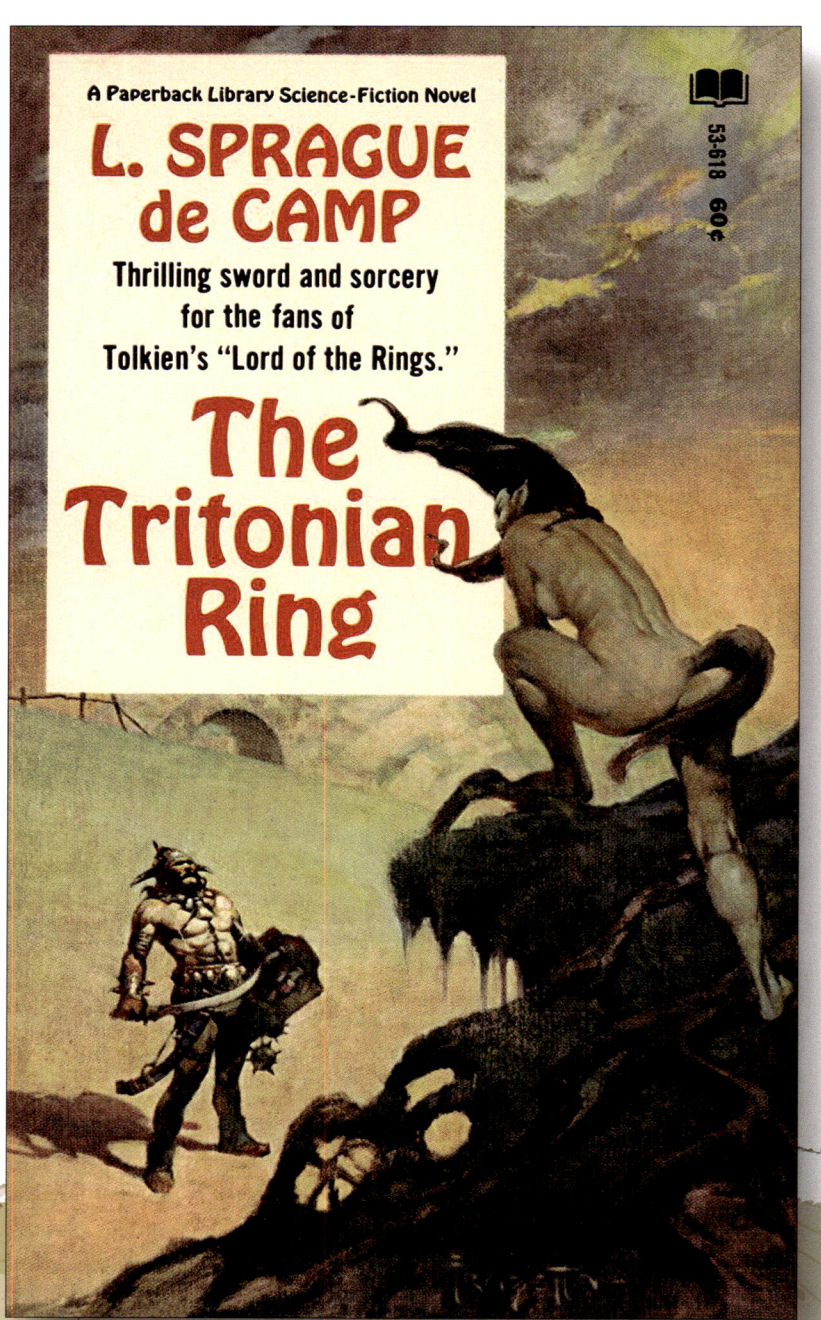

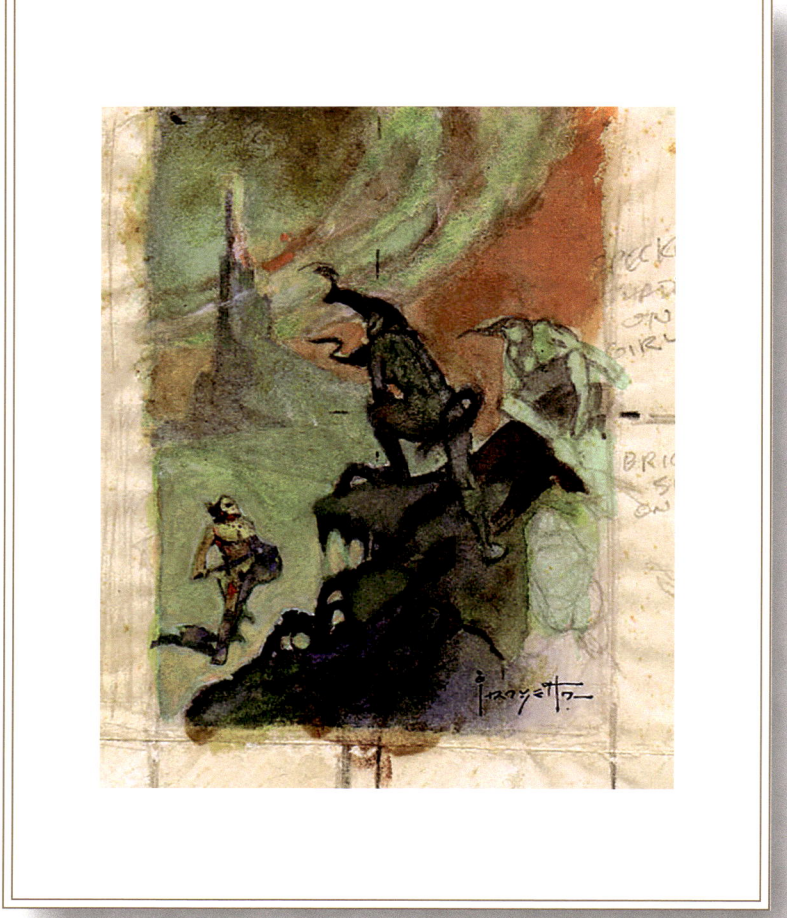

PONY TAIL
Oil on academy board, 1967
First printed as the cover to The Tritonian Ring
(Paperback Library, 1968)

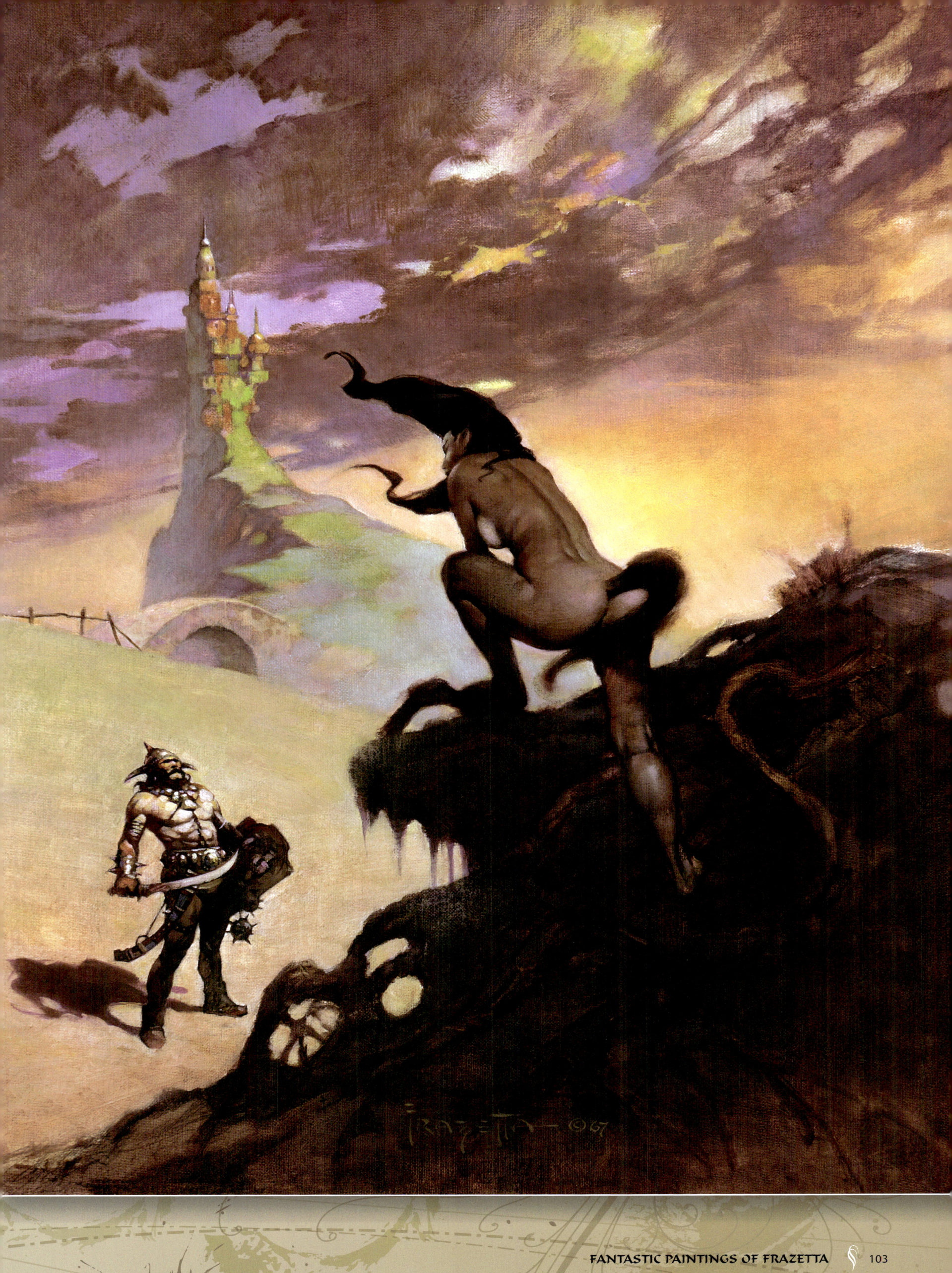

Ellie called me in 1974 to talk about the possibility of trading me another painting for the cover painting for Creepy #9. *Ellie mentioned a handful of paintings that she and Frank would be willing to trade, but I didn't care for any of them enough to trade. Before I thought of Tarzan and The Ant Men, I asked Ellie if the April 1971* National Lampoon *cover might be available for the trade; it was one of my favorite paintings by Frank and I would have really liked to have had it. But Frank wouldn't hear of it, saying that he really liked it and had plans for it. So I ended up with the Tarzan painting and I was/am completely satisfied!*

ROBERT R. BARRETT

Frank Frazetta Facebook group, April 25, 2013

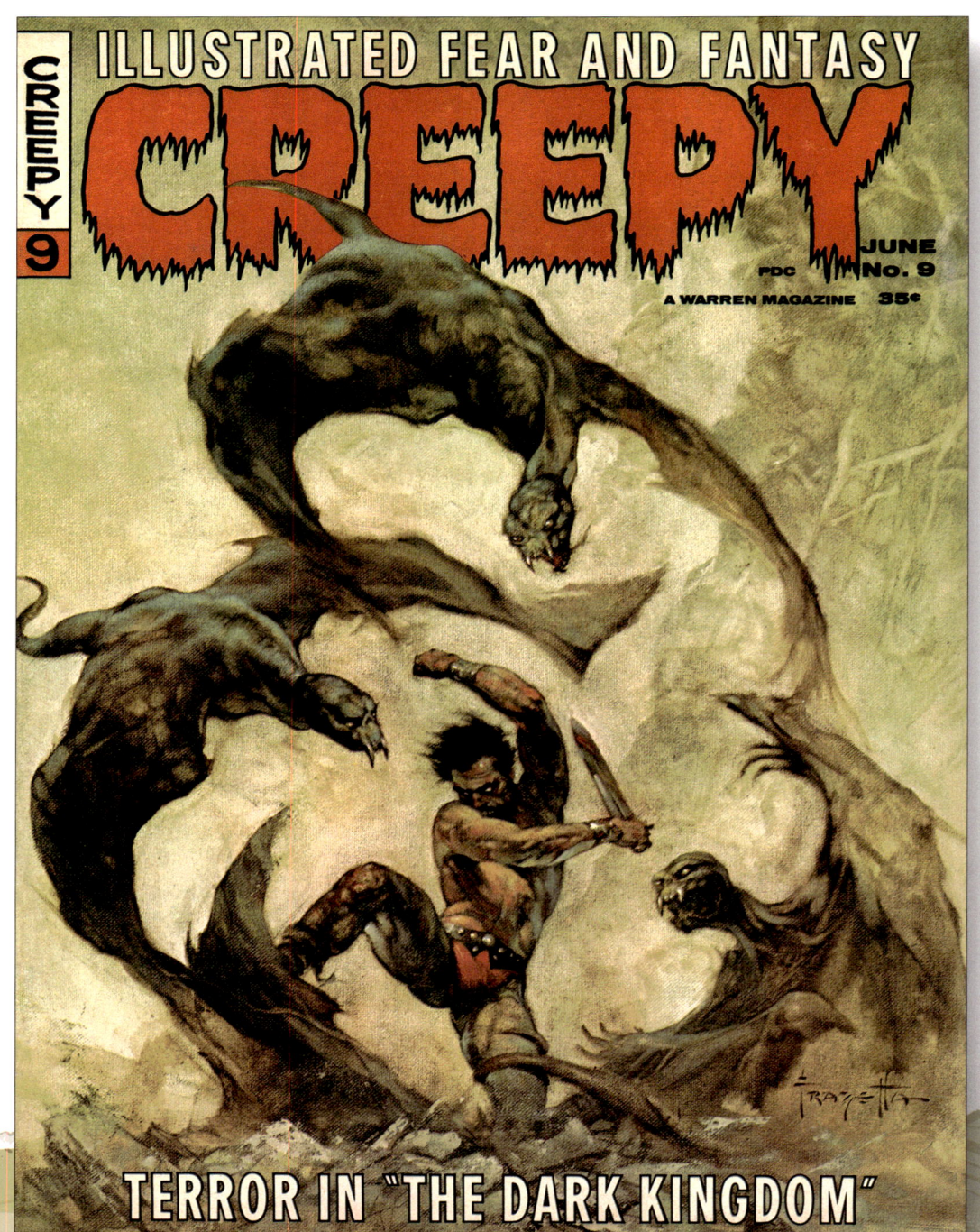

WINGED TERROR
Oil on academy board, 1965
First printed as the cover to Creepy #9
(Warren, 1966)

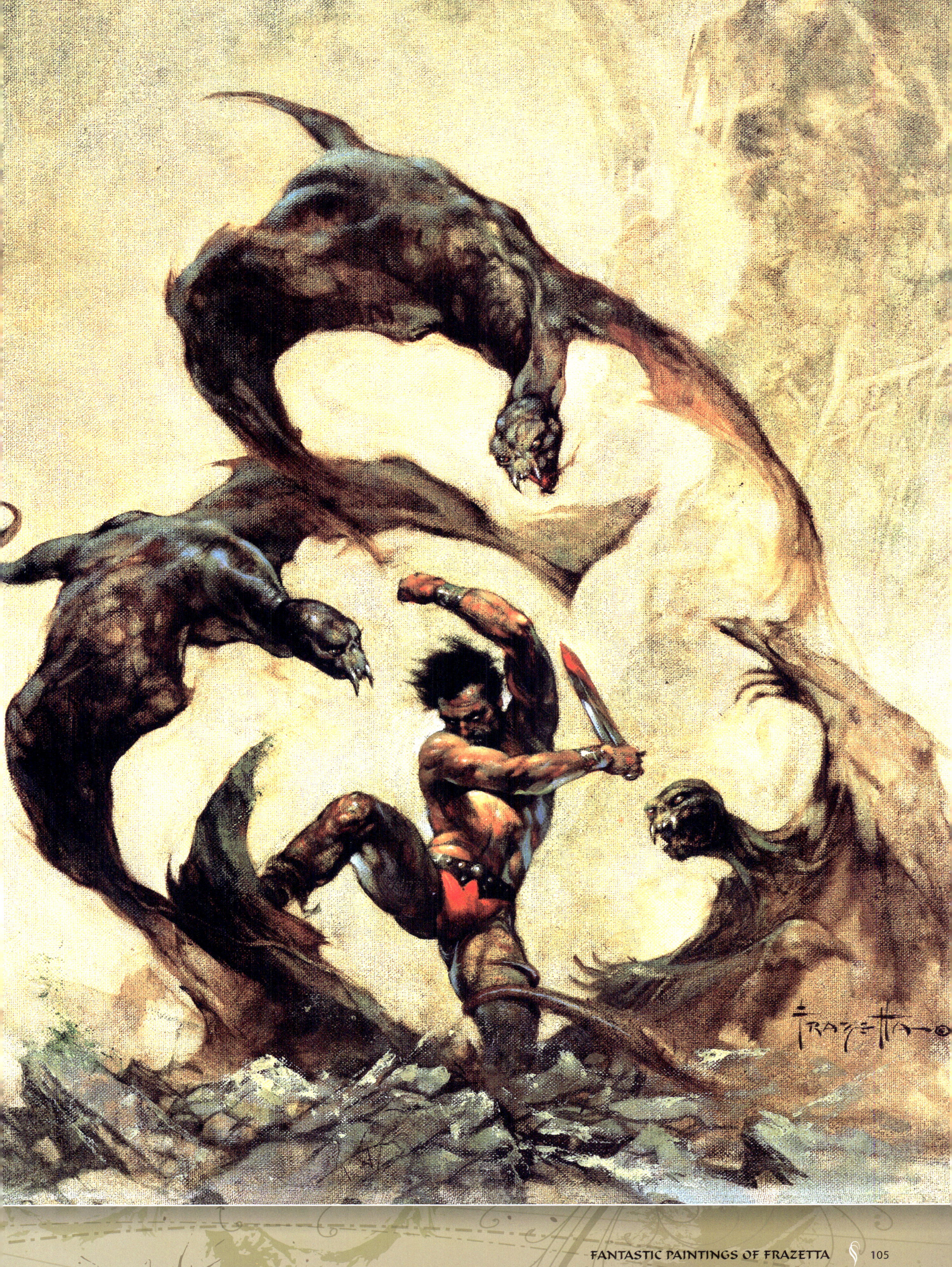

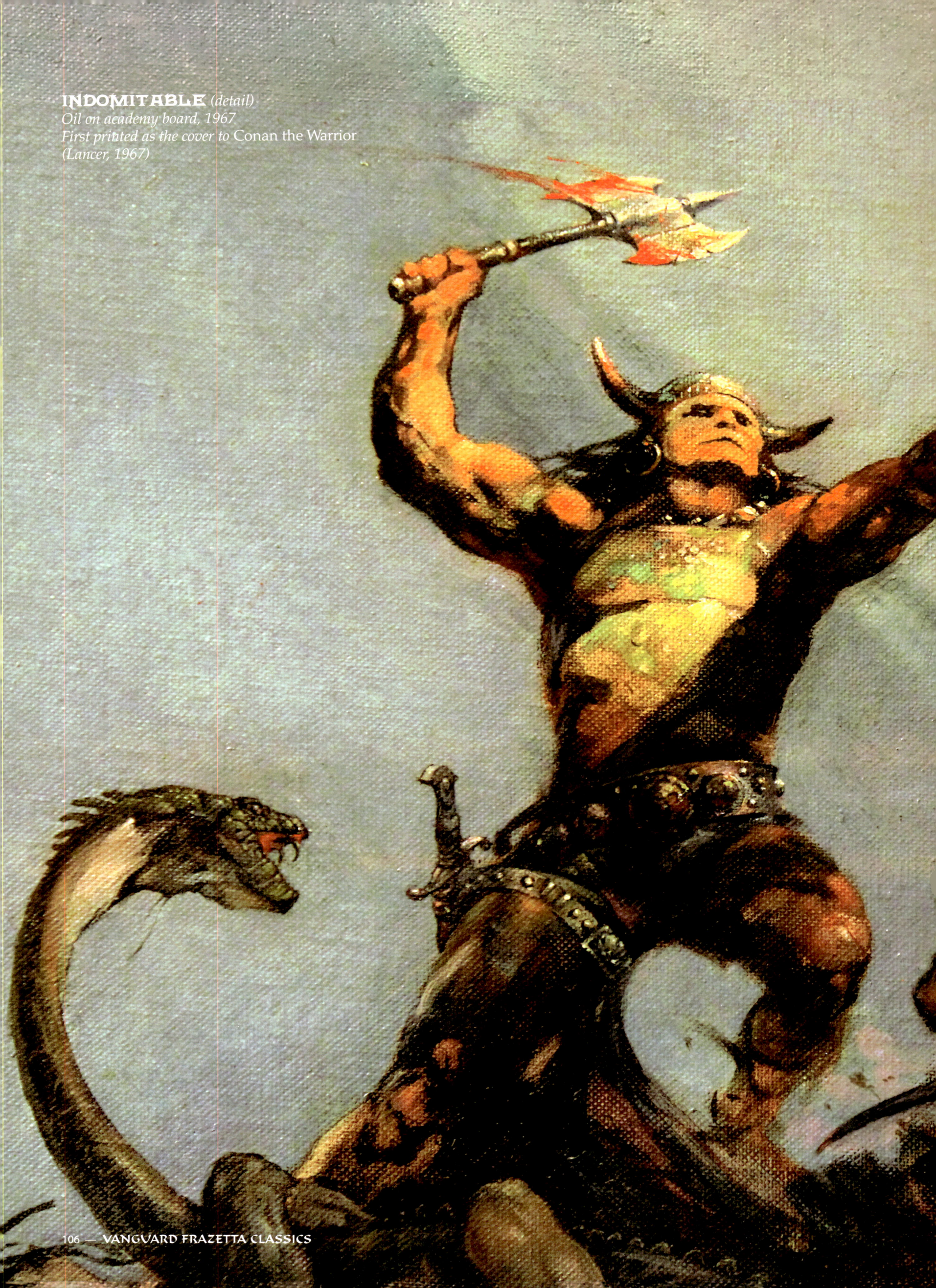

INDOMITABLE *(detail)*
Oil on academy board, 1967
First printed as the cover to Conan the Warrior
(Lancer, 1967)

AFTERWORD BY FRANK FRAZETTA, JR.

For over six decades, Frank Frazetta's art has touched and inspired fans and art lovers around the world. Newly published books pertaining to Frank Frazetta continue to broaden his exposure to generations of all ages and preserve his legacy. Though he is no longer with us, his spirit lives on through the masterful work he left behind.

My parents were extremely appreciative of his loyal fans that made him one of the most influential illustrators of the 20th century and they knew that, without a fan base, he could not have reached this level of success. The only way my parents could show their appreciation and gratitude for the loyalty of his global fan base was to give back with the construction of the Frazetta Art Museum. Sadly, with both parents no longer with us, we too want to honor their wishes and strive to keep the Museum doors open for you as well. This is our way to thank you for making him one of the most recognized and inspirational fantasy illustrators of the 20th century and beyond.

Today, my wife, Lori, my son, William, and I continue to keep the Museum open, welcoming fans and art lovers from all parts of the world to visit with us year round. To view some of his most iconic illustrations that are displayed on the walls of the Museum is unlike anything you've ever seen before.

My father's art enthralls us, his creations are like a brilliantly produced film, and his personal visions remove us from the real world to escape reality and the stress associated with our daily lives. To stand before his original art for the very first time is unlike anything you could imagine. Books and magazines cannot capture the vibrant colors and subtle brush strokes the original art possesses. Most reproductions are four-color separations, not justifying the magnificent blending of colors and tones which the original art employs. His original work entails literally thousands of color combinations to allure us, making it difficult to walk away from his work. My father always said, "What separates a good artist from the great ones is his ability to be creative, the gift of imagination." Sure there was a process in his work, many years of drawing and dedication to develop his raw talent and the gift he was blessed with. Yet from a very young age he was able to reach deep down and access his abyss of endless ideas. He dipped directly into that hidden chamber of imagination for most of his iconic creations. He could access it any time he chose, yet the most remarkable thing was he was best under extreme pressure. Starting the night prior to the deadline date, working through the evening hours and finishing some of his most famous work in one sitting.

Early the next day he'd jump in a cab and bring the finished work to the publisher while the paint was still wet. It did not seem possible when my father tucked us into bed only to wake up dumbfounded and see a finished painting sitting on the kitchen table. What made his art so remarkable is that it connects us to life itself, making the unbelievable believable. He embellishes the narrative beyond our wildest dreams, yet it enthralls us to become part of the world he brings forth through the art and we never want to let go. My father consciously eliminated what was non-essential which he knew diminished the power of his intention and instead choose to present a single idea as forcefully and powerful as possible. Though most of his paintings are masterfully dynamic, his genius came from energy through suggestion with something about to enter the scene then your mind takes it to the

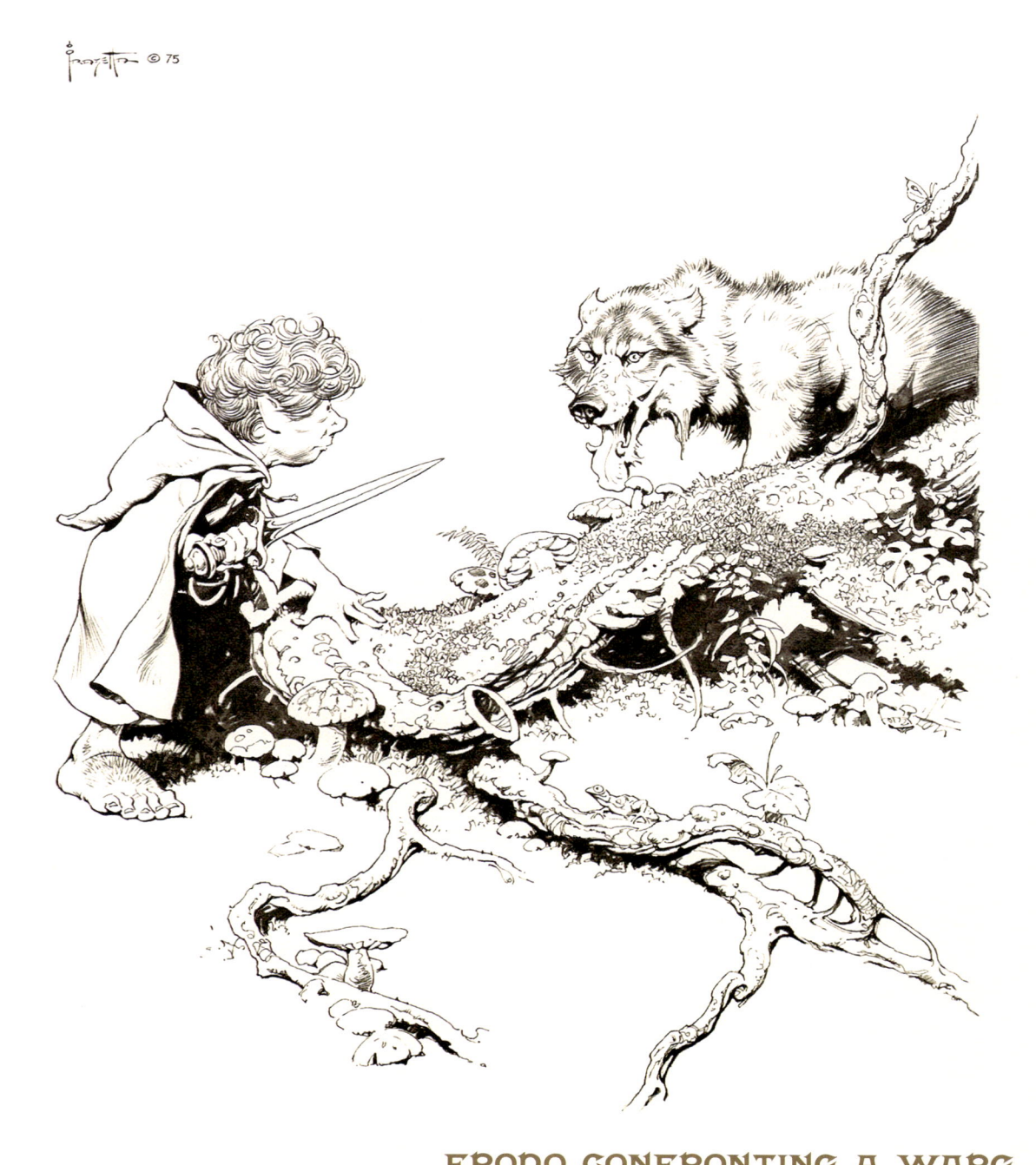

FRODO CONFRONTING A WARG
Pen and ink, 1975
From the Lord of the Rings Portfolio
(Middle Earth, 1975)

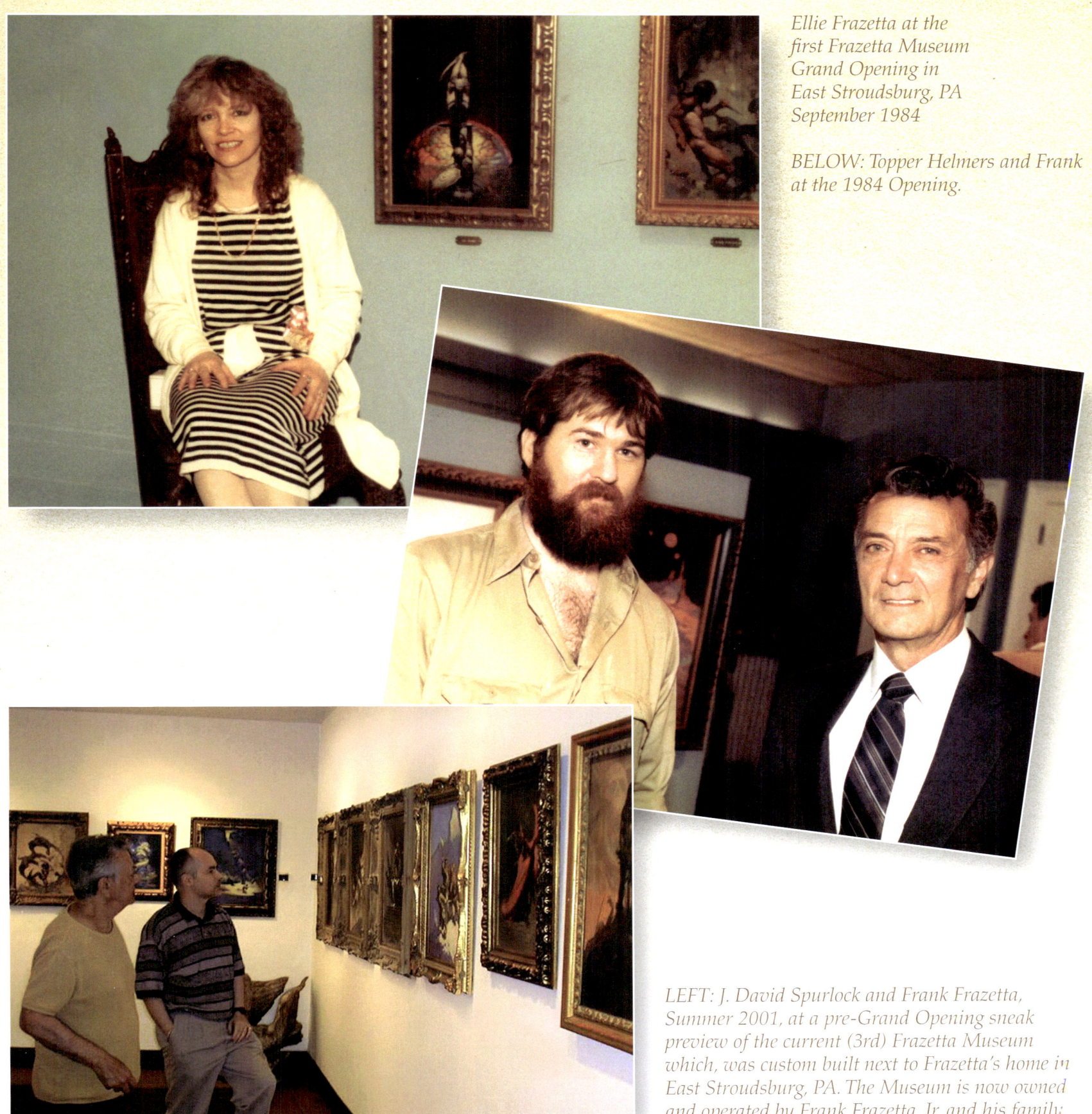

Ellie Frazetta at the first Frazetta Museum Grand Opening in East Stroudsburg, PA September 1984

BELOW: Topper Helmers and Frank at the 1984 Opening.

LEFT: J. David Spurlock and Frank Frazetta, Summer 2001, at a pre-Grand Opening sneak preview of the current (3rd) Frazetta Museum which, was custom built next to Frazetta's home in East Stroudsburg, PA. The Museum is now owned and operated by Frank Frazetta, Jr. and his family.

For information pertaining to the museum or purchasing merchandise, please call or visit the official Frazetta Museum website, frazettaartmuseum.com or the Museum is within 90 minutes of both New York and Philadelphia.

next step and leaves it up to the viewer's discretion and why his art will continue to fascinate us for years to come. One thing he was adamant about while teaching me to draw was knowing when to stop and not continually trying to make it better by adding more content or refine areas that have little or no importance with the focal point. He told me many times over the years, "Sometimes less is more and what could be the difference between a great piece of art and just another one in your portfolio."

My father was not a prisoner to his art and by no means was it anything other than his way of putting food on the table and supporting his family. Fame, fortune and material things never had a place in his life and though he could have had anything his heart desired, his family came first at all costs. He was a private and sensitive individual enjoying the company of friends and family more than anything. As a young man his true passion came from baseball and while being approached by the New York Giants to play professional ball in 1947 and 1948, he felt leaving life without his friends and family for months at a time was not something he could get accustomed to, so he stuck with his art. Working on his own terms was a far better career choice in life than being away seven months a year playing baseball. On occasion he did regret not playing ball, but in the end, where would our world of fantasy be today if his art never came to be? I guess we'll never know, but I'm most certain every Frazetta fan is eternally grateful he made the right decision.

For those not aware, the Frazetta Museum has reopened. Originally constructed and opened in 2001, it was temporarily closed after the passing of my beloved parents in 2010. Honoring my parent's final wishes, my wife Lori and I purchased the estate property, their home and the museum that resides in the beautiful Pocono mountains of Pennsylvania. After the estate and the remaining artwork was settled between the siblings, we decided to reopen the museum and display my personal collection of artwork as a thank you to all the fans that have made my father one of the most recognized and celebrated fantasy illustrators in the world today. We are open all year long, weather permitting, for anyone to visit and have the opportunity to stand before his breathtaking illustrations.

Frank Frazetta, Jr., Lori Supers Frazetta, William Frazetta in front of the Museum in East Stroudsburg, PA October 2019

The museum incorporates many of his most iconic illustrations, yet offers an intriguing insight to the man behind the art with drawings dating back to 1931. We have a wonderful arrangement of his art and personal memorabilia to give the visitor a better understanding of who my father was. Personal tours by a family member tells of a special individual that was not affected by his worldwide fame and popularity. Everyone that visits will have a chance to see and hear what was most important in his life to an individual that could have had anything his heart desired. With hundreds of illustrations, family photos, personal memorabilia and much, much more, this museum is unlike any other pertaining to one man. This is the largest and only display of Frazetta work in the world with all proceeds and revenue generated with sales going directly back into the preservation of the Frazetta Museum and estate grounds.

In closing; he was a gifted and very special individual. One of the most inspiring and influential artist that ever picked up a brush; However, the man behind the art, the lean, athletic and handsome man I only knew as dad, was a far better father than an artist.

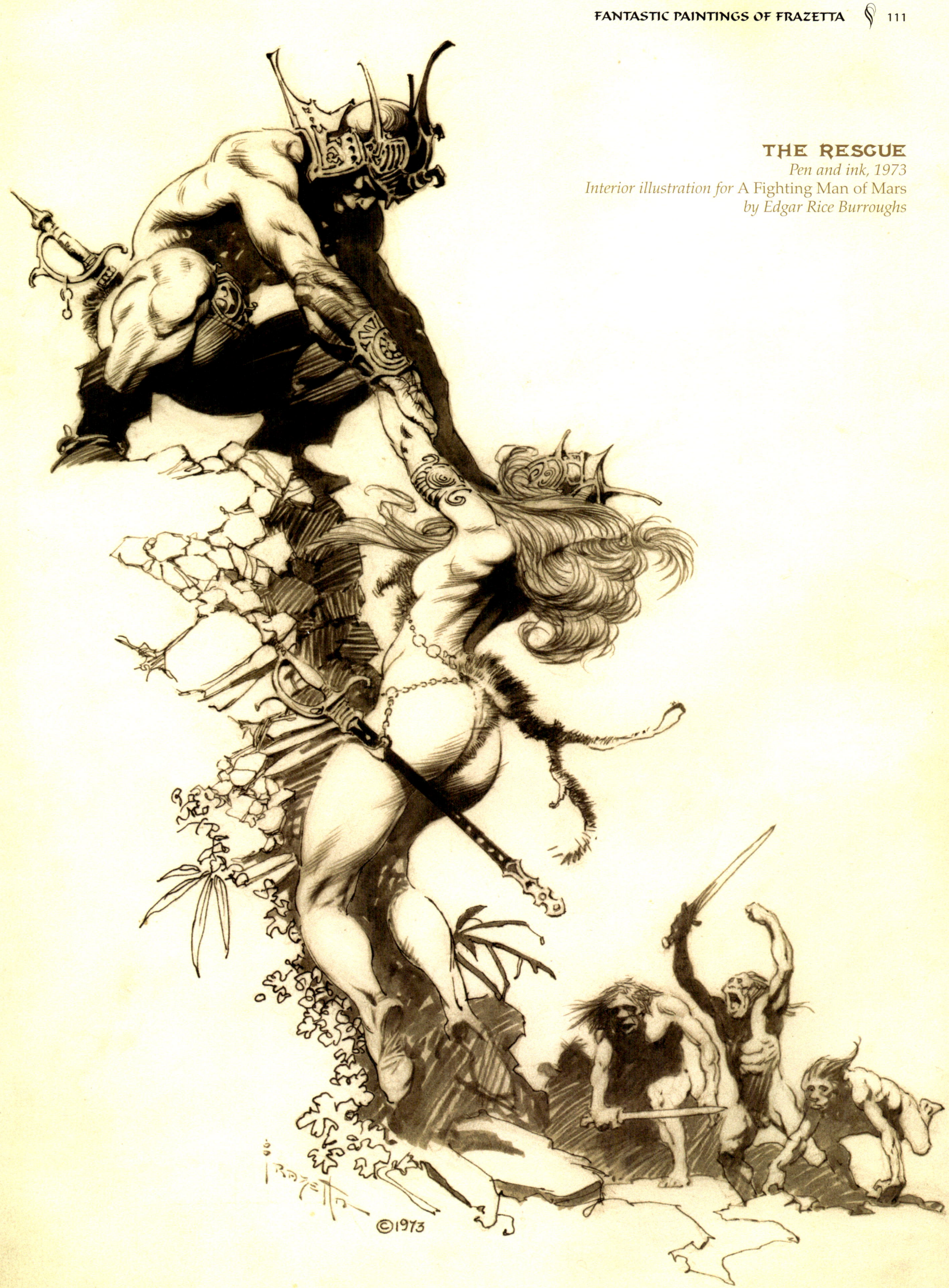

THE RESCUE
Pen and ink, 1973
Interior illustration for A Fighting Man of Mars
by Edgar Rice Burroughs

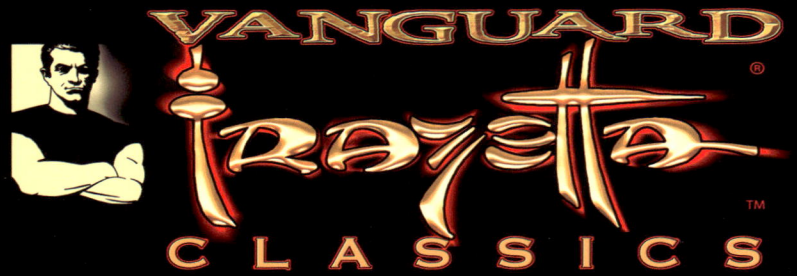

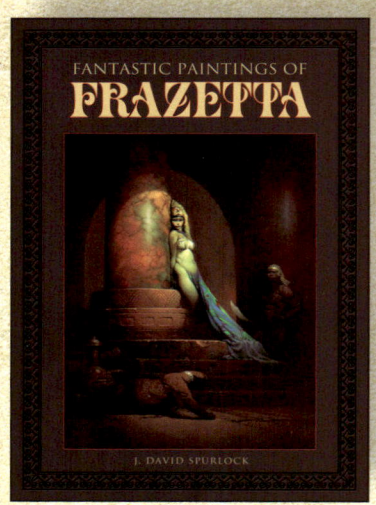

Fantastic Paintings HC

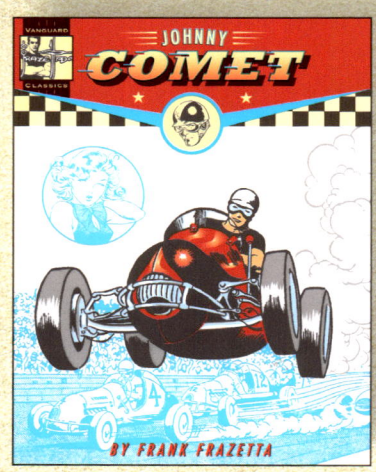

Johnny Comet SC

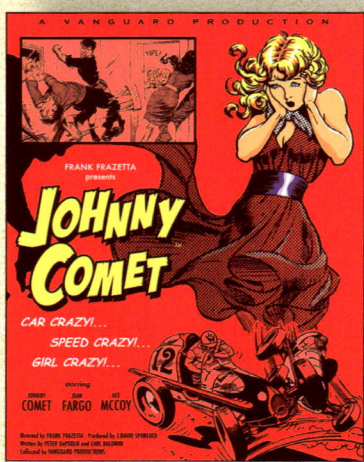

Johnny Comet DLX

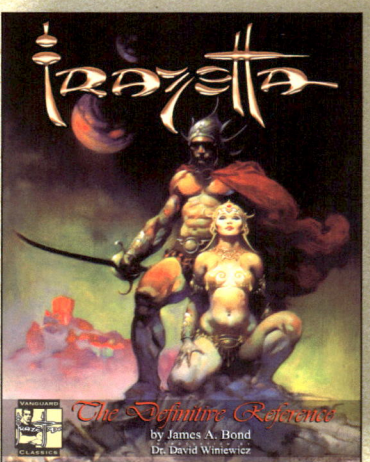

Definitive Reference

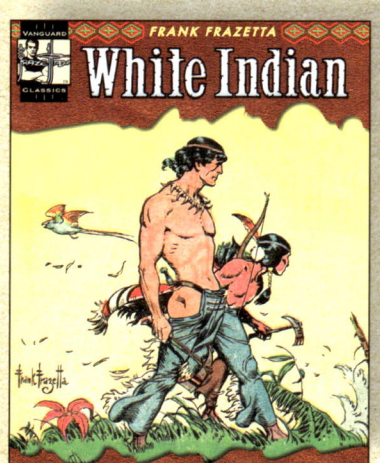

White Indian SC

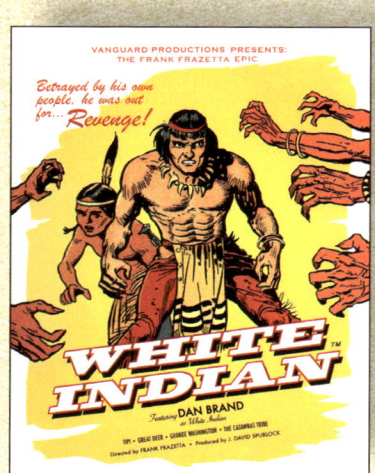

White Indian DLX

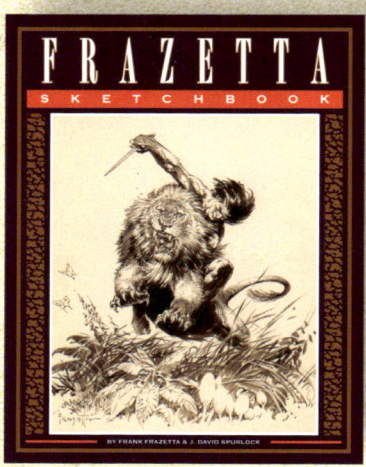

Sketchbook I SC

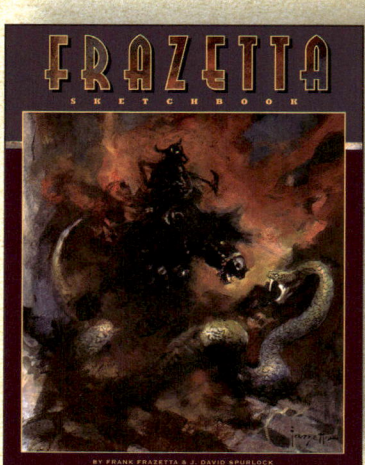

Sketchbook I DLX

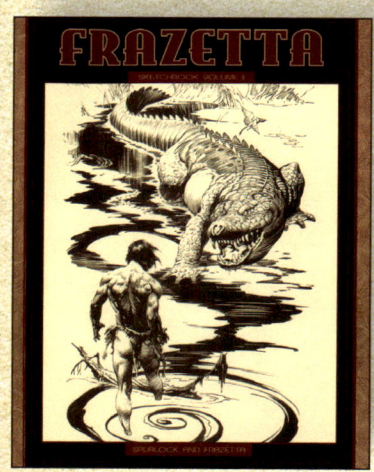

Sketchbook II SC

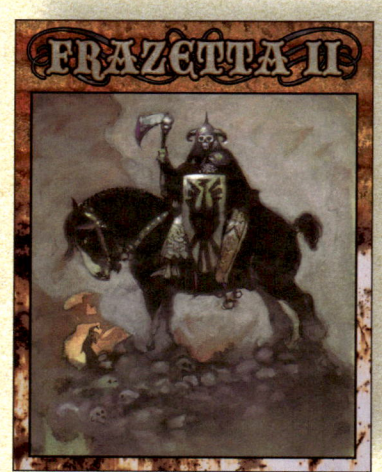

Sketchbook II DLX

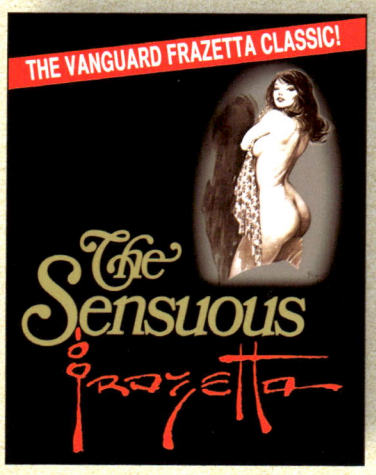

Sensuous Frazetta SC

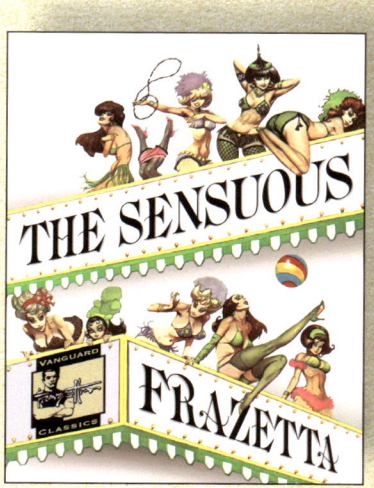

Sensuous Frazetta DLX

www.VANGUARDPUBLISHING.com

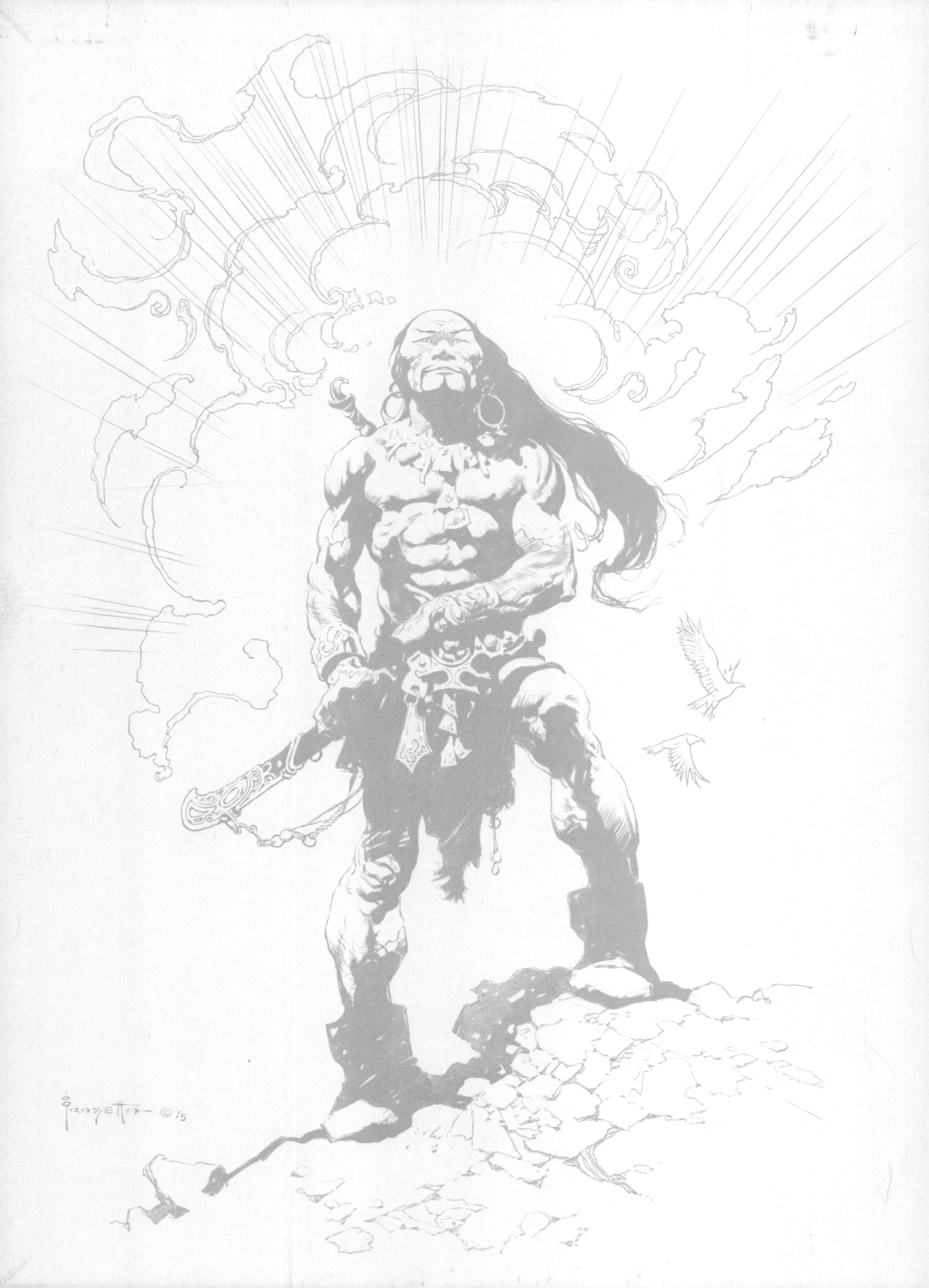